MASS MEDIA
AND MASS MAN

MASS MEDIA

AND

MASS MAN

Alan Casty

Santa Monica City College

HOLT, RINEHART AND WINSTON, INC.

New York Chicago San Francisco Atlanta
Dallas Montreal Toronto

Preface

In *Mass Media and Mass Man,* I have collected materials that focus on the media as processors and conveyors of culture and information. In their dual role, the mass media create and shape not only the values, tastes, attitudes, and the art and entertainment experiences of their audience, but also the patterns of fact and opinion about the world of that audience. Although the organization of the book separates these two roles, they are, of course, interrelated: The communication of information does produce values, attitudes, and emotions that are intricately connected to those communicated by art and entertainment; and conversely, art and entertainment do provide facts and produce opinions.

The materials selected for the book will provide a survey of the approaches being made and what is said about the media today. These materials can also serve as a practical guide for the reader and viewer of the media. With this guide the student can develop an understanding of such significant points as the roles and influences of the media, their methods and performances, and their relationship to political life and private life, to individuals and to the public. And he can also learn to make more valuable use of the media, to read and view intelligently, and to judge with valid critical standards the performances of the media.

The student reader and viewer is also a writer. These selections can act as models or subject matter for his own writing about the media, as well as provide a valuable sampling of writing styles and rhetorical strategies.

To achieve these purposes, I have combined a variety of pieces. Both Part One, "The Mass Media and Culture," and Part Two, "The Mass Media and Information," are divided into three parallel sections. In each part, Section I gives the overview. From the perspectives of journalism, criticism, political science, sociology, psychology, and anthropology, these readings give the backgrounds and suggest the theories and approaches. Section II discusses individual media, while Section III furnishes analyses and critiques of specific cases and media events. In Part Two, Section III also includes a sampling of readings *from* the media for an application of the approaches and methods illustrated. Part Three supplies topics and questions and a bibliography for further study, analysis, and research.

The imaginative editorial advice of both Kenney Withers and Richard Beal was a valuable aid in giving this book its final form. They have my thanks.

A.C.

Santa Monica, California
March 1968

Contents

MASS MEDIA
AND MASS MAN

PART ONE

THE MASS MEDIA
AND CULTURE

I · Backgrounds and Perspectives

CULTURE CAN BE DEFINED in many ways. One view of the meaning of culture includes everything that occurs in a society, from its social habits and manners to its religious rites and practices, from its techniques of preparing food or making love to its customs of marriage and the family, from its commonplaces of transportation or conversation to its conceptions of time, birth, and death. This all-encompassing definition is generally used by anthropologists. At the other extreme is the more limited interpretation of culture of the aestheticians and critics who refer to the aesthetic, philosophic, theological, and intellectual areas of society and its achievements, and to the arts, the deep values, and the past guidelines a society produces and lives by.

Somewhere between the two, but perhaps closer to a broadly defined aesthetic-intellectual view, is the definition of culture assumed by most of the selections in this book. The traditional view of the fine arts and the higher reaches of learning as the repository of culture has been altered to a compromise by the variety of arts and types of learning present in our time—a variety produced and provided, in the main, by the mass media of communication. The response to the changes in culture produced by the mass media is the burden of this section, "Backgrounds and Perspectives." This response has been no less various than the elements of the new culture themselves.

The initial response of professional critics and scholars of culture to these changes was negative. The approaches of Ernest van den Haag and Dwight MacDonald are representative of this first wave of criticism which crested and struck following World War II. Although writing from opposite political positions (conservative and liberal, respectively), van den Haag and MacDonald share a deep distaste for—even fear of—mass culture and its products. Writing as a sociologist, van den Haag emphasizes the psychological effects of mass culture that he believes are produced on the audience: alienation and impoverishment of emotion. MacDonald, on the other hand, stresses the effects on art itself as well as on the audience, the deepening split between low and high culture, and the threat posed by mass culture to both high art and folk art.

3

In the next selection, David Manning White counters this negative thinking with several sanguine theories and interpretations, and. he makes numerous references to the variety of fare offered by the media. A longer, more theoretical approach to the defense of the media can be found in an article by Edward Shils.[1]

The selection by C. Wright Mills focuses on the more limited concept of "psychological illiteracy" that he sees resulting from the media. He examines this illiteracy in terms of both culture and information about the world.

In recent years a new approach to the media and their effects has assumed a dominant position in the field. This approach is best exemplified by the writings of Marshall McLuhan. McLuhan's belief that "the medium is the message" emphasizes the effect that the *form* of communication produces on human consciousness both in structure and in content. He views the current changes in form and their outcomes with sympathy, even elation. In the selections presented, McLuhan's colleague Edmund Carpenter defines both the nature of this approach and the new kind of language and consciousness now being produced by the new media, and McLuhan narrows the focus to an examination of the psychological attributes and effects of two kinds of media, which he labels "hot" and "cold."

The new movement has not been without its critics, and the selection by Benjamin DeMott is representative of these in its attack not only on McLuhan's ideas, but also on their implications. He uses McLuhan's writing style as an indication of the weaknesses of the concepts themselves.

[1] Edward Shils, "Daydreams and Nightmares: Reflections on the Criticism of Mass Culture," *Sewanee Review,* 65 (Autumn 1957), 597–608.

Of Happiness and of Despair
We Have No Measure

Ernest van den Haag

All mass media in the end alienate people from personal experience and, though appearing to offset it, intensify their moral isolation from each other, from reality and from themselves. One may turn to the mass media when lonely or bored. But mass media, once they become a habit, impair the capacity for meaningful experience. Though more diffuse and not as gripping, the habit feeds on itself, establishing a vicious circle as addictions do.

The mass media do not physically replace individual activities and contacts—excursions, travel, parties, etc. But they impinge on all. The portable radio is taken everywhere—from seashore to mountaintop—and everywhere it isolates the bearer from his surroundings, from other people, and from himself. Most people escape being by themselves at any time by voluntarily tuning in on something or somebody. Anyway, it is nearly beyond the power of individuals to escape broadcasts. Music and public announcements are piped into restaurants, bars, shops, cafes, and lobbies, into public means of transportation, and even taxis. You can turn off your radio but not your neighbor's, nor can you silence his portable or the set at the restaurant. Fortunately, most persons do not seem to miss privacy, the cost of which is even more beyond the average income than the cost of individuality.

People are never quite in one place or group without at the same time, singly or collectively, gravitating somewhere else, abstracted, if not transported by the mass media. The incessant announcements, arpeggios, croonings, sobs, bellows, brayings and jingles draw to some faraway world at large and by weakening community with immediate surroundings make people lonely even when in a crowd and crowded even when alone.

We have already stressed that mass media must offer homogenized fare to meet an average of tastes. Further, whatever the quality of the offerings, the very fact that one after the other is absorbed continuously, indiscriminately and casually, trivializes all. Even the most profound

Excerpts from "Of Happiness and of Despair We Have No Measure" by Ernest van den Haag, in *The Fabric of Society* by Ernest van den Haag and Ralph Ross. © 1957 by Harcourt, Brace & World, Inc. and reprinted with their permission.

of experiences, articulated too often on the same level, is reduced to a
cliché. The impact of each of the offerings of mass media is thus weakened by the next one. But the impact of the stream of all mass-media
offerings is cumulative and strong. It lessens people's capacity to experience life itself.

Sometimes it is argued that the audience confuses actuality with mass-
media fiction and reacts to the characters and situations that appear in
soap operas or comic strips as though they were real. For instance, wed-
ding presents are sent to fictional couples. It seems more likely, however,
that the audience prefers to invest fiction with reality—as a person might
prefer to dream—without actually confusing it with reality. After all,
even the kids know that Hopalong Cassidy is an actor and the adults
know that "I Love Lucy" is fiction. Both, however, may attempt to live
the fiction because they prefer it to their own lives. The significant effect
is not the (quite limited) investment of fiction with reality, but the de-
realization of life lived in largely fictitious terms. Art can deepen the
perception of reality. But popular culture veils it, diverts from it, and
becomes an obstacle to experiencing it. It is not so much an escape from
life but an invasion of life first, and ultimately evasion altogether.

Parents, well knowing that mass media can absorb energy, often lighten
the strain that the attempts of their children to reach for activity and
direct experience would impose; they allow some energy to be absorbed
by the vicarious experience of the television screen. Before television, the
cradle was rocked, or poppy juice given, to inhibit the initiative and
motility of small children. Television, unlike these physical sedatives,
tranquillizes by means of substitute gratifications. Manufactured activities and plots are offered to still the child's hunger for experiencing
life. They effectively neutralize initiative and channel imagination. But
the early introduction of de-individualized characters and situations and
early homogenization of taste on a diet of meaningless activity hardly
foster development. Perhaps poppy juice, offering no models in which
to cast the imagination, was better.

The homogenizing effect of comic books or television, the fact that
they neither express nor appeal to individuality, seems far more injurious
to the child's mind and character than the violence they feature, though
it is the latter that is often blamed for juvenile delinquency. The blame
is misplaced. Violence is not new to life or fiction. It waxed large in
ancient fables, fairy tales, and in tragedies from Sophocles to Shakespeare.

Mom always knew that "her boy could not have thought of it," that

the other boys must have seduced him. The belief that viewing or reading about violence persuades children to engage in it is Mom's ancient
conviction disguised as psychiatry. Children are quite spontaneously
bloodthirsty and need both direct and fantasy outlets for violence. What
is wrong with the violence of the mass media is not that it is violence,
but that it is not art—that it is meaningless violence which thrills but
does not gratify. The violence of the desire for life and meaning is displaced and appears as a desire for meaningless violence. But the violence
which is ceaselessly supplied cannot ultimately gratify it because it does
not meet the repressed desire. . . .

The gist of any culture is an ethos which gives meaning to the lives of
those who dwell in it. If this be the purport of popular culture, it is
foiled. We have suggested how it comes to grief in various aspects. What
makes popular culture as a whole so disconcerting is best set forth now
by exploring the relationship among diversion, art and boredom.

Freud thought of art as a diversion, "an illusion in contrast to reality,"
a "substitute gratification" like a dream. In this he fully shared what
was and still is the popular view of art. It is a correct view—of popular
"art," of pseudo-art produced to meet the demand for diversion. But it
is a mistaken, reductive definition of art.

Freud finds the "dreamwork" attempting to hide or disguise the
dreamer's true wishes and fears so that they may not alarm his consciousness. The "substitute gratification" produced by the dreamwork, mainly
by displacements, helps the dreamer continue sleeping. However, one
major function of art is precisely to undo this dreamwork, to see through
disguises, to reveal to our consciousness the true nature of our wishes and
fears. The dreamwork covers, to protect sleep. Art discovers and attempts
to awaken the sleeper. Whereas the dreamwork tries to aid repression,
the work of art intensifies and deepens perception and experience of the
world and of the self. It attempts to pluck the heart of the mystery, to
show where "the action lies in its true nature."

Though dreams and art both may disregard literal reality, they do
so to answer opposite needs. The dream may ignore reality to keep
the sleeper's eyes closed. Art transcends immediate reality to encompass
wider views, penetrate into deeper experience and lead to a fuller confrontation of man's predicament. The dreamwork even tries to cover
upsetting basic impulses with harmless immediate reality. Art, in contrast, ignores the immediate only to uncover the essential. Artistic revelation need not be concerned with outer or with social reality. It may be

purely aesthetic. But it can never be an illusion if it is art. Far from distracting from reality, art is a form of reality which strips life of the fortuitous to lay bare its essentials and permit us to experience them.

In popular culture, however, "art" is all that Freud said art is, and no more. Like the dreamwork, popular culture distorts human experience to draw "substitute gratifications" or reassurances from it. Like the dream-work, it presents "an illusion in contrast to reality." For this reason, popular "art" falls short of satisfaction. And all of popular culture leaves one vaguely discontented because, like popular art, it is only a "substitute gratification"; like a dream, it distracts from life and from real gratification.

Substitute gratifications are uneconomic, as Freud often stressed. They do not in the end gratify as much, and they cost more psychologically than the real gratifications which they shut out. This is why sublimation and realistic control are to be preferred to substitution and repression. That is why reality is to be preferred to illusion, full experience to symptomatic displacements and defense mechanisms. Yet substitute gratifications, habitually resorted to, incapacitate the individual for real ones. In part they cause or strengthen internalized hindrances to real and gratifying experience; in part they are longed for because internal barriers have already blocked real gratification of the original impulses.

Though the specific role it plays varies with the influence of other formative factors in the life of each individual, popular culture must be counted among the baffling variety of causes and effects of defense mechanisms and repressions. It may do much damage, or do none at all, or be the only relief possible, however deficient. But whenever popular culture plays a major role in life significant repressions have taken (or are taking) place. Popular culture supplants those gratifications, which are no longer sought because of the repression of the original impulses. But it is a substitute and spurious. It founders and cannot succeed because neither desire nor gratification are true. "Nought's had, all's spent/ where desire is got without content."

It may seem paradoxical to describe popular culture in terms of repression. Far from repressed, it strikes one as uninhibited. Yet the seeming paradox disappears if we assume that the uproarious din, the raucous noise and the shouting are attempts to drown the shriek of unused capacities, of repressed individuality, as it is bent into futility.

Repression bars impulses from awareness without satisfying them. This damming up always generates a feeling of futility and apathy or, in defense against it, an agitated need for action. The former may be called listless, the latter restless boredom. They may alternate and they may enter consciousness only through anxiety and a sense of meaninglessness, fatigue and nonfulfillment. Sometimes there is such a general numbing of the eagerness too often turned aside that only a dull feeling of dreariness and emptiness remains. More often, there is an insatiable longing for things to happen. The external world is to supply these events to fill the emptiness. Yet the bored person cannot designate what would satisfy a craving as ceaseless as it is vague. It is not satisfied by any event supplied.

The yearning for diversion to which popular culture caters cannot be sated by diversion "whereof a little more than a little is by much too much," because no displaced craving can be satisfied by catering to it in its displaced form. Only when it becomes possible to experience the desire in its true form and to dispense with the internalized processes that balked and displaced it does actual gratification become possible. Diversion at most, through weariness and fatigue, can numb and distract anxiety.

For instance, in many popular movies the tear ducts are massaged and thrills are produced by mechanized assaults on the centers of sensation. We are diverted temporarily and in the end perhaps drained—but not gratified. Direct manipulation of sensations can produce increases and discharges of tension, as does masturbation, but it is a substitute. It does not involve the whole individual as an individual, it does not involve reality but counterfeits it. Sensations directly stimulated and discharged without being intensified and completed through feelings sifted and acknowledged by the intellect are debasing because they do not involve the whole individual in his relation to reality. When one becomes inured to bypassing reality and individuality in favor of meaningless excitement, ultimate gratification becomes impossible.

Once fundamental impulses are thwarted beyond retrieving, once they are so deeply repressed that no awareness is left of their aims, once the desire for a meaningful life has been lost as well as the capacity to create it, only a void remains. Life fades into tedium when the barrier between impulses and aims is so high that neither penetrates into consciousness and no sublimation whatever takes place. Diversion, however frantic, can overwhelm temporarily but not ultimately relieve the boredom which oozes from nonfulfillment.

Though the bored person hungers for things to happen to him, the disheartening fact is that when they do he empties them of the very meaning he unconsciously yearns for by using them as distractions. In popular culture even the second coming would become just another barren "thrill" to be watched on television till Milton Berle comes on. No distraction can cure boredom, just as the company so unceasingly pursued cannot stave off loneliness. The bored person is lonely for himself, not, as he thinks, for others. He misses the individuality, the capacity for experience from which he is debarred. No distraction can restore it. Hence he goes unrelieved and insatiable.

The popular demand for "inside" stories, for vicarious sharing of the private lives of "personalities" rests on the craving for private life—even someone else's—of those who are dimly aware of having none whatever, or at least no life that holds their interest. The attempts to allay boredom are as assiduous as they are unavailing. Countless books pretend to teach by general rules and devices what cannot be learned by devices and rules. Individual personalities cannot be mass produced (with happiness thrown in or your money back). Nevertheless, the message of much popular culture is "you, too, can be happy" if you only buy this car or that hair tonic; you will be thrilled, you will have adventure, romance, popularity—you will no longer be lonely and left out if you follow this formula. And success, happiness or at least freedom from anxiety is also the burden of popular religion, as unchristian in these its aims as it is in its means. From Dale Carnegie to Norman Vincent Peale to Harry and Bonaro Overstreet only the vocabulary changes. The principle remains the same. The formula is well illustrated in the following.

Warm Smile Is an Attribute of Charm

For this, train the upper lip by this method:

1. Stretch the upper lip down over the teeth. Say "Mo-o-o-o."
2. Hold the lip between the teeth and smile.
3. Purse the lips, pull them downward and grin.
4. Let the lower jaw fall and try to touch your nose with your upper lip.

Months of daily practice are necessary to eliminate strain from the new way of smiling, but it, too, can become as natural as all beguiling smiles must be.

Whatever the formula, nothing can be more tiresome than the tireless, cheerless pursuit of pleasure. Days go slowly when they are empty; one cannot tell one from the other. And yet the years go fast. When time is endlessly killed, one lives in an endless present until time ends without ever having passed, leaving a person who never lived to exclaim, "I wasted time and now doth time waste me."

To the Christian, despair is a sin not because there is anything to be hoped for in this life, but because to despair is to lack faith in redemption from it—in the life everlasting. As for the pleasures of this life, they are not worth pursuing. Lancelot Andrewes described them: ". . . though they fade not of themselves yet to us they fade. We are hungry and we eat. Eat we not till that fades and we are as weary of our fulness as we were of our fasting? We are weary and we rest. Rest we not till that fades and we are as weary of our rest as ever we were of our weariness?" Our bodies and minds themselves fade as do their pleasures. The insults of time are spared to none of us. Such is the human predicament.

In *Civilization and Its Discontents,* Freud pointed to the additional burdens that civilization imposes on human beings. They, too, are inevitable, for civilization, despite its cost, eases the total burden we bear.

A little more than a hundred years ago, Henry David Thoreau wrote in *Walden:* "The mass of men lead lives of quiet desperation. . . . A stereotyped but unconscious despair is concealed even under what are called the games and amusements of mankind." Despair, we find, is no longer quiet. Popular culture tries to exorcise it with much clanging and banging. Perhaps it takes more noise to drone it out. Perhaps we are less willing to face it. But whether wrapped in popular culture, we are less happy than our quieter ancestors, or the natives of Bali, must remain an open question despite all romanticizing. (Nor do we have a feasible alternative to popular culture. Besides, a proposal for "the mass of men" would be unlikely to affect the substance of popular culture. And counsel to individuals must be individual.)

There have been periods happier and others more desperate than ours. But we don't know which. And even an assertion as reasonable as this is a conjecture like any comparison of today's bliss with yesterday's. The happiness felt in disparate groups, in disparate periods and places cannot be measured and compared. Our contention is simply that by distracting from the human predicament and blocking individuation and experience, popular culture impoverishes life without leading to contentment. But whether "the mass of men" felt better or worse without the mass-production techniques of which popular culture is an ineluctable part, we shall never know. Of happiness and of despair, we have no measure.

A Theory of Mass Culture

Dwight MacDonald

For about a century, Western culture has really been two cultures: the traditional kind—let us call it "High Culture"—that is chronicled in the textbooks, and a "Mass Culture" manufactured wholesale for the market. In the old art forms, the artisans of Mass Culture have long been at work: in the novel, the line stretches from Eugène Sue to Lloyd C. Douglas; in music, from Offenbach to Tin-Pan Alley; in art from the chromo to Maxfield Parrish and Norman Rockwell; in architecture, from Victorian Gothic to suburban Tudor. Mass Culture has also developed new media of its own, into which the serious artist rarely ventures: radio, the movies, comic books, detective stories, science fiction, television.

It is sometimes called "Popular Culture," but I think "Mass Culture" a more accurate term, since its distinctive mark is that it is solely and directly an article for mass consumption, like chewing gum. A work of High Culture is occasionally popular, after all, though this is increasingly rare. Thus Dickens was even more popular than his contemporary, G. A. Henty, the difference being that he was an artist, communicating his individual vision to other individuals, while Henty was an impersonal manufacturer of an impersonal commodity for the masses.

THE NATURE OF MASS CULTURE

The historical reasons for the growth of Mass Culture since the early 1800's are well known. Political democracy and popular education broke down the old upper-class monopoly of culture. Business enterprise found a profitable market in the cultural demands of the newly awakened masses, and the advance of technology made possible the cheap production of books, periodicals, pictures, music, and furniture, in sufficient quantities to satisfy this market. Modern technology also created new media such as the movies and television which are specially well adapted to mass manufacture and distribution.

The phenomenon is thus peculiar to modern times and differs radically from what was hitherto known as art or culture. It is true that Mass

Excerpts from "A Theory of Mass Culture" by Dwight MacDonald, in *Diogenes*, No. 3, Summer 1953, pp. 1–17. Reprinted by permission of the author.

Culture began as, and to some extent still is, a parasitic, a cancerous growth on High Culture. As Clement Greenberg pointed out in "Avant-garde and *Kitsch*" (*Partisan Review*, Fall, 1939): "The precondition of *kitsch* (a German term for 'Mass Culture') is the availability close at hand of a fully matured cultural tradition, whose discoveries, acquisitions, and perfected self-consciousness *kitsch* can take advantage of for its own ends." The connection, however, is not that of the leaf and the branch but rather that of the caterpillar and the leaf. *Kitsch* "mines" High Culture the way improvident frontiersmen mine the soil, extracting its riches and putting nothing back. Also, as *kitsch* develops, it begins to draw on its own past, and some of it evolves so far away from High Culture as to appear quite disconnected from it.

It is also true that Mass Culture is to some extent a continuation of the old Folk Art which until the Industrial Revolution was the culture of the common people, but here, too, the differences are more striking than the similarities. Folk Art grew from below. It was a spontaneous, autochthonous expression of the people, shaped by themselves, pretty much without the benefit of High Culture, to suit their own needs. Mass Culture is imposed from above. It is fabricated by technicians hired by business; its audiences are passive consumers, their participation limited to the choice between buying and not buying. The Lords of *kitsch*, in short, exploit the cultural needs of the masses in order to make a profit and/or to maintain their class rule—in Communist countries, only the second purpose obtains. (It is very different to *satisfy* popular tastes, as Robert Burns' poetry did, and to exploit them, as Hollywood does.) Folk Art was the people's own institution, their private little garden walled off from the great formal park of their masters' High Culture. But Mass Culture breaks down the wall, integrating the masses into a debased form of High Culture and thus becoming an instrument of political domination. If one had no other data to go on, the nature of Mass Culture would reveal capitalism to be an exploitive class society and not the harmonious commonwealth it is sometimes alleged to be. The same goes even more strongly for Soviet Communism and *its* special kind of Mass Culture. . . .

GRESHAM'S LAW IN CULTURE

The separation of Folk Art and High Culture in fairly watertight compartments corresponded to the sharp line once drawn between the common people and the aristocracy. The eruption of the masses onto the political stage has broken down this compartmentation, with disastrous cultural results. Whereas Folk Art had its own special quality, Mass Culture is at best a vulgarized reflection of High Culture. And whereas High Culture could formerly ignore the mob and seek to please only the *cognoscenti*, it must now compete with Mass Culture or be merged into it.

The problem is acute in the United States and not just because a prolific Mass Culture exists here. If there were a clearly defined cultural *élite*, then the masses could have their *kitsch* and the *élite* could have its High Culture, with everybody happy. But the boundary line is blurred. A statistically significant part of the population, I venture to guess, is chronically confronted with a choice between going to the movies or to a concert, between reading Tolstoy or a detective story, between looking at old masters or at a TV show; i.e., the pattern of their cultural lives is "open" to the point of being porous. Good art competes with *kitsch*, serious ideas compete with commercialized formulae—and the advantage lies all on one side. There seems to be a Gresham's Law in cultural as well as monetary circulation: bad stuff drives out the good, since it is more easily understood and enjoyed. It is that facility of access which at once sells *kitsch* on a wide market and also prevents it from achieving quality. Clement Greenberg writes that the special aesthetic quality of *kitsch* is that it "predigests art for the spectator and spares him effort, provides him with a shortcut to the pleasures of art that detours what is necessarily difficult in genuine art" because it includes the spectator's reactions in the work of art itself instead of forcing him to make his own responses. Thus "Eddie Guest and the Indian Love Lyrics are more 'poetic' than T. S. Eliot and Shakespeare." And so, too, our "collegiate Gothic" such as the Harkness Quadrangle at Yale is more picturesquely Gothic than Chartres, and a pinup girl smoothly airbrushed by Petty is more sexy than a real naked woman.

When to this ease of consumption is added *kitsch's* ease of production because of its standardized nature, its prolific growth is easy to understand. It threatens High Culture by its sheer pervasiveness, its brutal, overwhelming *quantity*. The upper classes, who begin by using it to make money from the crude tastes of the masses and to dominate them politically, end by finding their own culture attacked and even threatened with destruction by the instrument they have thoughtlessly employed. (The same irony may be observed in modern politics, where most swords seem to have two edges; thus Nazism began as a tool of the big bourgeoisie and the army *Junkers* but ended by using *them* as *its* tools.)

HOMOGENIZED CULTURE

Like nineteenth-century capitalism, Mass Culture is a dynamic, revolutionary force, breaking down the old barriers of class, tradition, taste, and dissolving all cultural distinctions. It mixes and scrambles everything together, producing what might be called homogenized culture, after another American achievement, the homogenization process that distributes the globules of cream evenly throughout the milk instead of allowing them to float separately on top. It thus destroys all values, since value judgments imply discriminations. Mass Culture is very, very democratic: it absolutely refuses to discriminate against, or between, anything or anybody. All is grist to its mill, and all comes out finely ground indeed.

Consider *Life*, a typical homogenized mass-circulation magazine. It appears on the mahogany library tables of the rich, the glass end-tables of the middle-class and the oilcloth-covered kitchen tables of the poor. Its contents are as thoroughly homogenized as its circulation. The same issue will contain a serious exposition of atomic theory alongside a disquisition on Rita Hayworth's love life; photos of starving Korean children picking garbage from the ruins of Pusan and sleek models wearing adhesive brassieres; an editorial hailing Bertrand Russell on his eightieth birthday ("A GREAT MIND IS STILL ANNOYING AND ADORNING OUR AGE") across from a full-page photo of a housewife arguing with an umpire at a baseball game ("MOM GETS THUMB"); a cover announcing in the same size type "A NEW FOREIGN POLICY, BY JOHN FOSTER DULLES" and "KERIMA: HER MARATHON KISS IS A MOVIE SENSATION"; nine color pages of Renoirs plus a memoir by his son, followed by a full-page picture of a roller-skating horse. The advertisements, of course, provide even more scope for the editor's homogenizing talents, as when a full-page photo of a ragged Bolivian peon grinningly drunk on coca leaves (which Mr. Luce's conscientious reporters tell us he chews to narcotize his chronic hunger pains) appears opposite an ad of a pretty, smiling, well-dressed American mother with her two pretty, smiling, well-dressed children (a boy and a girl, of course —children are always homogenized in American ads) looking raptly at a clown on a TV set ("RCA VICTOR BRINGS YOU A NEW KIND OF TELEVISION—SUPER SETS WITH 'PICTURE POWER'"). The peon would doubtless find the juxtaposition piquant if he could afford a copy of *Life*, which, fortunately for the Good Neighbor Policy, he cannot.

ACADEMICISM AND AVANTGARDISM

Until about 1930, High Culture tried to defend itself against the encroachments of Mass Culture in two opposite ways: Academicism, or an attempt to compete by imitation; and Avantgardism, or a withdrawal from competition.

Academicism is *kitsch* for the *élite:* spurious High Culture that is outwardly the real thing but actually as much a manufactured article as the cheaper cultural goods produced for the masses. It is recognized at the time for what it is only by the Avantgardists. A generation or two later, its real nature is understood by everyone and it quietly drops into the same oblivion as its franker sister-under-the-skin. Examples are painters such as Bougereau and Rosa Bonheur, critics such as Edmund Clarence Stedman and Edmund Gosse, the Beaux Arts school of architecture, composers such as the late Sir Edward Elgar, poets such as Stephen Phillips, and novelists such as Alphonse Daudet, Arnold Bennett, James Branch Cabell and Somerset Maugham.

The significance of the Avantgarde movement (by which I mean poets such as Rimbaud, novelists, such as Joyce, composers such as Stravinsky, and painters such as Picasso) is that it simply refused to compete. Rejecting Academicism—and thus, at a second remove, also Mass Culture —it made a desperate attempt to fence off some area where the serious artist could still function. It created a new compartmentation of culture, on the basis of an intellectual rather than a social *élite.* The attempt was remarkably successful: to it we owe almost everything that is living in the art of the last fifty or so years. In fact, the High Culture of our times is pretty much identical with Avantgardism. The movement came at a time (1890–1930) when bourgeois values were being challenged both culturally and politically. (In this country, the cultural challenge did not come until World War I, so that our Avantgarde flourished only in the twenties.) In the thirties the two streams mingled briefly, after each had spent its real force, under the aegis of the Communists, only to sink together at the end of the decade into the sands of the wasteland we still live in. The rise of Nazism and the revelation in the Moscow Trials of the real nature of the new society in Russia inaugurated the present period, when men cling to the evils they know rather than risk possibly greater ones by pressing forward. Nor has the chronic state of war, hot or cold, that the world has been in since 1939 encouraged rebellion or experiment in either art or politics.

A MERGER HAS BEEN ARRANGED

In this new period, the competitors, as often happens in the business world, are merging. Mass Culture takes on the color of both varieties of the old High Culture, Academic and Avantgarde, while these latter are increasingly watered down with Mass elements. There is slowly emerging a tepid, flaccid Middlebrow Culture that threatens to engulf everything in its spreading ooze. Bauhaus modernism has at last trickled down, in a debased form of course, into our furniture, cafeterias, movie theatres, electric toasters, office buildings, drug stores, and railroad trains. Psychoanalysis is expounded sympathetically and superficially in popular magazines, and the psychoanalyst replaces the eccentric millionaire as the *deus ex machina* in many a movie. T. S. Eliot writes *The Cocktail Party* and it becomes a Broadway hit. (Though in some ways excellent, it is surely inferior to his *Murder in the Cathedral*, which in the unmerged thirties had to depend on WPA to get produced at all.)

The typical creator of *kitsch* today, at least in the old media, is an indeterminate specimen. There are no widely influential critics so completely terrible as, say, the late William Lyon Phelps was. Instead we have such gray creatures as Clifton Fadiman and Henry Seidel Canby. The artless numbers of an Eddie Guest are drowned out by the more sophisticated though equally commonplace strains of Benet's *John Brown's Body*. Maxfield Parrish yields to Rockwell Kent, Arthur Brisbane to Walter Lippman, Theda Bara to Ingrid Bergman. We even have what might be called *l'avantgarde pompier* (or, in American "phoney Avantgardism"), as in the buildings of Raymond Hood and the later poetry of Archibald MacLeish, as there is also an academic Avantgardism in *belles lettres* so that now the "little" as well as the big magazines have their hack writers.

All this is not a raising of the level of Mass Culture, as might appear at first, but rather a corruption of High Culture. There is nothing more vulgar than sophisticated *kitsch*. Compare Conan Doyle's workmanlike and unpretentious Sherlock Holmes stories with the bogus "intellectuality" of Dorothy M. Sayers, who, like many contemporary detective-story writers, is a novelist *manquée* who ruins her stuff with literary attitudinizing. Or consider the relationship of Hollywood and Broadway. In the twenties, the two were sharply differentiated, movies being produced for the masses of the hinterland, theatre for an upper-class New York audience. The theatre was High Culture, mostly of the Academic variety (Theatre Guild) but with some spark of the Avantgarde fire (the "little" or "experimental" theatre movement). The movies were definitely Mass Culture, mostly very bad but with some leaven of Avantgardism (Griffith, Stroheim) and Folk Art (Chaplin and other comedians). With the sound film, Broadway and Hollywood drew closer together. Plays are now produced mainly to sell the movie rights, with many being directly financed by the film companies. The merge has standardized the theatre to such an extent that even the early Theatre Guild seems vital in retrospect, while hardly a trace of the "experimental" theatre is left. And what have the movies gained? They are more sophisticated, the acting is subtler, the sets in better taste. But they too have become standardized: they are never as awful as they often were in the old days, but they are never as good either. They are better entertainment and worse art. The cinema of the twenties occasionally gave us the fresh charm of Folk Art or the imaginative intensity of Avantgardism. The coming of sound, and with it Broadway, degraded the camera to a recording instrument for an alien art form, the spoken play. The silent film had at least the *theoretical possibility*, even within the limits of Mass Culture, of being artistically significant. The sound film, within those limits, does not.

DIVISION OF LABOR

The whole field could be approached from the standpoint of the division of labor. The more advanced technologically, the greater the division. Cf. the great Blackett-Semple-Hummert factory—the word is accurate—for the mass production of radio "soap operas." Or the fact that in Hollywood a composer for the movies is not *permitted* to make his own orchestrations any more than a director can do his own cutting. Or the "editorial formula" which every big-circulation magazine tailors its fiction and articles to fit, much as automobile parts are machined in Detroit. *Time* and *Newsweek* have carried specialization to its extreme: their writers don't even sign their work, which in fact is not properly theirs, since the gathering of data is done by a specialized corps of researchers and correspondents and the final article is often as much the result of the editor's blue-penciling and rewriting as of the original author's efforts. The *"New Yorker* short story" is a definite genre— smooth, minor-key, casual, suggesting drama and sentiment without ever being crude enough to actually create it—which the editors have established by years of patient, skilful selection the same way a gardener develops a new kind of rose. They have, indeed, done their work all too well: would-be contributors now deluge them with lifeless imitations, and they have begun to beg writers not to follow the formula *quite* so closely.

Such art workers are as alienated from their brainwork as the industrial worker is from his handwork. The results are as bad qualitatively as they are impressive quantitatively. The only great films to come out of Hollywood, for example, were made before industrial elephantiasis had reduced the director to one of a number of technicians all operating at about the same level of authority. Our two great directors, Griffith and Stroheim, were artists, not specialists; they did everything themselves, dominated everything personally: the scenario, the actors, the camera work, and above all the cutting (or montage). Unity is essential in art; it cannot be achieved by a production line of specialists, however competent. There have been successful collective creations (Greek temples, Gothic churches, perhaps the *Iliad*) but their creators were part of a tradition which was strong enough to impose unity on their work. We have no such tradition today, and so art—as against *kitsch*—will result only when a single brain and sensibility is in full command. In the movies, only the director can even theoretically be in such a position; he was so in the pre-1930 cinema of this country, Germany, and the Soviet Union.

Griffith and Stroheim were both terrific egoists—crude, naïve, and not without charlatanry—who survived until the industry became highly enough organized to resist their vigorous personalities. By about 1925, both were outside looking in; the manufacture of commodities so costly to make and so profitable to sell was too serious a matter to be intrusted to artists.

"One word of advice, Von," Griffith said to Stroheim, who had been his assistant on *Intolerance*, when Stroheim came to him with the news that he had a chance to make a picture himself. "Make your pictures in your own way. Put your mark on them. Take a stand and stick to your guns. You'll make some enemies, but you'll make good pictures." Could that have been only thirty years ago?

ADULTIZED CHILDREN
AND INFANTILE ADULTS

The homogenizing effects of *kitsch* also blurs age lines. It would be interesting to know how many adults read the comics. We do know that comic books are by far the favorite reading matter of our soldiers and sailors, that some forty million comic books are sold a month, and that some seventy million people (most of whom must be adults, there just aren't that many kids) are estimated to read the newspaper comic strips every day. We also know that movie Westerns and radio and TV programs such as "The Lone Ranger" and "Captain Video" are by no means enjoyed only by children. On the other hand, children have access to such grown-up media as the movies, radio and TV. (Note that these newer arts are the ones which blur age lines because of the extremely modest demands they make on the audience's cultural equipment; thus there are many children's books but few children's movies.)

This merging of the child and grown-up audience means: (1) infantile regression of the latter, who, unable to cope with the strains and complexities of modern life, escape via *kitsch* (which in turn, confirms and enhances their infantilism); (2) "overstimulation" of the former, who grow up too fast. Or, as Max Horkheimer well puts it: "Development has ceased to exist. The child is grown up as soon as he can walk, and the grown-up in principle always remains the same." Also note (a) our cult of youth, which makes 18–22 the most admired and desired period of life, and (b) the sentimental worship of Mother ("Momism") as if we couldn't bear to grow up and be on our own. Peter Pan might be a better symbol of America than Uncle Sam.

IDOLS OF CONSUMPTION

Too little attention has been paid to the connection of our Mass Culture with the historical evolution of American Society. In *Radio Research, 1942–43* (Paul F. Lazarsfeld, ed.), Leo Lowenthal compared the biographical articles in *Collier's* and *The Saturday Evening Post* for 1901 and 1940–41 and found that in the forty-year interval the proportion of articles about business and professional men and political leaders had declined while those about entertainers had gone up 50 per cent. Furthermore, the 1901 entertainers are mostly serious artists—opera singers, sculptors, pianists, etc.—while those of 1941 are *all* movie stars, baseball players, and such; and even the "serious" heroes in 1941 aren't so very serious after all; the businessmen and politicians are freaks, oddities, not the really powerful leaders as in 1901. The 1901 *Satevepost* heroes he calls "idols of production," those of today "idols of consumption."

Lowenthal notes that the modern *Satevepost* biographee is successful not because of his own personal abilities so much as because he "got the breaks." The whole competitive struggle is presented as a lottery in which a few winners, no more talented or energetic than any one else, drew the lucky tickets. The effect on the mass reader is at once consoling (it might have been me) and deadening to effort, ambition (there are no rules, so why struggle?). It is striking how closely this evolution parallels the country's economic development. Lowenthal observes that the "idols of production" maintained their dominance right through the twenties. The turning point was the 1929 depression when the problem became how to consume goods rather than how to produce them, and also when the arbitrariness and chaos of capitalism was forcefully brought home to the mass man. So he turned to "idols of consumption," or rather these were now offered him by the manufacturers of Mass Culture, and he accepted them.

SHERLOCK HOLMES TO MIKE HAMMER

The role of science in Mass Culture has similarly changed from the rational and the purposive to the passive, accidental, even the catastrophic. Consider the evolution of the detective story, a genre which can be traced back to the memoirs of Vidocq, the master-detective of the Napoleonic era. Poe, who was peculiarly fascinated by scientific method, wrote the first and still best detective stories: *The Purloined Letter, The Gold Bug, The Mystery of Marie Roget, The Murders in the Rue Morgue.* Conan Doyle created the great folk hero, Sherlock Holmes, like Poe's Dupin a sage whose wizard's wand was scientific deduction (Poe's "ratiocination"). Such stories could only appeal to—in fact, only be comprehensible to—an audience accustomed to think in scientific terms: to survey the data, set up a hypothesis, test it by seeing whether it caught the murderer. The very idea of an art genre cast in the form of a problem to be solved by purely intellectual means could only have arisen in a scientific age. This kind of detective fiction, which might be called the "classic" style, is still widely practiced (well by Agatha Christie and John Dickson Carr, badly by the more popular Erle Stanley Gardiner) but of late it has been overshadowed by the rank, noxious growth of works in the "sensational" style. This was inaugurated by Dashiel Hammett (whom André Gide was foolish enough to admire) and has recently been enormously stepped up in voltage by Mickey Spillane, whose six books to date have sold thirteen million copies. The sensationalists use what for the classicists was the point—the uncovering of the criminal— as a mere excuse for the minute description of scenes of bloodshed, brutality, lust, and alcoholism. The cool, astute, subtle Dupin-Holmes is replaced by the crude man of action whose prowess is measured not by intellectual mastery but by his capacity for liquor, women, and mayhem (he can "take it" as well as "dish it out"—Hammett's *The Glass Key* is largely a chronicle of the epic beatings absorbed by the hero before he finally staggers to the solution). Mike Hammer, Spillane's aptly named hero, is such a monumental blunderer that even Dr. Watson would have seen through him. According to Richard W. Johnston (*Life*, June 23, 1952), "Mike has one bizarre and memorable characteristic that sets him apart from all other fictional detectives: sheer incompetence. In the five Hammer cases, 48 people have been killed, and there is reason to believe that if Mike had kept out of the way, 34 of them—all innocent of the original crime—would have survived." A decade ago, the late George Orwell, apropos a "sensationalist" detective story of the time, *No Orchids for Miss Blandish*, showed how the brutalization of this genre mirrors the general degeneration in ethics from nineteenth-century standards. What he would have written had Mickey Spillane's works been then in existence I find it hard to imagine.

FRANKENSTEIN TO HIROSHIMA

The real heirs of the "classic" detective story today, so far as the exploitation of science is concerned, are the writers of science fiction, where the marvels and horrors of the future must always be "scientifically possible"—just as Sherlock Holmes drew on no supernatural powers. This is the approach of the bourgeoisie, who think of science as their familiar instrument. The masses are less confident, more awed in their approach to science, and there are vast lower strata of science fiction where the marvellous is untrammeled by the limits of knowledge. To the masses, science is the modern *arcanum arcanorum*, at once the supreme mystery and the philosopher's stone that explains the mystery. The latter concept appears in comic strips such as "Superman" and in the charlatan-science exploited by "health fakers" and "nature fakers." Taken this way, science gives man mastery over his environment and is beneficent. But science itself is not understood, therefore not mastered, therefore terrifying because of its very power. Taken *this* way, as the supreme mystery, science becomes the stock in trade of the "horror" pulp magazines and comics and movies. It has got to the point, indeed, that if one sees a laboratory in a movie, one shudders, and the white coat of the scientist is as blood-chilling a sight as Count Dracula's black coat. These "horror" films have apparently an indestructible popularity: *Frankenstein* is still shown, after twenty-one years, and the current revival of *King Kong* is expected to gross over 2 million dollars.

If the scientist's laboratory has acquired in Mass Culture a ghastly atmosphere, is this perhaps not one of those deep popular intuitions? From Frankenstein's laboratory to Maidenek and Hiroshima is not a long journey. Was there a popular suspicion, perhaps only half conscious, that the nineteenth-century trust in science, like the nineteenth-century trust in popular education, was mistaken, that science can as easily be used for antihuman as for prohuman ends, perhaps even more easily? For Mrs. Shelley's Frankenstein, the experimenter who brought disaster by pushing his science too far, is a scientific folk hero older than and still as famous as Mr. Doyle's successful and beneficent Sherlock Holmes.

THE PROBLEM OF THE MASSES

Conservatives such as Ortega y Gasset and T. S. Eliot argue that since "the revolt of the masses" has led to the horrors of totalitarianism (and of California roadside architecture), the only hope is to rebuild the old class walls and bring the masses once more under aristocratic control. They think of the popular as synonymous with cheap and vulgar. Marxian radicals and liberals, on the other hand, see the masses as intrinsically healthy but as the dupes and victims of cultural exploitation by the Lords of *kitsch*—in the style of Rousseau's "noble savage" idea. If only the masses were offered good stuff instead of *kitsch*, how they would eat it up! How the level of Mass Culture would rise! Both these diagnoses seem to me fallacious: they assume that Mass Culture is (in the conservative view) or could be (in the liberal view) an expression of *people*, like Folk Art, whereas actually it is an expression of *masses*, a very different thing.

There are theoretical reasons why Mass Culture is not and can never be any good. I take it as axiomatic that culture can only be produced by and for human beings. But in so far as people are organized (more strictly, disorganized) as masses, they lose their human identity and quality. For the masses are in historical time what a crowd is in space: a large quantity of people unable to express themselves as human beings because they are related to one another neither as individuals nor as members of communities—indeed, they are not related to *each other* at all, but only to something distant, abstract, nonhuman: a football game, or bargain sale, in the case of a crowd, a system of industrial production, a party or a State in the case of the masses. The mass man is a solitary atom, uniform with and undifferentiated from thousands and millions of other atoms who go to make up "the lonely crowd," as David Riesman well calls American society. A folk or a people, however, is a community, i.e., a group of individuals linked to each other by common interests, work, traditions, values, and sentiments; something like a family, each of whose members has a special place and function as an individual while at the same time sharing the group's interests (family budget), sentiments (family quarrels), and culture (family jokes). The scale is small enough so that it "makes a difference" what the individual does, a first condition for human—as against mass—existence. He is at once more important as an individual than in mass society and at the same time more closely integrated into the community, his creativity nourished by a rich combination of individualism and communalism. (The great culture-bearing *élites* of the past have been communities of this kind.) In contrast, a mass society, like a crowd, is so undifferentiated and loosely structured that its atoms, in so far as human values go, tend to cohere only along the line of the least common denominator; its morality sinks to that of its most brutal and primitive members, its taste to that of the least sensitive and most ignorant. And in addition to everything else, the scale is simply too big, there are just *too many people.* . . .

Mass Culture in America:
Another Point of View

David Manning White

Is it really true that the media have transformed the greatest part of the American population into this nebulous "mass mind" one reads about so often? Do the media contrive with all their cunning, Madison Avenue, grey-flanneled wit to keep Mencken's *booboisie* on the thirteen-year-old level? Many serious and earnest critics of the American scene imply this is

Excerpt from "Mass Culture in America: Another Point of View" by David Manning White, in *Saturday Review*, Vol. 39, November 3, 1956, pp. 11–13. Reprinted by permission of the *Saturday Review* and the author.

so. In his book, *The Power Elite*, the noted sociologist C. Wright Mills decries what appears to him our inevitable trend to a mass society for which the mass media must be held to account. At the end of this road, on which we are travelling so precariously, Mills sees totalitarianism, as in Nazi Germany.

But, was the Germany of 1932 a "mass society" when it *voted* Hitler's party into power? To be sure, a dictator will grasp to his own use whatever mass media are available, but this is not the same as saying the mass media so weakened the people of Germany that they were helpless puppets in the hands of Goebbels. This is the country which had more symphony orchestras per capita, published more books, pioneered and developed a cinema industry whose productions were of first quality, etc. From the eighteenth century its lead in the world of music had never been challenged—from Bach through titanic Beethoven to the serene Brahms. In its vaunted gymnasia what German youth could not cite or recite innumerable portions of such giants of the literary world as Goethe, Schiller or Lessing? Yet with all this great cultural buttress its best seller of all time was *Mein Kampf*, with its 10 million copies.

I am not suggesting that Hitlerism with its psychotic misanthropy was in any sense correlated with the high level of German culture. But is this any more illogical than the arguments of those who see us heading directly for an Orwellian 1984 (or worse) because of our mass media?

There was nothing to preclude an Ilse Koch from listening to the 2nd Brandenburg Concerto on her gramophone (as Eliot so nicely puts it, "When lovely woman stoops to folly. . . .") while she practiced her hobby of tanning the human skin of some unfortunate Jew who was placed in Belsen. We are told that she made lamp shades from some of the skins, or perhaps book covers to rebind her collected works of Nietzsche. The thread of psyche that spread between Attila and Adolf apparently was not weakened *or* strengthened by the cultural growth of the German people. Misanthropy and race hatred can be the common heritage of a musical genius like Wagner and a political demagogue like Senator Bilbo. No one could applaud the exquisite work of the Ballet at the Bolshoi Theater louder and longer than Comrade Stalin, but his appreciation of the arts did not stand in the way of the most utter ruthlessness. To equate sane and beneficent government with *haut culture* is to open a magic casement upon a scene that has no real basis in man's experience.

To imply that there is some kind of mysterious compact on the part of the executives of our television networks, large book publishers, cinema studios, *et al.,* to mongrelize the sensibilities of the mass of Americans, is not only a canard but logically untrue. Admittedly, the media are Big Business, and they must show profits at the end of the fiscal year in order to stay in business. Yet the facts are in plain view that on March 11, 1956, the National Broadcasting Company invested $500,000 to present a three-hour-long première of Sir Laurence Olivier's *Richard III*. This production, which drama critics have extolled in highest terms, was viewed by the largest daytime audience in television's history. Trendex surveys indicated that more than 50 million people watched some part of what is surely not one of Shakespeare's better-known plays. Conservative estimates place the number of viewers who stayed with the intrigues of the last of the Plantagenets throughout the three plot-laden hours at 20 to 25 million. The reassuring success of the venture will probably encourage the network to offer more entertainment of this caliber.

Television is capable of contributing its share to the best in our popular arts, as seen clearly in the Academy-Award-winning movie, *Marty*, originally a television play. That its author, Paddy Chayevsky, should go from television to the legitimate theater of New York, where his successful drama was staged by Joshua Logan, is but another example of the mobility of an artist who has something worthwhile to say, no matter the medium.

Surely there is a great deal that is mediocre, repetitious and patronizing in television, or the movies. Yet in closing their eyes to the significant contributions of the mass media, the detractors encourage the very banality they purport to despise. For example, it is not difficult for them to look down their noses at the phenomenally successful *Life*, with its emphasis on photo-journalism. But not to take heed when *Life* presents a superb series, such as *The World We Live In*, or when it gives its several million readers the initial publication of Hemingway's *Old Man and The Sea*, is to invite the media to lose respect for the good things they themselves try to do. To lionize Tennessee Williams when the *Rose Tattoo* is available to the relatively few who attend its stage presentations but ignore it when he writes the same story into a movie of rich comic force, is to invite the cinema industry to cater to the lowest elements within itself rather than the best.

In the grim Orwellian world of 1984 which the critics of the mass society prophesy for us (if we continue to opiate ourselves with the mass media) there will be little reading done. By then we shall have gone through 3-D television, smellevision and on to Huxley's feelevision. Yet an interested party on the side of good reading, Bennett Cerf, the publisher of Random House, recently had this to say:

Television apparently has not been the destructive ogre that publishers feared so short a time ago. But then publishers always have been expecting *something* to end the practice of reading in America. Fifty years ago, believe it or not, a publisher seriously announced that so many devil-may-care citizens were risking life and limb on *interurban trolley cars* that they had no more time to peruse a book! Then came the menace of the tandem bicycle, followed in turn, by cheap automobiles, the movies, and radio. The fact is, of course, that nothing can replace a really good book.

Very well, the book publishing business has never had a better year than 1955, but what about the youngsters who spend innumerable hours watching television? Dr. Robert Goldenson, a psychology professor at Hunter College reports:

> Instead of the adverse effect they feared, librarians and teachers report that the cultural values communicated by children's television programs are responsible for much wider exploration of the world of books by children than in pre-television days.

In 1955 youngsters set a record for borrowing books from public libraries, and much of this is due to their desire to delve more and more into literature dealing with exploration, general science, space travel and life in other countries. Professor Goldenson adds "the youngsters are often far ahead of many producers who think all that children want is blood and thunder." Children will, of course, watch what the programmers give them. But if every program of violence (and let the behavioral scientist define what is deleterious) were taken off the air tomorrow, there wouldn't be enough protest to give an agency man a heartburn.

In the minds of certain critics of mass culture the people will invariably choose the mediocre and the meretricious. This mixture of noblese oblige and polite contempt for anyone outside of university circles, or avant-garde literary groups, seems to me just as authoritarian as the anti-intellectualism that the "masses" direct against the scholastics.

One gets the impression that those who find the mass media anathema would feel more secure if we could go back to a period that had no radios or television sets, no motion pictures, an era in which books were the possessions of the few and the newspapers were priced beyond the means of all but the élite whose class interests were catered to. Short of going back to this pre-media era, which is palpably impossible, they would remove from the "average" man's leisure anything that didn't meet their self-styled standards of high culture. If the "average" man is not quite ready to accept the best that art and literature have to offer him (and again I ask, in what period has he?) these critics turn their anger on the media.

Yet it is just these mass media that hold out the greatest promise to the "average" man that a cultural richness no previous age could give him is at hand. If television (or the other media) provided only a diet of the tried and true stereotyped programs, that is, allowed the majority taste to mandate every choice, then I would agree with these critics in their fear for the future. But the variety and quality of what is available to *national* audiences show this is not the case.

Take, for example, the offerings of the television networks on Sunday, March 18, 1956, a Sunday which I chose at random. The televiewer would have been able to see on this day a discussion of the times and works of Toulouse-Lautrec by three prominent art critics; an inspiring interview with Dr. Paul Tillich, the noted theologian; a sensitive adaptation of Walter von Tilburg Clark's "Hook," a story of a hawk's life; a powerful documentary on mental illness with Orson Welles and Dr. William Menninger; an interview with the Secretary of Health, Welfare and Education; an interview with the Governor of Minnesota on the eve of the primary elections in his state; an hour and a half performance of *Taming of the Shrew* in color with Maurice Evans and Lilli Palmer.

While the above may not be of same cultural status as the works of Kant or the music of Bartok, it's a pretty substantial diet—certainly not pap. Very well, reply the detractors, so there is a modicum of cultural programs available on Sunday. How do you know that people look at them? This can be answered in two ways: (1) Most of these programs are in a series, some sponsored and others maintained year after year by the networks. If they were not being watched they would have been replaced. (2) This is not a fair question. Nobody can force anyone to watch anything that does not interest him, except in a totalitarian state in which one watches or else! The important thing is that the networks *offer* these programs for those who do wish to watch. It is not the network's or anyone else's duty, to create the publics who will watch these programs.

To be sure, the editing and abridgment of Shakespeare's *Taming of the Shrew* to the hour-and-a-half period might be considered a watered down version of the sacred text by some. But Shakespeare himself was a player who had as good an eye on the house as on posterity. The skillful elimination of some of the tedious subplots by Mr. Evans (surely one of the great modern interpreters of Shakespeare) not only increased the pace of the play but made it more understandable.

There are dedicated groups of people in this country who instead of damning the media blanketly do something about improving what they dislike. Typical of such groups is the National Citizens' Committee for Educational Television, who have done more than cry about the low level of American culture. It is significant to note that by the end of 1956 there will be twenty-six educational television stations on the air. The eighteen stations now in operation are programming 340 hours weekly to a potential audience of 40 million. The new stations will bring an additional seven million viewers within the educational TV orbit. According to a recent survey by the Committee, 57 per cent of the programs were live and locally produced, the remainder were kinescopes and film. Through this medium many courses are being offered, the most popular of which are history and languages, with music appreciation high on the list.

An outstanding example of an educational television station in operation is WQED in Pittsburgh, which is on the air sixty-seven and a half hours a week. Recently one of its programs, the "Children's Corner," was signed for a three-year National Broadcasting contract. The commercial networks are watching the efforts of their educational confreres with more and more interest. It was also from WQED that Dr. Benjamin Spock, the well-known children's specialist, went to a network show on the National Broadcasting Company. As educational television networks develop throughout the states there will be few communities in America where the audiences do not have their choice any evening between Berle or Bach, Godfrey or Goya, the *$64,000 Question* or a discussion of Thucydides' historical method.

But to get back to books. As Clifton Fadiman pointed out recently, we are in the midst of a reprint revolution that may be the greatest boon since Gutenberg. This revolution, which started in 1939 when Pocket Books experimented with twenty-five cent reprints, saw 300 million paperbound books printed last year! Since 1939 we've consumed about two billion copies.

The encouraging aspect of the paperbound books is that the quality of the titles is constantly improving. Whereas a few years ago the first association that came to one's mind was Mickey Spillane, today one thinks of the very successful *Anchor* books published by Doubleday, Harcourt Brace's *Harvest* books, Knopf's *Vintage* books, the Beacon Press paperbacks, Penguin books, to mention only a few. There appears to be a very substantial public for these modestly priced reprints of works by Tocqueville, Ernst Cassirer, Stendhal. Take, for example, Saul Bellow's novel *Augie March*. Although it won the National Book Award in 1954, its trade edition sold only a moderate number of copies. In its paperbound edition, Bellow's novel has sold more than a million copies.

One further area we might look into before we call America a cultural wasteland is serious music. In the special fiftieth anniversary edition of *Variety*, which might appear to some as a most unlikely publication to present facts and figures about "longhair" art, Arthur Bronson has compiled some extremely significant data. In the fifty-year period covered by *Variety's* life serious musical expression has made extraordinary progress. Where in 1905 opera was the province of the few, today the listening audience of the Metropolitan Opera's Saturday afternoon broadcast alone is 15 million. To contrast with the half-dozen major symphony orchestras of a half-century ago, today we have thirty-two American symphonies. Ballet, which virtually was unknown in this country fifty years ago, now has three major American companies.

But, rejoins the detractor of American mass culture, what about the small cities? True, there may be four radio stations in Boston that broadcast a combined thirty to thirty-five hours *daily* of the finest classical music, but what about the hinterland? The answer to that is partly to be found in the fact that in 1940 there were 1,000 towns in this country offering concert series. Today there are some 2,500. As the sale of recordings of serious music by our symphony orchestras and noted artists have continued to grow, almost in direct correlation we have seen a growth in concert series. The two events are not without a causal relationship.

Since 1920 more than 20 million recordings of Arturo Toscanini alone have been sold, nor is it without significance that since 1903 when the first recordings were made of Mozart's work, more than 60 million records of his music have been sold.

Where 1916 saw the renowned Diaghilev ballet with Nijinsky come to America and cost its backers about $400,000, by 1954 the Sadler's Wells company of London arrived here and in twenty weeks of a national tour earned more than $2,500,000. More noteworthy, perhaps, is that the National Broadcasting Company on December 12, 1955, presented the Sadler's Wells ballet with Margot Fonteyn in an hour-and-a-half performance of Tchaikovsky's *Sleeping Beauty*. With the kind of courage that puts the lie to the adage that the giants of the mass media are afraid to buck the stereotype of the "thirteen-year-old mind," Producers' Showcase matched Fonteyn and company against CBS' Burns and Allen, Arthur Godfrey and *I Love Lucy* on the intensely competitive Monday night hours.

Millions of Americans were introduced to ballet for the first time that evening, but to me the significant factor is that they were provided with the opportunity to choose between Godfrey and the Sadler's Wells. If, as was the case, Godfrey's Talent Scouts program retained a higher audience rating, this is no cause to despair and decry the low tastes of the American people. Rather, such programs as Richard III, the Sadler's Wells ballet, Omnibus and scores more give me confidence that the media, as they, too, grow in stature and understanding, will offer more and more substantial fare.

Perhaps it is an invidious comparison to point out that in 1955 about 35 million people paid to attend classical music events as against the 15 million who attended baseball games. But it is no *non sequitur* to note that the 1955 attendance at serious music events is about double that of 1940.

That the performance of symphonic music is not restricted to larger cities may be seen when in the last dozen years orchestras have sprung up in such places as Phoenix, Arizona, San Jose, California, Great Falls, Montana, and even the atomic town of Oak Ridge, Tennessee. The 200 symphony orchestras in this country (80 per cent more than fifteen years ago and ten times as many as in the early 1920's) indicate a musical awareness such as we have never known.

Surely no one will claim that all (if any) of our small-town symphonies have the musicianship of a Boston, Philadelphia or St. Louis orchestra, but the members of these groups are donating their musical services free for the most part. In the city of Peoria, Illinois, for example, where I once lived, it was stimulating to be part of an orchestra where one colleague in the string section was a prominent attorney, another a chemistry professor and perhaps a third the owner of a small but profitable dry goods store. The strains of the Franck *D minor* symphony were meaningful to each of the citizen-musicians.

Mass culture in America. If I have presented a hopeful picture of our future as we go into the era of extended leisure that Americans will share in the next decade or two, it is because I see substantial amelioration in the uses of our mass media. There has been such a rehearsal of all that is ugly and bathetic in our popular arts by critics whose sincerity cannot be questioned that it is time that the other side of the coin be examined.

Some Effects of Mass Media

C. Wright Mills

Early observers believed that the increase in the range and volume of the formal means of communication would enlarge and animate the primary public. In such optimistic views—written before radio and television and movies—the formal media are understood as simply multiplying the scope and pace of personal discussion. Modern conditions, Charles Cooley wrote, "enlarge indefinitely the competition of ideas, and whatever has owed its persistence merely to lack of comparison is likely to go, for that which is really congenial to the choosing mind will be all the more cherished and increased." Still excited by the break-up of the conventional consensus of the local community, he saw the new means of communication as furthering the conversational dynamic of classic democracy, and with it the growth of rational and free individuality.

No one really knows all the functions of the mass media, for in their entirety these functions are probably so pervasive and so subtle that they cannot be caught by the means of social research now available. But we do now have reason to believe that these media have helped less to enlarge and animate the discussion of primary publics than to transform them into a set of media markets in mass-like society. I do not refer merely to the higher ratio of deliverers of opinion to receivers and to the decreased chance to answer back; nor do I refer merely to the violent banalization and stereotyping of our very sense organs in terms of which these media now compete for "attention." I have in mind a sort of psychological illiteracy that is facilitated by the media, and that is expressed in several ways:

I. Very little of what we think we know of the social realities of the world have we found out first-hand. Most of "the pictures in our heads" we have gained from these media—even to the point where we often do not really believe what we see before us until we read about it in the paper or hear about it on the radio. The media not only give us information; they guide our very experiences. Our standards of credulity, our standards of reality, tend to be set by these media rather than by our own fragmentary experience.

Accordingly, even if the individual has direct, personal experience of events, it is not really direct and primary: it is organized in stereotype. It takes long and skillful training to so uproot such stereotypes that an individual sees things freshly, in an unstereotyped manner. One might suppose, for example, that if all the people went through a depression they would all "experience it," and in terms of this experience, that they would all debunk or reject or at least refract what the media say about it. But experience of such a *structural* shift has to be organized and interpreted if it is to count in the making of opinion.

The kind of experience, in short, that might serve as a basis for resistance to mass media is not an experience of raw events, but the experience of meanings. The fleck of interpretation must be there in the experience if we are to use the word experience seriously. And the capacity for such experience is socially implanted. The individual does not trust his own experience, as I have said, until it is confirmed by others or by the media. Usually such direct exposure is not accepted if it disturbs loyalties and beliefs that the individual already holds. To be accepted, it must relieve or justify the feelings that often lie in the back of his mind as key features of his ideological loyalties.

Stereotypes of loyalty underlie beliefs and feelings about given symbols and emblems; they are the very ways in which men see the social world and in terms of which men make up their specific opinions and views of events. They are the results of previous experience which affect present and future experience. It goes without saying that men are often unaware of these loyalties, that often they could not formulate them explicitly. Yet such general stereotypes make for the acceptance or the rejection of specific opinions not so much by the force of logical consistency as by their emotional affinity and by the way in which they relieve anxieties. To accept opinions in their terms is to gain the good solid feeling of being correct without having to think. When ideological stereotypes and specific opinions are linked in this way, there is a lowering of the kind of anxiety which arises when loyalty and belief are not in accord. Such ideologies lead to a willingness to accept a given line of belief; then there is no need, emotionally or rationally, to overcome resistance to given items in that line; cumulative selections of specific opinions and feelings become the pre-organized attitudes and emotions that shape the opinion-life of the person.

These deeper beliefs and feelings are a sort of lens through which men experience their worlds, they strongly condition acceptance or rejection of specific opinions, and they set men's orientation toward prevailing authorities. Three decades ago, Walter Lippmann saw such prior convictions as biases: they kept men from defining reality in an adequate way.

They are still biases. But today they can often be seen as "good biases"; inadequate and misleading as they often are, they are less so than the crackpot realism of the higher authorities and opinion-makers. They are the lower common sense and as such a factor of resistance. But we must recognize, especially when the pace of change is so deep and fast, that common sense is more often common than sense. And, above all, we must recognize that "the common sense" of our children is going to be less the result of any firm social tradition than of the stereotypes carried by the mass media to which they are now so fully exposed. They are the first generation to be so exposed.

II. So long as the media are not entirely monopolized, the individual can play one media off against another; he can compare them, and hence resist what any one of them puts out. The more genuine competition there is among the media, the more resistance the individual might be able to command. But how much is this now the case? *Do* people compare reports on public events or policies, playing one medium's content off against another's?

The answer is: generally no, very few do: (1) We know that people tend strongly to select those media which carry contents with which they already agree. There is a kind of selection of new opinions on the basis of prior opinions. No one seems to search out such counter-statements as may be found in alternative media offerings. Given radio programs and magazines and newspapers often get a rather consistent public, and thus reinforce their messages in the minds of that public. (2) This idea of playing one medium off against another assumes that the media really have varying contents. It assumes genuine competition, which is not widely true. The media display an apparent variety and competition, but on closer view they seem to compete more in terms of variations on a few standardized themes than of clashing issues. The freedom to raise issues effectively seems more and more to be confined to those few interests that have ready and continual access to these media.

III. The media have not only filtered into our experience of external realities, they have also entered into our very experience of our own selves. They have provided us with new identities and new aspirations of what we should like to be, and what we should like to appear to be. They have provided in the models of conduct they hold out to us a new and larger and more flexible set of appraisals of our very selves. In terms of the modern theory of the self, we may say that the media bring the reader, listener, viewer into the sight of larger, higher reference groups—groups, real or imagined, up-close or vicarious, personally known or distractedly glimpsed—which are looking glasses for his self-image. They have multiplied the groups to which we look for confirmation of our self-image.

More than that: (1) the media tell the man in the mass who he is—they give him identity; (2) they tell him what he wants to be—they give him aspirations; (3) they tell him how to get that way—they give him technique; and (4) they tell him how to feel that he is that way even when he is not—they give him escape. The gaps between the identity and aspiration lead to technique and/or to escape. That is probably the basic psychological formula of the mass media today. But, as a formula, it is not attuned to the development of the human being. It is the formula of a pseudo-world which the media invent and sustain.

IV. As they now generally prevail, the mass media, especially television, often encroach upon the small-scale discussion, and destroy the chance for the reasonable and leisurely and human interchange of opinion. They are an important cause of the destruction of privacy in its full human meaning. That is an important reason why they not only fail as an educational force, but are a malign force: they do not articulate for the viewer or listener the broader sources of his private tensions and anxieties, his inarticulate resentments and half-formed hopes. They neither enable the individual to transcend his narrow milieu nor clarify its private meaning. . . .

The New Languages

Edmund Carpenter

Brain of the New World,
What a task is thine,
To formulate the modern
. . . to recast poems, churches, art

WHITMAN

English is a mass medium. All languages are mass media. The new mass media—film, radio, TV—are new languages, their grammars as yet unknown. Each codifies reality differently; each conceals a unique metaphysics. Linguists tell us it's possible to say anything in any language if you use enough words or images, but there's rarely time; the natural course is for a culture to exploit its media biases.

Writing, for example, didn't record oral language; it was a new language, which the spoken word came to imitate. Writing encouraged an analytical mode of thinking with emphasis upon lineality. Oral languages tended to be polysynthetic, composed of great, tight conglomerates, like twisted knots, within which images were juxaposed, inseparably fused; written communications consisted of little words chronologically ordered. Subject became distinct from verb, adjective from noun, thus separating actor from action, essence from form. Where preliterate man imposed form diffidently, temporarily—for such transitory forms lived but temporarily on the tip of his tongue, in the living situation—the printed word was inflexible, permanent, in touch with eternity: it embalmed truth for posterity.

This embalming process froze language, eliminated the art of ambiguity, made puns "the lowest form of wit," destroyed word linkages. The word became a static symbol, applicable to and separate from that which it symbolized. It now belonged to the objective world; it could be seen. Now came the distinction between being and meaning, the dispute as to whether the Eucharist *was* or only *signified* the body of the Sacrifice. The word became a neutral symbol, no longer an inextricable part of a creative process.

Gutenberg completed the process. The manuscript page with pictures, colors, correlation between symbol and space, gave way to uniform type, the black-and-white page, read silently, alone. The format of the book favored lineal expression, for the argument ran like a thread from cover to cover: subject to verb to object, sentence to sentence, paragraph to paragraph, chapter to chapter, carefully structured from beginning to end, with value embedded in the climax. This was not true of great poetry and drama, which retained multi-perspective, but it was true of most books, particularly texts, histories, autobiographies, novels. Events were arranged chronologically and hence, it was assumed, causally; relationship, not being, was valued. The author became an *authority;* his data were serious, that is, *serially* organized. Such data, if sequentially ordered and printed, conveyed value and truth; arranged any other way, they were suspect.

The newspaper format brought an end to book culture. It offers short, discrete articles that give important facts first and then taper off to incidental details, which may be, and often are, eliminated by the make-up man. The fact that reporters cannot control the length of their articles means that, in writing them, emphasis can't be placed on structure, at least in the traditional linear sense, with climax or conclusion at the end. Everything has to be captured in the headline; from there it goes down the pyramid to incidentals. In fact there is often more in the headline than in the article; occasionally, no article at all accompanies the banner headline.

The position and size of articles on the front page are determined by interest and importance, not content. Unrelated reports from Moscow, Sarawak, London, and Ittipik are juxtaposed; time and space, as separate concepts, are destroyed and the *here* and *now* presented as a single Gestalt. Subway readers consume everything on the front page, then turn to page 2 to read, in incidental order, continuations. A Toronto banner headline ran: TOWNSEND TO MARRY PRINCESS; directly beneath this was a second headline: *Fabian Says This May Not Be Sex Crime*. This went unnoticed by eyes and minds conditioned to consider each newspaper item in isolation.

Such a format lends itself to simultaneity, not chronology or lineality. Items abstracted from a total situation aren't arranged in casual sequence, but presented holistically, as raw experience. The front page is a cosmic *Finnegans Wake*.

The disorder of the newspaper throws the reader into a producer role. The reader has to process the news himself; he has to co-create, to cooperate in the creation of the work. The newspaper format calls for the direct participation of the consumer.

In magazines, where a writer more frequently controls the length of his article, he can, if he wishes, organize it in traditional style, but the majority don't. An increasingly popular presentation is the printed symposium, which is little more than collected opinions, pro and con. The magazine format as a whole opposes lineality; its pictures lack tenses. In *Life*, extremes are juxtaposed: space ships and prehistoric monsters, Flemish monasteries and dope addicts. It creates a sense of urgency and uncertainty: the next page is unpredictable. One encounters rapidly a riot in Teheran, a Hollywood marriage, the wonders of the Eisenhower administration, a two-headed calf, a party on Jones beach, all sandwiched between ads. The eye takes in the page as a whole (readers may pretend this isn't so, but the success of advertising suggests it is), and the page—indeed, the whole magazine—becomes a single Gestalt where association, though not causal, is often lifelike.

The same is true of the other new languages. Both radio and TV offer short, unrelated programs, interrupted between and within by commercials. I say "interrupted," being myself an anachronism of book culture, but my children don't regard them as interruptions, as breaking continuity. Rather, they regard them as part of a whole, and their reaction is neither one of annoyance nor one of indifference. The ideal news broadcast has half a dozen speakers from as many parts of the world on as many subjects. The London correspondent doesn't comment on what the Washington correspondent has just said; he hasn't even heard him.

The child is right in not regarding commercials as interruptions. For the only time anyone smiles on TV is in commercials. The rest of life, in news broadcasts and soap operas, is presented as so horrible that the only way to get through life is to buy this product: then you'll smile. Aesop never wrote a clearer fable. It's heaven and hell brought up to date: Hell in the headline, Heaven in the ad. Without the other, neither has meaning.

There's pattern in these new media—not line, but knot; not lineality or causality or chronology, nothing that leads to a desired climax; but a Gordian knot without antecedents or results, containing within itself carefully selected elements, juxtaposed, inseparably fused; a knot that can't be united to give the long, thin cord of lineality.

This is especially true of ads that never present an ordered, sequential, rational argument but simply present the product associated with desirable things or attitudes. Thus Coca-Cola is shown held by a beautiful blonde, who sits in a Cadillac, surrounded by bronze, muscular admirers, with the sun shining overhead. By repetition these elements become associated, in our minds, into a pattern of sufficient cohesion so that one element can magically evoke the others. If we think of ads as designed solely to sell products, we miss their main effect: to increase pleasure in the consumption of the product. Coca-Cola is far more than a cooling drink; the consumer participates, vicariously, in a much larger experience. In Africa, in Melanesia, to drink a Coke is to participate in the American way of life.

Of the new languages, TV comes closest to drama and ritual. It combines music and art, language and gesture, rhetoric and color. It favors simultaneity of visual and auditory images. Cameras focus not on speakers but on persons spoken to or about; the audience *hears* the accuser but *watches* the accused. In a single impression it hears the prosecutor, watches the trembling hands of the big-town crook, and sees the look of moral indignation on Senator Tobey's face. This is real drama, in process, with the outcome uncertain. Print can't do this; it has a different bias.

Books and movies only pretend uncertainty, but live TV retains this vital aspect of life. Seen on TV, the fire in the 1952 Democratic Convention threatened briefly to become a conflagration; seen on newsreel, it was history, without potentiality.

The absence of uncertainty is no handicap to other media, if they are properly used, for their biases are different. Thus it's clear from the beginning that Hamlet is a doomed man, but, far from detracting in interest, this heightens the sense of tragedy.

Now, one of the results of the time-space duality that developed in Western culture, principally from the Renaissance on, was a separation within the arts. Music, which created symbols in time, and graphic art, which created symbols in space, became separate pursuits, and men gifted in one rarely pursued the other. Dance and ritual, which inherently combined them, fell in popularity. Only in drama did they remain united.

It is significant that of the four new media, the three most recent are dramatic media, particularly TV, which combines language, music, art, dance. They don't, however, exercise the same freedom with time that the stage dares practice. An intricate plot, employing flash backs, multiple time perspectives and overlays, intelligible on the stage, would mystify on the screen. The audience has no time to think back, to establish relations between early hints and subsequent discoveries. The picture passes before the eyes too quickly; there are no intervals in which to take stock of what has happened and make conjectures of what is going to happen. The observer is in a more passive state, less interested in subtleties. Both TV and film are nearer to narrative and depend much more upon the episodic. An intricate time construction can be done in film, but in fact rarely is. The soliloquies of *Richard III* belong on the stage; the film audience was unprepared for them. On stage Ophelia's death was described by three separate groups: one hears the announcement and watches the reactions simultaneously. On film the camera flatly shows her drowned where "a willow lies aslant a brook."

Media differences such as these mean that it's not simply a question of communicating a single idea in different ways but that a given idea or insight belongs primarily, though not exclusively, to one medium, and can be gained or communicated best through that medium.

Thus the book was ideally suited for discussing evolution and progress. Both belonged, almost exclusively, to book culture. Like a book, the idea of progress was an abstracting, organizing principle for the interpretation and comprehension of the incredibly complicated record of human experience. The sequence of events was believed to have a direction, to follow a given course along an axis of time; it was held that civilization, like the reader's eye (in J. B. Bury's words), "has moved, is moving, and will move in a desirable direction. Knowledge will advance, and with that advance, reason and decency must increasingly prevail among men." Here we see the three main elements of book lineality: the line, the point moving along that line, and its movement toward a desirable goal.

The Western conception of a definite moment in the present, of the present as a definite moment or a definite point, so important in book-dominated languages, is absent, to my knowledge, in oral languages. Absent as well, in oral societies, are such animating and controlling ideas as Western individualism and three-dimensional perspective, both related to this conception of the definite moment, and both nourished, probably bred, by book culture.

Each medium selects its ideas. TV is a tiny box into which people are crowded and must live; film gives us the wide world. With its huge screen, film is perfectly suited for social drama, Civil War panoramas, the sea, land erosion, Cecil B. DeMille spectaculars. In contrast, the TV screen has room for two, at the most three, faces, comfortably. TV is closer to stage, yet different. Paddy Chayefsky writes:

> The theatre audience is far away from the actual action of the drama. They cannot see the silent reactions of the players. They must be told in a loud voice what is going on. The plot movement from one scene to another must be marked, rather than gently shaded as is required in television. In television, however, you can dig into the most humble, ordinary relationships; the relationship of bourgeois children to their mother, of middle-class husband to his wife, of white-collar father to his secretary—in short, the relationships of the people. We relate to each other in an incredibly complicated manner. There is far more exciting drama in the reasons why a man gets married than in why he murders someone. The man who is unhappy in his job, the wife who thinks of a lover, the girl who wants to get into television, your father, your mother, sister, brothers, cousins, friends—all these are better subjects for drama than Iago. What makes a man ambitious? Why does a girl always try to steal her kid sister's boy friends? Why does your uncle attend his annual class reunion faithfully every year? Why do you always find it depressing to visit your father? These are the substances of good television drama; and the deeper you probe into and examine the twisted, semi-formed complexes of emotional entanglements, the more exciting your writing becomes.[1]

This is the primary reason, I believe, why Greek drama is more readily adapted to TV than to film. The boxed-in quality of live TV lends itself to static literary tragedy with greater ease than does the elastic, energetic, expandable movie. Guthrie's recent movie of *Oedipus* favored the panoramic shot rather than the selective eye. It consisted of a succession of tableaux, a series of elaborate, unnatural poses. The effect was of congested groups of people moving in tight formation as though they had

[1] *Television Plays*, New York, Simon and Schuster, 1955, pp. 176–78.

trained for it by living for days together in a self-service elevator. With the lines, "I grieve for the City, and for myself and you . . . and walk through endless ways of thought," the inexorable tragedy moved to its horrible "come to realize" climax as though everyone were stepping on everyone else's feet.

The tight, necessary conventions of live TV were more sympathetic to Sophocles in the Aluminium Hour's *Antigone*. Restrictions of space are imposed on TV as on the Greek stage by the size and inflexibility of the studio. Squeezed by physical limitations, the producer was forced to expand the viewer's imagination with ingenious devices.

When T. S. Eliot adapted *Murder in the Cathedral* for film, he noted a difference in realism between cinema and stage:

> Cinema, even where fantasy is introduced, is much more realistic than the stage. Especially in an historical picture, the setting, the costume, and the way of life represented have to be accurate. Even a minor anachronism is intolerable. On the stage much more can be overlooked or forgiven; and indeed, an excessive care for accuracy of historical detail can become burdensome and distracting. In watching a stage performance, the member of the audience is in direct contact with the actor playing a part. In looking at a film, we are much more passive; as audience, we contribute less. We are seized with the illusion that we are observing an actual event, or at least a series of photographs of the actual event; and nothing must be allowed to break this illusion. Hence the precise attention to detail.[2]

If two men are on a stage in a theatre, the dramatist is obliged to motivate their presence; he has to account for their existing on the stage at all. Whereas if a camera is following a figure down a street or is turned to any object whatever, there is no need for a reason to be provided. Its grammar contains that power of statement of motivation, no matter what it looks at.

In the theatre, the spectator sees the enacted scene as a whole in space, always seeing the whole of the space. The stage may present only one corner of a large hall, but that corner is always totally visible all through the scene. And the spectator always sees that scene from a fixed, unchanging distance and from an angle of vision that doesn't change. Perspective may change from scene to scene, but within one scene it remains constant. Distance never varies.

But in film and TV, distance and angle constantly shift. The same

2 George Hoellering and T. S. Eliot, *Film of Murder in the Cathedral*, New York, Harcourt, Brace & World, 1952, p. vi; London, Faber & Faber, 1952.

scene is shown in multiple perspective and focus. The viewer sees it from here, there, then over here; finally he is drawn inexorably into it, becomes part of it. He ceases to be a spectator. Balázs writes:

> Although we sit in our seats, we do not see Romeo and Juliet from there. We look up into Juliet's balcony with Romeo's eyes and look down on Romeo with Juliet's. Our eye and with it our consciousness is identified with the characters in the film, we look at the world out of their eyes and have no angle of vision of our own. We walk amid crowds, ride, fly or fall with the hero and if one character looks into the other's eyes, he looks into our eyes from the screen, for, our eyes are in the camera and become identical with the gaze of the characters. They see with our eyes. Herein lies the psychological act of identification. Nothing like this "identification" has ever occurred as the effect of any other system of art and it is here that the film manifests its absolute artistic novelty.
>
> . . . Not only can we see, in the isolated "shots" of a scene, the very atoms of life and their innermost secrets revealed at close quarters, but we can do so without any of the intimate secrecy being lost, as always happens in the exposure of a stage performance or of a painting. The new theme which the new means of expression of film art revealed was not a hurricane at sea or the eruption of a volcano: it was perhaps a solitary tear slowly welling up in the corner of a human eye.
>
> . . . Not to speak does not mean that one has nothing to say. Those who do not speak may be brimming over with emotions which can be expressed only in forms and pictures, in gesture and play of feature. The man of visual culture uses these not as substitutes for words, as a deaf-mute uses his fingers.[3]

The gestures of visual man are not intended to convey concepts that can be expressed in words, but inner experiences, nonrational emotions, which would still remain unexpressed when everything that can be told has been told. Such emotions lie in the deepest levels. They cannot be approached by words that are mere reflections of concepts, any more than musical experiences can be expressed in rational concepts. Facial expression is a human experienced rendered immediately visible without the intermediary of word. It is Turgenev's "living truth of the human face."

Printing rendered illegible the faces of men. So much could be read from paper that the method of conveying meaning by facial expression fell into desuetude. The press grew to be the main bridge over which the more remote interhuman spiritual exchanges took place; the immediate, the personal, the inner, died. There was no longer need for the subtler

[3] Béla Balázs, *Theory of Film*, New York, Roy Publishers, 1953, pp. 48, 31, 40; London, Denis Dobson, 1952.

means of expression provided by the body. The face became immobile; the inner life, still. Wells that dry up are wells from which no water is dipped.

Just as radio helped bring back inflection in speech, so film and TV are aiding us in the recovery of gesture and facial awareness—a rich, colorful language, conveying moods and emotions, happenings and characters, even thoughts, none of which could be properly packaged in words. If film had remained silent for another decade, how much faster this change might have been!

Feeding the product of one medium through another medium creates a new product. When Hollywood buys a novel, it buys a title and the publicity associated with it: nothing more. Nor should it.

Each of the four versions of the *Caine Mutiny*—book, play, movie, TV—had a different hero: Willie Keith, the lawyer Greenwald, the United States Navy, and Captain Queeg, respectively. Media and audience biases were clear. Thus the book told, in lengthy detail, of the growth and making of Ensign William Keith, American man, while the movie camera with its colorful shots of ships and sea, unconsciously favored the Navy as hero, a bias supported by the fact the Navy cooperated with the movie makers. Because of stage limitations, the play was confined, except for the last scene, to the courtroom, and favored the defense counsel as hero. The TV show, aimed at a mass audience, emphasized patriotism, authority, allegiance. More important, the cast was reduced to the principals and the plot to its principles; the real moral problem—the refusal of subordinates to assist an incompetent, unpopular superior—was clear, whereas in the book it was lost under detail, in the film under scenery. Finally, the New York play, with its audience slanted toward Expense Account patronage—Mr. Sampson, Western Sales Manager for the Cavity Drill Company—became a morality play with Willie Keith, innocent American youth, torn between two influences: Keefer, clever author but moral cripple, and Greenwald, equally brilliant but reliable, a businessman's intellectual. Greenwald saves Willie's soul.

The film *Moby Dick* was in many ways an improvement on the book, primarily because of its explicitness. For *Moby Dick* is one of those admittedly great classics, like *Robinson Crusoe* or Kafka's *Trial,* whose plot and situation, as distilled apart from the book by time and familiarity, are actually much more imposing than the written book itself. It's the drama of Ahab's defiance rather than Melville's uncharted leviathan meanderings that is the greatness of *Moby Dick*. On film, instead of laborious tacks through leagues of discursive interruptions, the most vivid descriptions of whales and whaling become part of the action. On

film, the viewer was constantly aboard ship: each scene an instantaneous
shot of whaling life, an effect achieved in the book only by illusion, by
constant, detailed reference. From start to finish, all the action of the
film served to develop what was most central to the theme—a man's
magnificent and blasphemous pride in attempting to destroy the brutal,
unreasoning force that maims him and turns man-made order into chaos.
Unlike the book, the film gave a spare, hard, compelling dramatization,
free of self-conscious symbolism.

Current confusion over the respective roles of the new media comes
largely from a misconception of their function. They are art forms, not
substitutes for human contact. Insofar as they attempt to usurp speech
and personal, living relations, they harm. This, of course, has long been
one of the problems of book culture, at least during the time of its
monopoly of Western middle-class thought. But this was never a legitimate function of books, nor of any other medium. Whenever a medium
goes claim jumping, trying to work areas where it is ill-suited, conflicts
occur with other media, or, more accurately, between the vested interests
controlling each. But, when media simply exploit their own formats,
they become complementary and cross-fertile.

Some people who have no one around talk to cats, and you can hear
their voices in the next room, and they sound silly, because the cat
won't answer, but that suffices to maintain the illusion that their world
is made up of living people, while it is not. Mechanized mass media reverse this: now mechanical cats talk to humans. There's no genuine feed-
back.

This charge is often leveled by academicians at the new media, but it
holds equally for print. The open-mouthed, glaze-eyed TV spectator is
merely the successor of the passive, silent, lonely reader whose head
moved back and forth like a shuttlecock.

When we read, another person thinks for us: we merely repeat his
mental process. The greater part of the work of thought is done for us.
This is why it relieves us to take up a book after being occupied by our
own thoughts. In reading, the mind is only the playground for another's
ideas. People who spend most of their lives in reading often lose the
capacity for thinking, just as those who always ride forget how to walk.
Some people read themselves stupid. Chaplin did a wonderful take-off of
this in City Lights, when he stood up on a chair to eat the endless con-
fetti that he mistook for spaghetti.

Eliot remarks: "It is often those writers whom we are lucky enough to
know whose books we can ignore; and the better we know them personally, the less need we may feel to read what they write."

Frank O'Connor highlights a basic distinction between oral and written traditions:

"By the hokies, there was a man in this place one time by name of Ned Sullivan, and he had a queer thing happen to him late one night and he coming up the Valley Road from Durlas." This is how a folk story begins, or should begin. . . . Yet that is how no printed short story should begin, because such a story seems tame when you remove it from its warm nest by the cottage fire, from the sense of an audience with its interjections and the feeling of terror at what may lurk in the darkness outside.

Face-to-face discourse is not as selective, abstract, nor explicit as any mechanical medium; it probably comes closer to communicating an unabridged situation than any of them, and, insofar as it exploits the give-take of dynamic relationship, it's clearly the most indispensable human one.

Of course, there can be personal involvement in the other media. When Richardson's *Pamela* was serialized in 1741, it aroused such interest that in one English town, upon receipt of the last installment, the church bell announced that virtue had been rewarded. Radio stations have reported receiving quantities of baby clothes and bassinets when, in a soap opera, a heroine had a baby. One of the commonest phrases used by devoted listeners to daytime serials is that they "visited with" Aunt Jenny or Big Sister. BBC and *News Chronicle* report cases of women viewers who kneel before TV sets to kiss male announcers good night.

Each medium, if its bias is properly exploited, reveals and communicates a unique aspect of reality, of truth. Each offers a different perspective, a way of seeing an otherwise hidden dimension of reality. It's not a question of one reality being true, the others distortions. One allows us to see from here, another from there, a third from still another perspective; taken together they give us a more complete whole, a greater truth. New essentials are brought to the fore, including those made invisible by the "blinders" of old languages.

This is why the preservation of book culture is as important as the development of TV. This is why new languages, instead of destroying old ones, serve as a stimulant to them. Only monopoly is destroyed. When actor-collector Edward G. Robinson was battling actor-collector Vincent Price on art on TV's *$64,000 Challenge,* he was asked how the quiz had affected his life; he answered petulantly, "Instead of looking at the pictures in my art books, I now have to read them." Print, along with all old languages, including speech, has profited enormously from the development of the new media. "The more the arts develop," writes E. M.

Forster, "the more they depend on each other for definition. We will borrow from painting first and call it pattern. Later we will borrow from music and call it rhythm." . . .

Media Hot and Cold

Marshall McLuhan

"The rise of the waltz," explained Curt Sachs in the *World History of the Dance,* "was a result of that longing for truth, simplicity, closeness to nature, and primitivism, which the last two-thirds of the eighteenth century fulfilled." In the century of jazz we are likely to overlook the emergence of the waltz as a hot and explosive human expression that broke through the formal feudal barriers of courtly and choral dance styles.

There is a basic principle that distinguishes a hot medium like radio from a cool one like the telephone, or a hot medium like the movie from a cool one like TV. A hot medium is one that extends one single sense in "high definition." High definition is the state of being well filled with data. A photograph is, visually, "high definition." A cartoon is "low definition," simply because very little visual information is provided. Telephone is a cool medium, or one of low definition, because the ear is given a meager amount of information. And speech is a cool medium of low definition, because so little is given and so much has to be filled in by the listener. On the other hand, hot media do not leave so much to be filled in or completed by the audience. Hot media are, therefore, low in participation, and cool media are high in participation or completion by the audience. Naturally, therefore, a hot medium like radio has very different effects on the user from a cool medium like the telephone.

A cool medium like hieroglyphic or ideogrammic written characters has very different effects from the hot and explosive medium of the phonetic alphabet. The alphabet, when pushed to a high degree of abstract visual intensity, became typography. The printed word with its specialist intensity burst the bonds of medieval corporate guilds and monasteries, creating extreme individualistic patterns of enterprise and monopoly. But the typical reversal occurred when extremes of monopoly brought back the corporation, with its impersonal empire over many lives. The hotting-up of the medium of writing to repeatable print intensity led to nationalism and the religious wars of the sixteenth century. The heavy and unwieldy media, such as stone, are time binders. Used for writing, they are very cool indeed, and serve to unify the ages; whereas paper is a hot medium that serves to unify spaces horizontally, both in political and entertainment empires.

Any hot medium allows of less participation than a cool one, as a lecture makes for less participation than a seminar, and a book for less than dialogue. With print many earlier forms were excluded from life and art, and many were given strange new intensity. But our own time is crowded with examples of the principle that the hot form excludes, and the cool one includes. When ballerinas began to dance on their toes a century ago, it was felt that the art of the ballet had acquired a new "spirituality." With this new intensity, male figures were excluded from ballet. The role of women had also become fragmented with the advent of industrial specialism and the explosion of home functions into laundries, bakeries, and hospitals on the periphery of the community. Intensity or high definition engenders specialism and fragmentation in living as in entertainment, which explains why any intense experience must be "forgotten," "censored," and reduced to a very cool state before it can be "learned" or assimilated. The Freudian "censor" is less of a moral function than an indispensable condition of learning. Were we to accept fully and directly every shock to our various structures of awareness, we would soon be nervous wrecks, doing double-takes and pressing panic buttons every minute. The "censor" protects our central system of values, as it does our physical nervous system by simply cooling off the onset of experience a great deal. For many people, this cooling system brings on a lifelong state of psychic *rigor mortis,* or of somnambulism, particularly observable in periods of new technology.

An example of the disruptive impact of a hot technology succeeding a cool one is given by Robert Theobald in *The Rich and the Poor.* When Australian natives were given steel axes by the missionaries, their culture, based on the stone axe, collapsed. The stone axe had not only been scarce but had always been a basic status symbol of male importance. The missionaries provided quantities of sharp steel axes and gave them to women and children. The men had even to borrow these from the women, caus-

ing a collapse of male dignity. A tribal and feudal hierarchy of traditional
kind collapses quickly when it meets any hot medium of the mechanical,
uniform, and repetitive kind. The medium of money or wheel or writing,
or any other form of specialist speedup of exchange and information,
will serve to fragment a tribal structure. Similarly, a very much greater
speed-up, such as occurs with electricity, may serve to restore a tribal
pattern of intense involvement such as took place with the introduction
of radio in Europe, and is now tending to happen as a result of TV in
America. Specialist technologies detribalize. The nonspecialist electric
technology retribalizes. The process of upset resulting from a new distribution of skills is accompanied by much culture lag in which people
feel compelled to look at new situations as if they were old ones, and
come up with ideas of "population explosion" in an age of implosion.
Newton, in an age of clocks, managed to present the physical universe
in the image of a clock. But poets like Blake were far ahead of Newton
in their response to the challenge of the clock. Blake spoke of the need
to be delivered "from single vision and Newton's sleep," knowing very
well that Newton's response to the challenge of the new mechanism was
itself merely a mechanical repetition of the challenge. Blake saw Newton
and Locke and others as hypnotized Narcissus types quite unable to meet
the challenge of mechanism. W. B. Yeats gave the full Blakean version
of Newton and Locke in a famous epigram:

> Locke sank into a swoon;
> The garden died;
> God took the spinning jenny
> Out of his side.[1]

Yeats presents Locke, the philosopher of mechanical and lineal associa-
tionism, as hypnotized by his own image. The "garden," or unified consciousness, ended. Eighteenth-century man got an extension of himself
in the form of the spinning machine that Yeats endows with its full sexual
significance. Woman, herself, is thus seen as a technological extension of
man's being.

Blake's counterstrategy for his age was to meet mechanism with organic
myth. Today, deep in the electric age, organic myth is itself a simple and
automatic response capable of mathematical formulation and expression,
without any of the imaginative perception of Blake about it. Had he
encountered the electric age, Blake would not have met its challenge

[1] Reprinted with permission of The Macmillan Company and A. P. Watt &
Son, London, from "Fragments" in *Collected Poems* by William Butler Yeats.
Copyright 1933 by The Macmillan Company, renewed 1961 by Bertha Georgie
Yeats.

with a mere repetition of electric form. For myth *is* the instant vision of a complex process that ordinarily extends over a long period. Myth is contraction or implosion of any process, and the instant speed of electricity confers the mythic dimension on ordinary industrial and social action today. We *live* mythically but continue to think fragmentarily and on single planes.

Scholars today are acutely aware of a discrepancy between their ways of treating subjects and the subject itself. Scriptural scholars of both the Old and New Testaments frequently say that while their treatment must be linear, the subject is not. The subject treats of the relations between God and man, and between God and the world, and of the relations between man and his neighbor—all these subsist together, and act and react upon one another at the same time. The Hebrew and Eastern mode of thought tackles problem and resolution, at the outset of a discussion, in a way typical of oral societies in general. The entire message is then traced and retraced, again and again, on the rounds of a concentric spiral with seeming redundancy. One can stop anywhere after the first few sentences and have the full message, if one is prepared to "dig" it. This kind of plan seems to have inspired Frank Lloyd Wright in designing the Guggenheim Art Gallery on a spiral, concentric basis. It is a redundant form inevitable to the electric age, in which the concentric pattern is imposed by the instant quality, and overlay in depth, of electric speed. But the concentric with its endless intersection of planes is necessary for insight. In fact, it is the technique of insight, and as such is necessary for media study, since no medium has its meaning or existence alone, but only in constant interplay with other media.

The new electric structuring and configuring of life more and more encounters the old lineal and fragmentary procedures and tools of analysis from the mechanical age. More and more we turn from the content of messages to study total effect. Kenneth Boulding put this matter in *The Image* by saying, "The meaning of a message is the change which it produces in the image." Concern with *effect* rather than *meaning* is a basic change of our electric time, for effect involves the total situation, and not a single level of information movement. Strangely, there is recognition of this matter of effect rather than information in the British idea of libel: "The greater the truth, the greater the libel."

The effect of electric technology had at first been anxiety. Now it appears to create boredom. We have been through the three stages of alarm, resistance and exhaustion that occur in every disease or stress of life, whether individual or collective. At least, our exhausted slump after the first encounter with the electric has inclined us to expect new problems. However, backward countries that have experienced little permeation with our own mechanical and specialist culture are much better able to confront and to understand electric technology. Not only have backward and nonindustrial cultures no specialist habits to overcome in their encounter with electromagnetism, but they have still much of their traditional oral culture that has the total, unified "field" character of our new electromagnetism. Our old industrialized areas, having eroded their oral traditions automatically, are in the position of having to rediscover them in order to cope with the electric age.

In terms of the theme of media hot and cold, backward countries are cool, and we are hot. The "city slicker" is hot, and the rustic is cool. But in terms of the reversal of procedures and values in the electric age, the past mechanical time was hot, and we of the TV age are cool. The waltz was a hot, fast mechanical dance suited to the industrial time in its moods of pomp and circumstance. In contrast, the Twist is a cool, involved and chatty form of improvised gesture. The jazz of the period of the hot new media of movie and radio was hot jazz. Yet jazz of itself tends to be a casual dialogue form of dance quite lacking in the repetitive and mechanical forms of the waltz. Cool jazz came in quite naturally after the first impact of radio and movie had been absorbed.

In the special Russian issue of *Life* magazine for September 13, 1963, it is mentioned that in Russian restaurants and night clubs, "though the Charleston is tolerated, the Twist is taboo." All this is to say that a country in the process of industrialization is inclined to regard hot jazz as consistent with its developing programs. The cool and involved form of the Twist, on the other hand, would strike such a culture at once as retrograde and incompatible with its new mechanical stress. The Charleston, with its aspect of a mechanical doll agitated by strings, appears in Russia as an avant-garde form. We, on the other hand, find the *avant-garde* in the cool and the primitive, with its promise of depth involvement and integral expression.

The "hard" sell and the "hot" line become mere comedy in the TV age, and the death of all the salesmen at one stroke of the TV axe has turned the hot American culture into a cool one that is quite unacquainted with itself. America, in fact, would seem to be living through the reverse process that Margaret Mead described in *Time* magazine (September 4, 1954):

> There are too many complaints about society having to move too fast to keep up with the machine. There is great advantage in moving fast if you move completely, if social, educational, and recreational changes keep pace. You must change the whole pattern at once and the whole group together— and the people themselves must decide to move.

Margaret Mead is thinking here of change as uniform speed-up of motion or a uniform hotting-up of temperatures in backward societies. We are certainly coming within conceivable range of a world automatically controlled to the point where we could say, "Six hours less radio in Indonesia next week or there will be a great falling off in literary attention." Or, "We can program twenty more hours of TV in South Africa next week to cool down the tribal temperature raised by radio last week." Whole cultures could now be programmed to keep their emotional climate stable in the same way that we have begun to know something about maintaining equilibrium in the commercial economies of the world.

In the merely personal and private sphere we are often reminded of how changes of tone and attitude are demanded of different times and seasons in order to keep situations in hand. British clubmen, for the sake of companionship and amiability, have long excluded the hot topics of religion and politics from mention inside the highly participational club. In the same vein, W. H. Auden wrote, ". . . this season the man of goodwill will wear his heart up his sleeve, not on it. . . . the honest manly style is today suited only to Iago" (Introduction to John Betjeman's *Slick But Not Streamlined*). In the Renaissance, as print technology hotted up the social *milieu* to a very high point, the gentleman and the courtier (Hamlet–Mercutio style) adopted, in contrast, the casual and cool nonchalance of the playful and superior being. The Iago allusion of Auden reminds us that Iago was the *alter ego* and assistant of the intensely earnest and very non-nonchalant General Othello. In imitation of the earnest and forthright general, Iago hotted up his own image and wore his heart on his sleeve, until General Othello read him loud and clear as "honest Iago," a man after his own grimly earnest heart.

Throughout *The City in History*, Lewis Mumford favors the cool or casually structured towns over the hot and intensely filled-in cities. The great period of Athens, he feels, was one during which most of the democratic habits of village life and participation still obtained. Then burst forth the full variety of human expression and exploration such as was later impossible in highly developed urban centers. For the highly developed situation is, by definition, low in opportunities of participation, and rigorous in its demands of specialist fragmentation from those who would control it. For example, what is known as "job enlargement" today in business and in management consists in allowing the employee more freedom to discover and define his function. Likewise, in reading a detective story the reader participates as co-author simply because so much has been left out of the narrative. The open-mesh silk stocking is far more sensuous than the smooth nylon, just because the eye must act as hand in filling in and completing the image, exactly as in the mosaic of the TV image.

Douglas Cater in *The Fourth Branch of Government* tells how the men of the Washington press bureaus delighted to complete or fill in the blank of Calvin Coolidge's personality. Because he was so like a mere cartoon, they felt the urge to complete his image for him and his public. It is instructive that the press applied the word "cool" to Cal. In the very sense of a cool medium, Calvin Coolidge was so lacking in any articulation of data in his public image that there was only one word for him. He was real cool. In the hot 1920s, the hot press medium found Cal very cool and rejoiced in his lack of image, since it compelled the participation of the press in filling in an image of him for the public. By contrast, F.D.R. was a hot press agent, himself a rival of the newspaper medium and one who delighted in scoring off the press on the rival hot medium of radio. Quite in contrast, Jack Paar ran a cool show for the cool TV medium, and became a rival for the patrons of the night spots and their allies in the gossip columns. Jack Paar's war with the gossip columnists was a weird example of clash between a hot and cold medium such as had occurred with the "scandal of the rigged TV quiz shows." The rivalry between the hot press and radio media, on one hand, and TV on the other, for the hot ad buck, served to confuse and to overheat the issues in the affair that pointlessly involved Charles Van Doren.

An Associated Press story from Santa Monica, California, August 9, 1962, reported how

> Nearly 100 traffic violators watched a police traffic accident film today to atone for their violations. Two had to be treated for nausea and shock. . . .
> Viewers were offered a $5.00 reduction in fines if they agreed to see the movie, *Signal 30,* made by Ohio State Police.
> It showed twisted wreckage and mangled bodies and recorded the screams of accident victims.

Whether the hot film medium using hot content would cool off the hot drivers is a moot point. But it does concern any understanding of media. The effect of hot media treatment cannot include much empathy or participation at any time. In this connection an insurance ad that featured Dad in an iron lung surrounded by a joyful family group did more to strike terror into the reader than all the warning wisdom in the world. It is a question that arises in connection with capital punishment. Is a severe penalty the best deterrent to serious crime? With regard to the bomb and the cold war, is the threat of massive retaliation the most effective means to peace? Is it not evident in every human situation that is pushed to a point of saturation that some precipitation occurs? When all the available resources and energies have been played up in an organism or in any structure there is some kind of reversal of pattern. The spectacle of brutality used as deterrent can brutalize. Brutality used in sports may humanize under some conditions, at least. But with regard to the bomb and retaliation as deterrent, it is obvious that numbness is the result of any prolonged terror, a fact that was discovered when the fallout shelter program was broached. The price of eternal vigilance is indifference.

Nevertheless, it makes all the difference whether a hot medium is used in a hot or a cool culture. The hot radio medium used in cool or non-literate cultures has a violent effect, quite unlike its effect, say in England or America, where radio is felt as entertainment. A cool or low literacy culture cannot accept hot media like movies or radio as entertainment. They are, at least, as radically upsetting for them as the cool TV medium has proved to be for our high literacy world.

And as for the cool war and the hot bomb scare, the cultural strategy that is desperately needed is humor and play. It is play that cools off the hot situations of actual life by miming them. Competitive sports between Russia and the West will hardly serve that purpose of relaxation. Such sports are inflammatory, it is plain. And what we consider entertainment or fun in our media inevitably appears as violent political agitation to a cool culture.

One way to spot the basic difference between hot and cold media uses is to compare and contrast a broadcast of a symphony performance with a broadcast of a symphony rehearsal. Two of the finest shows ever released by the CBC were of Glenn Gould's procedure in recording piano recitals, and Igor Stravinsky's rehearsing the Toronto symphony in some of his new work. A cool medium like TV, when really used, demands this involvement in process. The neat tight package is suited to hot media, like radio and gramophone. Francis Bacon never tired of contrasting hot and cool prose. Writing in "methods" or complete packages, he contrasted with writing in aphorisms, or single observations such as "Revenge is a kind of wild justice." The passive consumer wants packages, but those, he suggested, who are concerned in pursuing knowledge and in seeking causes will resort to aphorisms, just because they are incomplete and require participation in depth.

The principle that distinguishes hot and cold media is perfectly embodied in the folk wisdom: "Men seldom make passes at girls who wear glasses." Glasses intensify the outward-going vision, and fill in the feminine image exceedingly, Marion the Librarian notwithstanding. Dark glasses, on the other hand, create the inscrutable and inaccessible image that invites a great deal of participation and completion.

Again, in a visual and highly literate culture, when we meet a person for the first time his visual appearance dims out the sound of the name, so that in self-defense we add: "How do you spell your name?" Whereas, in an ear culture, the *sound* of a man's name is the overwhelming fact, as Joyce knew when he said in *Finnegans Wake,* "Who gave you that numb?" For the name of a man is a numbing blow from which he never recovers.

Another vantage point from which to test the difference between hot and cold media is the practical joke. The hot literary medium excludes the practical and participant aspect of the joke so completely that Constance Rourke, in her *American Humor,* considers it as no joke at all. To literary people, the practical joke with its total physical involvement is as distasteful as the pun that derails us from the smooth and uniform progress that is typographic order. Indeed, to the literary person who is quite unaware of the intensely abstract nature of the typographic medium, it is the grosser and participant forms of art that seem "hot," and the abstract and intensely literary form that seems "cool." "You may perceive, Madam," said Dr. Johnson, with a pugilistic smile, "that I am well-bred to a degree of needless scrupulosity." And Dr. Johnson was right in supposing that "well-bred" had come to mean a white-shirted stress on attire that rivaled the rigor of the printed page. "Comfort" consists in abandoning a visual arrangement in favor of one that permits casual participation of the senses, a state that is excluded when any one sense, but especially the visual sense, is hotted up to the point of dominant command of a situation.

On the other hand, in experiments in which all outer sensation is withdrawn, the subject begins a furious fill-in or completion of senses that is sheer hallucination. So the hotting-up of one sense tends to result in hallucination.

Against McLuhan

Benjamin DeMott

A marvy year for Marshall McLuhan, take it all in all. Tom Wolfe compared him with Darwin, Freud and Einstein, Susan Sontag said in public she thought he was swell. London saw him as an epoch maker and intellectual frontiersman (*Encounter* and the *Times Lit Supp*), and *The New Yorker* reviewed him rapt. What is more, academe—after a period of sitting tall but silent on his bandwagon—began talking out loud about his work. (One example: a recent international convocation of savants at Southern Illinois University spent days discussing the "communications revolution" in open session—mainly in McLuhanian terms.) Success being what it is, wasps and carpers were doubtless waiting for the man a piece or two up the road. But no amount of carping could obscure the facts of his rise. Overnight the author of *Understanding Media* had emerged as Midcult's Mr. Big. And ahead of him lay a shot at mass adulation and the title of Everyman's Favorite Brain.

The secret of this ascent isn't instantly visible to casual reportorial eyes. Marshall McLuhan is no literary old pro blessed with a power base and a rich experience at name-making. An English professor for most of his working life (Wisconsin, Assumption, St. Louis), he moved on from teaching only quite recently to his present post as director of Toronto University's Center for Culture and Technology. And despite long years in the classroom, he has no credit reserves in the trade—no stretch of unheralded, scholarly labor of the kind fellow professionals pant to puff. McLuhan avoided book-writing until he was forty. His first work, *The Mechanical Bride* (1951), was an analysis of the sex-power-horsepower ploy by which two generations of ad men have sold us our annual car. (Not much there for the Modern Language Association.) And after the *Bride* appeared, the author resumed his silence as a bookman and maintained it for another full decade and more.

Nor can it be said—still on the mystery of the McLuhanian boom—that here is a case of a late-blooming stylist, somebody who had to turn fifty to turn a slick phrase. In terms of style, this flower has yet to bud. Marshall McLuhan's present reputation rests on two books—*The Gutenberg Galaxy* (1962) and *Understanding Media* (1964); both are some-

From *Esquire Magazine,* August 1966. Reprinted by permission of *Esquire Magazine.* © 1966 by Esquire, Inc.

times stimulating, but neither is pretty prose. One problem is that of opacity (McLuhan's pages are dense with stoppers like "sense ratios," "interiorizations of alphabetic technology," and the like). Another is that the favored method of organization has a bit too much in common with that of an impresario squirrel. *The Gutenberg Galaxy* looks gathered, not written: a pasteup from a hundred histories of math, political theology, nationalism, and fur-trading, and from a thousand "other authorities." (Walt Whitman and Walt Whitman Rostow, Cicero and Father Ong, de Chardin and de Beauvoir, Rabelais, Riesman and Shakespeare, the Opies, Powys and Poe—name your hero, he surely is here.) The man's work reads for pages at a stretch like a Marboro clearance ad:

> Clagett [author of *The Science of Mechanics in the Middle Ages*] presents the treatise of Nicholas of Oresme *On the Configurations of Qualities* in which Oresme says: "Every measurable thing except numbers is conceived in the manner of continuous quantity." This recalls us to the Greek world in which as Tobias D. Dantzig points out in his *Number: The Language of Science* (pp. 141–2): "The attempt to apply rational arithmetic to a problem in geometry resulted in the first crisis in the history of mathematics. . . ." Number is the dimension of tactility, as Ivins explained in *Art and Geometry* (p. 7), etc.

Furthermore, the two leading articles of this thinker's gospel can't be called easy to grasp. The first is a theory of culture which contends that communications media impose a wide range of assumptions "subliminally." (The form of the media, not the content, structures men's values, according to McLuhan; the form also determines the content of the senses and the very look of the world.) The second is an interpretation of history which claims that revolutionary transformations of media occur periodically through the ages, and that one such transformation is in progress right now. (A five-hundred-year-old "typographic and mechanical" era is ending and an "electric galaxy of events" has begun; the new "galaxy" offers experiences of simultaneity and heightened interdependence in which traditional values—privacy, independence and so on—are engulfed.) Neither of these items is wholly lacking in interest, and McLuhan's historical chapters are often enlivened by canny, comprehensible remarks. But the key idea, to repeat—that of the centrality of *form* in the media as the determinant of social structure and individual minds—is to most men unfamiliar and abstract. An author who makes it into his dogma would ordinarily be ill-advised to brood overmuch about fame.

That Marshall McLuhan is now in position (if he chooses) to brood about nothing else owes a little to his skill with the magic of the modern. "Baby, it's what's happening" is a regularly sounded ground theme in his work. The basic language is video-mesh, circuits and data processing. Injunctions to *Think Modern!* appear on page after page. ("We still have our eyes fixed on the rearview mirror looking firmly and squarely at the job that is receding into the nineteenth-century past.") The right names —Cage, Camp, Bond, Van Der Beek, the whole of the switched-on mob —are fingered throughout like sacred medals. The Farthest-out Art— electric landscapes, Pop Happenings or whatever—is treated either as classic or already passé, and idols of the hour are probed intensely, like important neglected codes:

> The Beatles stare at us with eloquent messages of changed sensory modes for our whole population, and yet people merely think how whimsical, how bizarre, how grotesque. The Beatles are trying to tell us by the antienvironment they present just how we have changed and in what ways.

Old times and old-timers do turn up, as indicated—especially in *The Gutenberg Galaxy*. But even they swim into the reader's ken to a definite R-and-R beat. (Who was Christopher Marlowe? The man, says McLuhan, turning dead Kit hummingly on, who "set up a national P.A. system of blank verse." Who was Heidegger? A cat who "surfboards along on the electronic wave." What were the Middle Ages? *"The Late Show* for the Renaissance.")

Among other crowd-pleasing elements in the McLuhanian equation, the author's literary persona rates a word. At some moments this writer plays Inside Dopester (I called the Kennedy-Nixon election, he announces, I knew exactly why Jack would win). At others he's simply a Scrappy Little Professorial Guy. Enemies as various as George Bernard Shaw ("he lost his nerve") and General Sarnoff ("the voice of the current somnambulism") are worked over in his books; Lewis Mumford, Arnold Toynbee and dozens more are patronized, and English profs ("literary brahmins") come off naturally as jerks. The author also does a turn as Kitsch Cynic, mocker of Goodie-good types—and it is here that he shows his best stuff, speaking again and again with the clarity of last night's knowing cabby or this week's issue of *Time*. People who are easily shocked give him the laughing fits. ("The historian Daniel Boorstin was scandalized by the fact that celebrity in our information age was not due to a person's having done anything but simply to his being known for being well-known. Professor Parkinson is scandalized that the structure of human work now seems to be quite independent of any job to be done.") And he likes interrupting the argument to defend the innocent guilty and to lean on moralizing twerps:

So great was the audience participation in the quiz shows that the directors of the show were prosecuted as con men. Moreover, press and radio ad interests, bitter about the success of the new TV medium, were delighted to lacerate the flesh of their rivals. Of course, the riggers had been blithely unaware of the nature of their medium, and had given it the movie treatment of intense realism, instead of the softer mythic focus proper to TV. Charles Van Doren merely got clobbered as an innocent bystander, and the whole investigation elicited no insight into the nature or effects of the TV medium. Regrettably, it simply provided a field day for the earnest moralizers. A moral point of view too often serves as a substitute for understanding in technological matters.

A literary self that amounts to an amalgam of Bogie and Dr. Huer might not seem everybody's dish; but the thing obviously meets a felt need.

And the same can be said about McLuhan's gamesmanly ploys as a historian. A specialist in unnoticed causes, this scholar never delves into a historical situation without emerging with "major factors" nobody quite hit on before. The handling in *Understanding Media* of the advent of philanthropy a century ago is typical of his cunning moves. Why did "even the hardiest of the rich dwindle into modest ways of timid service to mankind"? Because of the invention of the telegraph, McLuhan explains—and does not stop for questions. What is the key factor in the Southern civil-rights struggle? The internal-combustion engine. ("The real integrator or leveler of white and Negro in the South was the private car and the truck, not the expression of moral points of view.") Why were the Jews murdered by the million? Because radio came before TV. ("Had TV come first there would have been no Hitler at all.") The talent in question isn't the kind treasured by trad historians, but it is what is called provocative and universally pleasing to wits.

In the end it won't do, though, to pretend that Marshall McLuhan's secret is a matter either of mere wit or mere newsiness or mere literary self-creation. The truth is more complicated—and more painful—than that. Grasping it means facing up to the dozen different kinds of stratagem by which this author empties facts and agonies from the world he thinks of as "Now." Some of these stratagems depend on tricks of futuristic projection, displacements of present-day reality which treat desperate hopes as facts. (Write that "the real integrator of the white and Negro *was*," and you imply that the struggle has already been won.) Other tricks include sudden weird tonal abstractions—see the flip comment about TV and Hitler—deadenings of feeling and sympathy that distance holocaust and shame. Still others con the reader into a frankly theatrical view of experience, a vision that insulates him from immediacies and shows forth all life as a production or stunt. Taken singly, needless to say, none of the stratagems would rank as original, amazing or troubling; taken in concert they have powerful and obnoxious effect. The complaint isn't that Professor McLuhan puts together a thoroughly fantastic account of the situation of contemporary man; it is that he sets himself up, speaking bluntly, as the constituted pardoner of this age—a purveyor of perfect absolution for every genuine kind of modern guilt.

Do I chide myself for trivial failings—my laxness as a parent, my sins of permissiveness, my failure to exact respect from the kids? Do I worry about rearing layabouts incapable of work or thought?—Oh but come *on*, says Marshall McLuhan, a benign forgiving face, the truth is your children are grand:

> Some people have estimated that the young person, the infant and the small child, growing up in our world today works harder than any child ever did in any previous human environment—only the work he has to perform is that of data processing. The small child in twentieth-century America does more data processing—more work—than any child in any previous culture in the history of the world. . . . We haven't really cottoned on to the fact that our children work furiously, processing data in an electrically structured world. . . .

Do I feel bad about my *own* laziness, say—my own unending belt of mindlessness in front of TV? Situation comedy, secret agents, mean mockeries of domestic life. . . . Has my intellectual appetite gone dead? My mind turned slush?—Forget it, says this Constant Comforter. The medium is the message, and whatever you think you are doing in front of the box, the fact is you're being expanded-extended-improved. "TV has opened the doors of audile-tactile perception to the nonvisual world of spoken languages and food and the plastic arts. . . ." TV has transformed "American innocence into depth sophistication, independently of 'content'. . . ." TV has "changed our sense-lives and our mental processes. It has created a taste for all experience in *depth*. . . . And oddly enough, with the demand for the depth, goes the demand for crash-programming [in education]. Not only deeper, but further, into all knowledge has become the normal popular demand since TV."

Or am I bugged by my pointless affluence, my guilt about having fat on my hide at a time when sores of starvation are the rule for hundreds of millions elsewhere?—But don't be *silly*, says my adviser, you're being ridiculous again. You're mired in outmoded thinking, you're the victim of moldy figs. Oh, yes, we've all heard about the underdeveloped nations, the "ascent into history," the necessity of hard labor, the problems of locating resources, building factories, educating work forces, creating credit systems and the like. But *we* know, don't we now, *we* know that we have it within us practically at this instant to do the miracle of our choice whenever we choose:

> The computer will be in a position to carry out orchestrated programming for the sensory life of entire populations. It can be programmed in terms of their total needs, not just in terms of the messages they should be hearing, but in terms of the total experience as picked up and patterned by all the senses at once. For example, if you were to write an ideal sensory program for Indonesia or some area of the world that you wanted to leapfrog across a lot of old technology, this would be possible if you knew in the first place its present sensory thresholds, and, second, if you had established what kind of sensory effect a given technology like radio or literacy had upon sensory life as a whole.

Or suppose I am simply worried about my *natural* self, my condition as part of the creation, my indecencies to the life around me that is coextensive with mine. I deface the garden, Earth, with cigarette butts, billboards, beer cans. I pollute the streams with uncycled wastes from my factory. Should I not then despise myself as a rapist?

Well, do what you like, answers Marshall McLuhan sniffishly, but you are a bit of a wag. Men may have been a bit hard on the planet in the past—but full amends are about to be made. If you'll just be patient a minute or two, you'll see us doing a kind of honor to this Little Old Earth that will more than make up for the past:

> If the planet itself has thus become the content of a new space created by its satellites, and its electronic extensions, if the planet has become the content and not the environment, then we can confidently expect to see the next few decades devoted to turning the planet into an art form. We will caress and shape and pattern every facet, every contour of this planet as if it were a work of art, just as surely as we put a new environment around it.

In sum: give it all over, is the message. Give over self-doubt, self-torment, self-hatred. Give over politics. Give over conscience. Relax, go soft and complacent, accept your subliminal perfectability. Before us, almost at hand, is a moment of revelation when it shall be shown that "we are living in a period richer" than that of Shakespeare, that our time is properly thought of as "the greatest of all human ages, whether in the arts or in the sciences." And while we are waiting, there are worthy acts to be done. We can cut ourselves off from our depressions. We can look beyond the trivia of daily life—beyond entanglements with wives and children and employers, beyond neighbors, bond issues, tax bills and the rest. We can overcome the tired sense that there are urgent local and international issues, and learn to see the dropout, the teach-in, even the casualty himself, as part of The Greater Showbiz:

> . . . we now experience simultaneously the dropout and the teach-in. The two forms are correlative. They belong together. The teach-in represents an attempt to shift education from instruction to discovery, from brainwashing students to brainwashing instructors. It is a big dramatic reversal. Vietnam, as the content of the teach-in, is a very small, misleading Red Herring. It really has nothing to do with the teach-in as such any more than with the dropout. The dropout represents a rejection of nineteenth-century technology as manifested in our educational establishments. The teach-in represents a creative effort to switch the educational process to discovery, from package to prove.

Thus will we rise to the certainty that Style and Method are all, that the visible—Vietnam or wherever—is not in any real sense *there*. And having done this we can take off absolutely, fly up from the non-world of consciousness into the broad sanctuaries of ecstasy and hope. ("The computer, in short, promises by technology a Pentecostal condition of universal understanding and unity . . . a perpetuity of collective harmony and peace.")

It is here, of course, precisely here—in the gift of oblivion—that the heart of the McLuhanian munificence is found. This writer does bestow on his reader a welcome grant of hip modernity. He stimulates in addition a voluptuous sense of mastery (to say "The Middle Ages were *The Late Show* for the Renaissance" is rather like cornering a Corvette). And whether or not the basis of his sunniness is sheer terror, his work does rank as the strongest incitement to optimism yet produced in this age. But the great gift offered is, ultimately, the release from consciousness itself. Those who accept it have clearly won a deliverance, a free way up and out.

Are they so reprehensible, it is asked? Poor men, the ignorant, the hopeless, have to buy *their* release from pushers. The Professor's enthusiasts spend less and get more. They buy a guarantee that the disorder, chaos and misery around them are but veils and shadows, lies told by the stupid conscious mind—yet they make no sacrifice whatever of their ability to function in the workaday world. In the act of discounting their own senses and anxieties, they rise up to form an elite—men dignified by their access to the knowledge that nobody knows what's what. If they are at bottom blind devotees of the subliminal dogma, they have at least kept their self-respect.

—And in any case what *is* the compulsion to Gloomsville that makes it shameful to smile with a Happy Prof? By what laws are we obliged to speak and act always as though tragedy, endless tragedy, were the perpetual human lot? Is it really a badge of reason to hold at every hour of day and night that—as Santayana claimed—"the only true dignity of man is his capacity to despise himself"?

The frustration that breathes in these questions, the boredom with canting pessimism, the thirst for a freshening of life, the longing for an inward sense of courage—these are doubtless the deepest secrets known by our new King of Popthink, the deepest needs his elixir is designed to meet. And making light of the needs is no less inhuman than exploiting them. The best that can be done is to repeat the questions that consciousness—were there any of it left around—would probably feel bound to raise, viz.:

How much can be said for an intellectual vision whose effect is to encourage abdication from all responsibility of mind?

Or: what good is this famous McLuhanacy if it makes men drunk as it makes them bold?

II · Individual Media

THE CONCEPT AND PROBLEM of stereotyping—so frequently discussed by critics of the mass media, such as C. Wright Mills—is here applied by T. W. Adorno to some of the particular psychological patterns developed by television, patterns that the contents and images of programs promote both consciously and unconsciously in their audience.

Henry M. Pachter, on the other hand, sees the psychological implications of television in a much brighter light. His piece, while initially a rebuttal to an earlier article by Gunther Anders,[1] is a broad defense of the effects and possibilities of television, and of the mass media as a whole.

A less optimistic analysis of the effects television produces in the character of its audience is presented by Eugene David Glynn. His selection also includes a glance at the potential values inherent in the medium.

The relationship between television and radio is examined by Philip Abrams. He sees the trivialization of experience as the chief problem to be faced and solved in both media.

Harold Mendelsohn's analysis of the roles radio plays in the lives of individuals examines the interaction of the media and its audience without making the strong value judgments that often are a part of such discussions.

While Vernon Young's approach to the film as an art form is not without value judgments, his emphasis is on an exposition of the way a film works and achieves its effects on the audience.

That the audience is growing and that the film plays a central role, if not *the* central role, in its cultural life—these are the starting assumptions for Stanley Kauffmann's definitions of the nature of the film today and the interrelationship of the film with its audience.

What the film means to one of its foremost artists is the core of the selection by Federico Fellini. This interview is particularly valuable for its illumination of the kinds of realism involved in the film medium.

---

[1] Gunther Anders, "The Phantom World of TV," *Dissent*, 3 (Spring 1956), 14–24.

Stereotyping on Television

T. W. Adorno

Only against psychological backdrops such as pseudo-realism and against implicit assumptions such as the normality of crime can the specific stereotypes of television plays be interpreted. The very standardization indicated by set frames of reference automatically produces a number of stereotypes. Also, the technology of television production makes stereotypy almost inevitable. The short time available for the preparation of scripts and the vast material continuously to be produced call for certain formulas. Moreover, in plays lasting only a quarter to half an hour each, it appears inevitable that the kind of person the audience faces each time should be indicated drastically through red and green lights. We are not dealing with the problem of the existence of stereotypes as such. Since stereotypes are an indispensable element of the organization and anticipation of experience, preventing us from falling into mental disorganization and chaos, no art can entirely dispense with them. Again, the functional change is what concerns us. The more stereotypes become reified and rigid in the present setup of cultural industry, the less people are likely to change their preconceived ideas with the progress of their experience. The more opaque and complicated modern life becomes, the more people are tempted to cling desperately to clichés which seem to bring some order into the otherwise ununderstandable. Thus, people may not only lose true insight into reality, but ultimately their very capacity for life experience may be dulled by the constant wearing of blue and pink spectacles.

In coping with this danger, we may not do full justice to the meaning of some of the stereotypes which are to be dealt with. We should never forget that there are two sides to every psychodynamic phenomenon, the unconscious or id element and the rationalization. Although the latter is psychologically defined as a defense mechanism, it may very well contain some nonpsychological, objective truth which cannot simply be pushed aside on account of the psychological function of the rationaliza-

From "How to Look at Television" by T. W. Adorno. © 1954 by The Regents of the University of California. Reprinted from the *Quarterly of Film, Radio, and Television* (now *Film Quarterly*) VIII, 229–235, by permission of The Regents.

tion. Thus some of the stereotypical messages, directed toward particularly weak spots in the mentality of large sectors of the population, may prove to be quite legitimate. However, it may be said with fairness that the questionable blessings of morals, such as "one should not chase after rainbows," are largely overshadowed by the threat of inducing people to mechanical simplifications by ways of distorting the world in such a way that it seems to fit into preestablished pigeonholes.

The example here selected, however, should indicate rather drastically the danger of stereotypy. A television play concerning a fascist dictator, a kind of hybrid between Mussolini and Peron, shows the dictator in a moment of crisis; and the content of the play is his inner and outer collapse. Whether the cause of his collapse is a popular upheaval or a military revolt is never made clear. But neither this issue nor any other of a social or political nature enters the plot itself. The course of events takes place exclusively on a private level. The dictator is just a heel who treats sadistically both his secretary and his "lovely and warmhearted" wife. His antagonist, a general, was formerly in love with the wife; and they both still love each other, although the wife sticks loyally to her husband. Forced by her husband's brutality, she attempts flight, and is intercepted by the general who wants to save her. The turning point occurs when the guards surround the palace to defend the dictator's popular wife. As soon as they learn that she has departed, the guards quit; and the dictator, whose "inflated ego" explodes at the same time, gives up. The dictator is nothing but a bad, pompous, and cowardly man. He seems to act with extreme stupidity; nothing of the objective dynamics of dictatorship comes out. The impression is created that totalitarianism grows out of character disorders of ambitious politicians, and is overthrown by the honesty, courage, and warmth of these figures with whom the audience is supposed to identify. The standard device employed is that of the spurious personalization of objective issues. The representatives of ideas under attack, as in the case of the fascists here, are presented as villains in a ludicrous cloak-and-dagger fashion, whereas those who fight for the "right cause" are personally idealized. This not only distracts from any real social issues but also enforces the psychologically extremely dangerous division of the world into black (the out group) and white (we, the in group). Certainly, no artistic production can deal with ideas or political creeds *in abstracto* but has to present them in terms of their concrete impact upon human beings; yet it would be utterly futile to present individuals as mere specimens of an abstraction, as puppets expressive of an idea. In order to deal with the concrete impact of totalitarian systems, it would be more commendable to show how the life of ordinary people is affected by terror and impotence than to cope with the phony psychology of the big-shots, whose heroic role is silently endorsed by such a treatment even if they are pictured as villains. There seems to be hardly any question of the importance of an analysis of pseudo-personalization and its effect, by no means limited to television.

Although pseudo-personalization denotes the stereotyped way of "looking at things" in television, we should also point out certain stereotypes in the narrower sense. Many television plays could be characterized by the sobriquet "a pretty girl can do no wrong." The heroine of a light comedy is, to use George Legman's term, "a bitch heroine." She behaves toward her father in an incredibly inhuman and cruel manner only slightly rationalized as "merry pranks." But she is punished very slightly, if at all. True, in real life bad deeds are rarely punished at all, but this cannot be applied to television. Here, those who have developed the production code for the movies seem right: what matters in mass media is not what happens in real life, but rather the positive and negative "messages," prescriptions, and taboos that the spectator absorbs by means of identification with the material he is looking at. The punishment given to the pretty heroine only nominally fulfills the conventional requirements of the conscience for a second. But the spectator is given to understand that the pretty heroine really gets away with everything just because she is pretty.

The attitude in question seems to be indicative of a universal penchant. In another sketch that belongs to a series dealing with the confidence racket, the attractive girl who is an active participant in the racket not only is paroled after having been sentenced to a long term, but also seems to have a good chance of marrying her victim. Her sex morality, of course, is unimpeachable. The spectator is supposed to like her at first sight as a modest and self-effacing character, and he must not be disappointed. Although it is discovered that she is a crook, the original identification must be restored, or rather maintained. The stereotype of the nice girl is so strong that not even the proof of her delinquency can destroy it; and, by hook or by crook, she must be what she appears to be. It goes without saying that such psychological models tend to confirm exploitative, demanding, and aggressive attitudes on the part of young girls—a character structure which has come to be known in psychoanalysis under the name of oral aggressiveness.

Sometimes such stereotypes are disguised as national American traits, a part of the American scene where the image of the haughty, egoistic, yet irresistible girl who plays havoc with poor dad has come to be a public institution. This way of reasoning is an insult to the American spirit.

High-pressure publicity and continuous plugging to institutionalize some obnoxious type does not make the type a sacred symbol of folklore. Many considerations of an apparently anthropological nature today tend only to veil objectionable trends, as though they were of an ethnological, quasi-natural character. Incidentally, it is amazing to what degree television material even on superficial examination brings to mind psychoanalytic concepts with the qualification of being a psychoanalysis in reverse. Psychoanalysis has described the oral syndrome combining the antagonistic trends of aggressive and dependent traits. This character syndrome is closely indicated by the pretty girl than can do no wrong, who, while being aggressive against her father exploits him at the same time, depending on him as much as, on the surface level, she is set against him. The difference between the sketch and psychoanalysis is simply that the sketch exalts the very same syndrome which is treated by psychoanalysis as a reversion to infantile developmental phases and which the psychoanalyst tries to dissolve. It remains to be seen whether something similar applies as well to some types of male heroes, particularly the super-he-man. It may well be that he too can do no wrong.

Finally, we should deal with a rather widespread stereotype which, inasmuch as it is taken for granted by television, is further enhanced. At the same time, the example may serve to show that certain psychoanalytic interpretations of cultural stereotypes are not really too far-fetched; the latent ideas that psychoanalysis attributes to certain stereotypes come to the surface. There is the extremely popular idea that the artist is not only maladjusted, introverted, and *a priori* somewhat funny; but that he is really an "aesthete," a weakling, and a "sissy." In other words, modern synthetic folklore tends to identify the artist with the homosexual and to respect only the "man of action" as a real, strong man. This idea is expressed in a surprisingly direct manner in one of the comedy scripts at our disposal. It portrays a young man who is not only the "dope" who appears so often on television but is also a shy, retiring, and accordingly untalented poet, whose moronic poems are ridiculed. He is in love with a girl but is too weak and insecure to indulge in the necking practices she rather crudely suggests; the girl, on her part, is caricatured as a boy-chaser. As happens frequently in mass culture, the roles of the sexes are reversed—the girl is utterly aggressive, and the boy, utterly afraid of her, describes himself as "woman-handled" when she manages to kiss him. There are vulgar innuendos of homosexuality of which one may be quoted: the heroine tells her boy friend that another boy is in love with someone, and the boy friend asks, "What's he in love with?" She answers, "A girl, of course," and her boy friend replies, "Why, of course? Once

before it was a neighbor's turtle, and what's more its name was Sam."
This interpretation of the artist as innately incompetent and a social
outcast (by the innuendo of sexual inversion) is worthy of examination.

We do not pretend that the individual illustrations and examples, or
the theories by which they are interpreted, are basically new. But in view
of the cultural and pedagogical problem presented by television, we do
not think that the novelty of the specific findings should be a primary
concern. We know from psychoanalysis that the reasoning, "But we know
all this!" is often a defense. This defense is made in order to dismiss insights as irrelevant because they are actually uncomfortable and make
life more difficult for us than it already is by shaking our conscience
when we are supposed to enjoy the "simple pleasures of life." The investigation of the television problems we have here indicated and illustrated by a few examples selected at random demands, most of all, taking
seriously notions dimly familiar to most of us by putting them into their
proper context and perspective and by checking them by pertinent material. We propose to concentrate on issues of which we are vaguely but
uncomfortably aware, even at the expense of our discomfort's mounting,
the further and the more systematically our studies proceed. The effort
here required is of a moral nature itself: knowingly to face psychological
mechanisms operating on various levels in order not to become blind
and passive victims. We can change this medium of far-reaching poten-
tialities only if we look at it in the same spirit which we hope will one
day be expressed by its imagery.

In Defense of Television

Henry M. Pachter

Casting an indulgent eye on the merry-making of Flemish peasants,
Breughel found it brutish, vulgar, lusty, gluttonous, bibulous and, possibly, dulling. Yet, nothing in his canvases suggests the suspicion that the
feudal lords might have devised the popular culture of their time the
better to keep the peasantry in submission. Pious monks might have believed that the Devil was to blame, but no serious historian would credit

From *Dissent,* Vol. 3, Summer 1956. Reprinted by permission of the author.

such views today. We condone superstition with reference only to our own culture. According to Gunther Anders (in *Dissent*, Winter 1956), e.g., a dark conspiracy has foisted television on us for the purposes of profit, deception and subjection:

1. "The mass producer . . . needs a mass broken up into the largest possible number of customers; he does not want all of his customers to consume one and the same product (as in looking at a movie together); he wants all to buy identical products" (as in watching television separately).

2. "The method allegedly intended to bring the object close to us, actually serves to veil the object, to alienate it or slowly to do away with it"; the implication is that capitalism needs unrealistic subjects who live in a "phantom world," as the title of the essay says.

3. "Mass production of the mass man himself was speeded up," meaning that by watching TV we acquire, without being aware of what is being done to us, the character of the crowd.

Assertion No. 1 obviously means to inform us of a more shattering discovery than the fact that the electronics industry is interested in the sale of television sets; after all, automobiles and refrigerators were sold without any "phantom" assisting. The real phantom which bothers our author is the little man behind the grey screen; isn't it difficult to realize how he got there, economically speaking? Someone paid to put him there, so he must be a "commodity"; and, reasoning further, one such commodity seen by a thousand people in a movie theatre must bring less profit, hence be less capitalistic than the same picture appearing a thousand times on a thousand little screens.

This is poor economics based on misunderstood technology, and primitive sociology too. A TV program supplies one identical product to a large mass, just as the movies; in both cases the admission price is calculated on the basis of cost and profit. Like any other enterprise, the entertainment industry does not count its customers, but the sales value of its product, no matter whether it is divided into many or few lumps. But worse: How did "the mass producer" convert his "need" into a desire of his customers? It is one thing to say that some modern inventions came as a boon to industry; Mr. Anders implies quite another thing—that these inventions were so conceived, and we consumers were so conditioned, that the greatest number of goods can be sold at the highest profit. He still believes in the omnipotence of the overlords; this new version of Jack London's Iron Heel even gives them credit for a far more ambitious scheme: mass production, Mr. Anders says, has been so devised that "mass consumption produces mass man." As a witticism the *aperçu* might be superb; as a theory, expounded at nauseating leisure, it is misleading. His reasoning is based on verbal tricks.

Consider this sentence: "The classical homeworker manufactures his wares in order to secure a minimum of consumer goods and leisure; the modern homeworker consumes a maximum of leisure products in order to help produce the mass man." The first "in order to" refers to the worker's intentions; the second "in order to," however, expresses the mystical power of the Iron Heel. An honest parallel to the latter statement would have been: "The classical homeworker manufactured goods in order to reproduce the social conditions which force him to manufacture more goods." Thus stated, we still have the primitive sociology, but at least the evil cycle of the producer society would be compared with the evil cycle of the consumer society.

Moreover, throughout his essay, as in the last quotation, Mr. Anders consistently idealizes and even idyllicizes the past. That noble worker in the Lord's vineyard seems never to have been conditioned by the ideologies of his terrestrial and spiritual overlords! That touching picture of the happy family, gathered around the big oaken table, seems never to have been marred by the tragedies which constitute up to 90 percent of the thematic material in nineteenth century literature. Those lovers, before radio, must all have been highly articulate Cyranos, and no Christian ever needed the voice of a poet or the song of a musician to conquer first his shyness and thereafter the bride. Those heroes of yesterday never saw politics as a spectacle but went in there to fight it out for themselves; they never went to a circus, never read novels, penny dreadfuls and Radcliffe, never relied on newspapers for their knowledge of the world, never believed a Napoleon or a Mussolini before radio. Finally, these intellectual giants had no occasion to look at the world in an "idealistic" way, but were always aware of the reality behind the pictures that supplied their limited opportunities of information. What nonsense! All the indictments against "mass culture" are at least as old as Gutenberg—not to speak of Ovid. Ortega y Gasset added elegance and Anders adds brilliant confusion, punning happily along Heidegger alley where all lights are fueled by free association.

Granted that the new inventions may create opportunities for manipulation or tend to cripple our sensorial experience of the world; it still does not follow that mass communication methods doom our intelligence to misorientation. The truth is that at all times most public events are experienced vicariously and that each society has its special means of communicating to its citizens the preferred picture of reality; at all times did people rely on teachers, travelers, pictures and other secondhand information to form their view of the world. Today's mass media and extreme mobility potentially increase our sources of information to the point of universality, where cross-checking has become easy and wilful distortion has become difficult. The walls of the city and the walls of the home have been laid down; the idols of the market and the idols of the cave have been blown to pieces—Mr. Anders claims that these old and wholesome walls, the protectors of the *penates,* have been replaced by a wide screen where the idols of the theatre simulate an unreal world.

I do not wish to belittle the difference between reading and viewing. Certainly the latter opens more opportunity to suggestion. Yet, not so long ago, the printed word was held almost sacred by the masses; from escapist literature to tabloids, people at all times preferred to read and believe what reassured them, rather than what might shake their complacency. Of their own volition they gave the manipulators a monopoly of information. Today nobody thinks that the picture on the little screen represents the real world; everybody knows that the President uses make-up and teleprompter; even the children who used to believe in Santa Claus know that Hopalong Cassidy is an actor.

But we have acquired, in this same process, a heightened sensibility for those illusory experiences which haunted modern writing long before TV. The camera has widened the range of this experience. It constantly prompts the experienced viewer to cheer the editor who switches to promising angles and selects the most interesting viewpoints. Mr. Anders is blind to the immense widening of our perceptive capacities through the camera.

While the possibility of deception is ever-present, the danger of deliberate manipulation and of "conditioning" through unconscious suggestion might even be declining. The ideals of our society may be less admirable than the virtues of ancient Rome; but if we live by them, not TV is to blame but the erosion of virtue that preceded popular culture. The loss of substance and certainty which characterizes the age began to be noticed eighty years ago by a generation of artists which did not call itself avant-garde but in relation to which our critics of TV are a sorry rear guard. They first revealed the surface character of our experience, but now we have run full circle: in popular experience, manipulation is visible or suspected everywhere. We know that our environment is being manufactured for us, and after some more years, TV-experienced people may tend to believe nothing, just as they have become fairly immune to propaganda of other sorts. The illusions which we buy—a perfume, a movie, a popular song, a comedian on TV—do not fool us; they are consciously presented and accepted as illusions, not as truth. Far from living in a world of phantoms, we are facing the danger of complete disillusionment.

Another facet of this development is our loss of values. I deplore it as much as Mr. Anders does. But again—is the display of profligacy on big and small screens a cause or a symptom of the decline in the stature of our heroes? What had Hitler or Stalin that Cromwell or Cortez did not have? Is Gary Cooper in *High Noon* less real than Robin Hood?

In this connection, Mr. Anders makes the shrewd remark that Socrates is being made over into a pal on TV and in popular science literature. The great men, he says, no longer are revered for their greatness but inserted into a world of appearances; they are known not for their unique substance but for that which the community of pals can understand. He might have addressed his reproach to Aristophanes, and he might have quoted in support of his own views any number of antique writers, beginning with Plato. They all complained that the *profanum vulgus* was taking over; they all hated themselves and others, begrudging the people their daily pleasures. I should have liked to meet Socrates; I understand he used to dine and wine with friends. He might not be less great for that. Plato's Socrates, whom Mr. Anders wishes to raise on a pedestal, is a completely phoney picture—a phantom, to use Mr. Anders's words. The mere fact that so many millions now can become familiar with him, makes Socrates a base commodity: "When the event can be . . . reproduced virtually any number of times, it acquires the characteristics of an assembly-line product; and when we pay for having it delivered to our homes, it is a commodity." Only professional philosophers turned theologians make such elementary mistakes in elementary logic. If I buy the print of a Rembrandt etching, not the meeting of Christ with the disciples at Emmaus is reproduced but its likeness; and neither the event nor Rembrandt's conception of it has become a commodity. What Mr. Anders means to say is much less mystical than the transubstantiation of an event into a commodity. Certain experiences—enjoying a work of art, meeting a great personality, reading a profound book—cannot be duplicated. The reproduction which pretends to be the original merely reminds us of it; the exciting moment of a live concert is not recorded along with the sound track; an "art appreciation course" substitutes learning for spontaneous perception. Manufacturers of such ersatz satisfaction surely would have us accept their wares for the real thing; clever producers even may exploit the real love affairs of a movie star or create suitable stories from whole cloth to provide vicarious experiences for an audience that increasingly likes to have the proper feelings preassembled and delivered along with the "event." Not multiplication of the event, but vulgarization of its stand-in, not communication of an experience but predigestion of experience results in the stunted sensibility of mass culture.

But before the hit song, folk music provided prefabricated sentimentality for emotionally underdeveloped people who had no feelings of their own. This possibility becomes a danger when a ruling class or state creates and directs the emotions. Worse—totalitarian governments may create an event or a seeming reality for political exploitation; their policies often are designed to confirm the dream world where they keep their subjects. Occasionally they fall for their own phantasmagoria and walk into an abyss where they had seen a road to glory. Strangely enough, the totalitarian implications are not discussed by Mr. Anders, though everywhere else he insists on the modern-age nature of his phantom world. In the German version of his essay, which is more complete, however, he speaks of important mimesis phenomena which belong here. "In the beginning, there was broadcasting," he says ironically, "and the world was made to suit it." He concludes: "Were one of us to try and go forth in quest of the real world . . . he soon would be disappointed. For out there he would find nothing but models modeled after the pictures of which they are supposed to be the originals." It may be unfair to polemicize against something that was not published; yet I feel that the published fragment does not do justice to Mr. Anders. He has developed an interesting theory of cognition which may apply to human nature. His may be a great discovery, occasioned by certain outstanding traits of perception which now are more visible than before. He is wrong, I submit, in trying to make a double discovery—namely, that these features are characteristic of the present society. A sociological analysis of knowledge must start out from sound sociology and careful use of history. Certainly, Orson Welles's famous radio invasion from Mars says something about the United States in the thirties—but have there not been panicky flights to the hills before, when a comet seemed to announce a new Flood? Certainly we pity the old ladies who start knitting baby clothes when their favorite soap opera heroine is pregnant; but did not Goethe get hundreds of letters from imaginary Lottes and did not would-be Werthers actually commit suicide?

Neither the economics nor the technical facilities of mass communication are to blame for the use which their owners make of them. We, on the other hand, are not helpless, powerless, and hopeless in front of inexorable forces unleashed by industry's ingenuity or the Iron Heel's clever scheming. These phantoms were built up by the pseudo-radicalism of the snobs to justify their flight into the cultural preserve, a Messianic religion, political or other nihilisms. Not popular culture but their own craving

for "alienation" keeps their eyes away from the realistic, "materialistic,"
Mr. Anders might say, conditions which must be changed. Mass entertainment can be debased by commercial or by political interests, but only
if and while these interests retain their monopoly of communication. The
ultra-left culture snobs from the start concede this monopoly to the interests. They have no real quarrel with the world as it is, except that they
pretend not to like it that way. The hypocrites! They like it exactly in
such a desperate state that they can lament about their impotence in
facing it.[1]

For the newest fashion in mass culture is to scorn mass culture. Everybody does, nowadays; those who don't either are writing a book on mass
culture or collect early jazz records. Conformism has come around full
circle; one dares no longer be "conformist," enjoy any product of the
entertainment industry, see differences between the two major parties,
admit opinions which might be shared by the multitude. Those who
cannot possibly be radicals on the left develop at least a radical or "new"
conservatism; these nonconformists in reverse usually get along with the
older variety of nonconformists in forward gear. In friendly competition,
the two élites are trying to outdo each other at deriding the "mass."
Members of their bipartisan club display in their home a copy of *Partisan
Review* together with a painting conceived in an advanced style (as to
records, progressives favor Bach while new-conservatives may boast a
Shostakovitch concerto played by Oistrakh), and are conversant with
words such as alienation, popular culture, pseudo-whatever-fashion-is,
anxiety, crowd, absurd and a few others, judicious use of which will
silence the uninitiated and bring recognition from those who belong;
many will grant you such recognition to be recognized themselves.

Nonconformist tolerance leaves a choice of many peculiar ways to
exquisiteness. One may be an existentialist, a Marxist, a surrealist, a
fascist—the crowd of frightened snobs will be so discriminating as not
to discriminate against him. They may differentiate, though; through
marginal differentiation between various crowds, each of them very distinctive, the crowd of the anti-crowds constitutes itself as an effective
instrument of terror. No one ever dares to defy its edicts. To be amused
by Groucho, to be excited by Armstrong, to be moved to tears by Molly
Goldberg (or Werther, for that matter), amounts to backwardness, lack

[1] Meanwhile, Marshall McLuhan has actually proclaimed the revolution of
the media, and not only likes it but secured a $100,000 professorship for saying
so. Academe, which Mr. Anders so valiantly defended, has capitulated before
brazen charlatanry.

of sensitivity, vulgarity and cultural treason. One has to be alienated to be counted. For here is art, there is entertainment.[2]

In their dread of being caught in a profane mood, would-be intellectuals alienate themselves from the sources of national experience and risk forfeiting their share in forming it. They refuse to see any transmission belt between popular and higher culture, or between popular ideologies and true ideals. Yet, popular culture may be a watered-down, vulgarized version of yesterday's class culture; it also may contain groping, unconscious adumbrations of tomorrow's means of expression. Contemporary indictments of jazz often are literal repetitions of similar pronouncements on the waltz 130 years ago. "Baroque" once had a meaning similar to our "kitsch," and already the suggestion has been made that the first half of this century may be known to, and admired by, posterity as the "Age of Kitsch." Kitsch, by the way, is most children's avenue to artistic expression—some never get beyond that stage, and much of the so-called folk culture, which often is favorably compared with our "mass culture," really is or was the mass culture of civilizations which knew few fashion changes. Though this difference may be decisive, it is precisely one where our mass culture and our nonconformists stand on the same side. Both fear nothing so much as yesterday's conformity. The mad chase for newness in "original creations" is fittingly aped on the assembly line of popular fashion. Mass production processes in the entertainment industries make its content repetitious, self-perpetuating, inflexible. It produces no original material but, on the contrary, transforms its consumer into a passive recipient of sense stimuli. There is no cross-fertilization, no participation in a creative process, but only the surrender to the narcotic effects of a merchandise. Popular culture no longer is entertainment which we provide for ourselves, but has become the supply of entertainment which we buy. All this is true, and serious, too. Our spectator sports, the Roman *circenses,* are opium for the crowds. Unable to escape the insanity of their existence, they purchase escape by the hour; incapable of facing their own feelings, they have sentimentality expressed for them; too sluggish to rebel against their impotence, they watch Superman conquer space and time.

Yet, these vicarious gratifications also express a yearning for a different world and reflect a search for a different humanity. The material content

---

[2] Ten years later, the above list will have to include beatniks, dharma boys, "Teddy boys," (England), "Gammler," (Germany), and hippies. And the "cool" fashion has made my outdated fondness of Groucho and Molly even more obsolete—who remembers now these sentimental heroes? The terrorism of nonconformist anti-mass mass cultists has wiped out their memory.

of some escape literature even points to preconscious states of rebellion. Sometimes in curiously inverted forms Al Capp, through his "Li'l Abner" cartoon, projects the immolated image of humanity into crudely ironical utopias. It is a gross overstatement that the alienation process in popular culture has gone too far for remedy and return. There is no conformistic material that cannot be turned into nonconformist outcries. Kung Fu changed a few words in a simple calendar to express his political criticism and everybody can think of many superb works of art issued from the new media. The technical characteristics of printing, photographing, filming, broadcasting, television, recording do not restrict, but enlarge the range of our experience and the possibilities of expression. Yet, like every other instrument, they may be used for laudable or for evil purposes. Like magic, they can be black or white.[3]

[3] Ten years later, I almost feel tempted to apologize to Mr. Anders. He has not deserved to be plundered and, in the same act, bowdlerized by Marshall McLuhan. The latter has had neither the grace nor the scholarship to acknowledge his debt to Mr. Anders; nor has Mr. Anders given credit to a pioneering essay by Walter Benjamin, published in 1936, "Das Kunstwerk im Zeitalter seiner technischen Reproduzier-barkeit."

Television and the American Character— A Psychiatrist Looks at Television

Eugene David Glynn, M.D.

To consider television as a shaping force on the American character, the attempt must be made to study it so far as possible purely as a form. Content and quality vary in a very great range, and while of great importance in the immediate and particular effects upon the viewer, there is a structure inherent in the very medium of television which must be seen completely in itself. It is this basic form which exerts the greatest influence upon the shaping of character when character is considered as the long-term expectations and responses of a person; automatic, repetitive, more or less conscious. This molding is almost completely outside of the aware-

From *Television's Impact on American Culture*, edited by William Y. Elliott. Copyright © 1956. Reprinted by permission of Michigan State University Press.

ness of the viewer. The customary repeated experience of television structures the viewer's whole idea of the world and his relation to it. It is here that permanent responses to television lie; it is here that character is formed, for these attitudes are what the viewer then takes into the rest of his experience.

What attitudes toward the world and what expectations of it does television bring about?

Certain types of adult illness—particularly the depressions, the oral character neuroses, the schizophrenias—and the use they make of television can be most valuable here. Those traits that sick adults now satisfy by television can be presumed to be those traits which children, exposed to television from childhood (infancy, really!), and all through the character forming years, may be expected to develop. Consider these actual clinical examples.

A twenty-five-year-old musician, daughter of an adoring, constantly present, constantly acting mother, quarrels with her parents and gives up her own quite busy professional life. She turns to the television set, and soon is spending ten to twelve hours a day watching it, constantly sitting before it, transfixed, drinking beer or eating ice cream, lost and desperate if the set is turned off. Making a joke one day, she said, "Boy, I don't know what I would do for a mother if that tube ever burned out." This girl, of real intellectual attainment, was completely indifferent as to what the programs actually were. A fifty-five-year-old man, hugely obese, all his life close to his three older sisters, who took care of him, becomes depressed after the death of one of them. His only activity for many months is to watch television, looking for interesting programs, but settling for anything. The staff of a hospital for schizophrenic adolescent girls finds that these girls, insatiable in their demands, and yet themselves incapable of sustaining activity, want nothing so much as to be allowed endless hours of television. Without it they are soon noisy, unruly and frequently destructive. Significantly, the only other control of these girls is an adult who constantly directs them or organizes their entertainment for them.

These examples could be multiplied endlessly. They all demonstrate quite clearly the special set of needs television satisfies, needs centering around the wish for someone to care, to nurse, to give comfort and solace. Adults, by their very age and status, can scarcely hope to find someone to take on this role, once their own mothers give it up. These infantile longings can be satisfied only symbolically, and how readily the television set fills in. Warmth, sound, constancy, availability, a steady giving without ever a demand for return, the encouragement to complete passive surrender and envelopment—all this and active fantasy besides. Watching these adults, one is deeply impressed by their acting out with the television set of their unconscious longings to be infants in mother's lap.

These, then, are traits television can so easily satisfy in adults, or foster in children; traits of passivity, receptiveness, being fed, taking in and absorbing what is offered. Activity, self-reliance, and aggression are notably absent. A great deal of activity and aggression may be present, but they are deceptive, for the demands and even rages are not to be doing, but to be getting. Very much energy can be spent, not in constructive accomplishment, but in trying to reestablish or keep a dependent relationship. The image is evident; the relationship clearly established. The musician's joke went to the core, for these are the relationships of a child to its mother; the relationship of a very young child who lives literally on its mother's bounty: her food, her warmth, her knowledge. This is the age described in Freudian psychology as the oral age; the age of intake and being fed, when the mouth is the vital organ in relation to the world. The extensions of this include such things as taking in the sound of others' voices through the ears or of absorbing others' ideas, as can easily be seen. The underlying pattern in whatever symbolic form is worked out will relate it to this oral character orientation: the counting on someone else to supply satisfaction and security rather than oneself. Typical, too, of this character structure are the intensity with which needs are felt, the poor tolerance of frustration and delay, the demand for immediate satisfaction. The television set is easily and agreeably a mother to whom the child readily turns with the same expectations as to her.

These traits, of course, are inherent in all spectator participation, be it sport or art or reading. What is crucially important about television is its ubiquitousness: there is so much television, so early, so steadily; five-year-olds watch television as a matter of course, and, increasingly, so do three-year-olds and even two-year-olds. Television at this age can, in the limited experience of the child, only be seen as a mother-substitute or a mother-extension. These needs of the child should be outgrown, and his relationship to his mother changed. Basically, this growth depends in great part on the mother's attitude toward the child; her encouraging him to greater activity and self-reliance, the lessening of her feeding functions. It is of the greatest importance in character formation that the child can now have these infantile wishes and needs satisfied by the always available television set. Indeed, to continue enjoying television, it becomes necessary these traits remain prominent. The danger is here: the passive dependent oral character traits become fixed. There are endless differences between children playing tag or cops and robbers and watching even the most action-filled Western; even between walking to the movies once a week and just switching on television by reaching out.

Hence, the chief effect of television is passivity and dependence in multiple shapes and forms. The world supplies and the individual feasts. In opposition to the point of view here expressed, the claim is made that aggression is not so much inhibited by television as displaced; that dormant aggressive forces are stimulated in the viewer, and that these forces result in increased activity of many kinds in other spheres. Similarly, television may release many new forces, aggressive or constructive in a direct way. This type of effect, however, depends almost entirely on the content of the particular program. Television might indeed arouse the viewer to extreme activity, but only by the portrayal of specific situations or specific messages. For example, some juvenile delinquency might be shaped by a television crime program, or a tree planting program be inspired. Again, attitudes toward parents, toward husbands and wives, toward social groups, attitudes which could lead to action of a most constructive kind can certainly be caused or influenced by television, but this, however, must always be specifically dependent on the content of the program. Action so aroused does not produce a characterological basis for further activity. The underlying structure, even here, is clear, for the stimulus to action, be it aggressive or sexual, comes from without. Deep characterological attitudes toward parents or family might be shaped, but only by specific propaganda content to programs.

The picture of the American character which emerges has a familiar look, for many students in the field have pointed out that the new American character is one of conformity; the search is for security, not glory, comfort in the group, not individual prominence. The whole present concept of the welfare state illustrates this. Americans today must be much more responsible to their society, much more aware of their group, much more conforming; the nonentrepreneur is rapidly becoming the necessary American character. It must look outside itself constantly for orientation so as to smoothly fit in. Television is simultaneously the result of and the instrument for producing the character needed to live in much of the current American world. To be responsive to and dependent on television, well trained in this, is to be able to live much more easily in our society.

There are other aspects of television's influence. It is used, certainly, in every hospital and in every institution as an extremely effective nonchemical sedative. An interesting parallel has been pointed out recently. It is well-known that fixing on a moving visual stimulus inhibits motor activity. The prime example of this is the situation in hypnosis, and the

concentration and stillness of television watchers certainly is reminiscent
of the hypnotized. Television-addiction certainly exists, and bears an immediate relation to the drug addicts, those who search for, in pills, what
they once found in mother's milk. A forty-four-year-old salesman, a
chronic alcoholic, tried to give up liquor. Every night he came home and
watched television, "drinking it in" (his words) until he fell asleep before
the set. Once off the wagon, he gave up television, too.

How lulling television can be has been widely observed. Most homes
soon give in to the temptation of using television to keep the children
quiet and out of mischief. It does this, but in a way much different from
playing games.

Marriage after marriage is preserved by keeping it drugged on television; television is used quite consistently to prevent quarreling from
breaking out by keeping people apart. This points up a somewhat less
obvious side of watching television: its schizoid-fostering aspects. Television seems to be a social activity, an activity performed by many people
together. Actually, though, it smothers contact, really inhibiting interpersonal exchange. A group watching television is frequently a group of
isolated people, not in real exchange at all. Television viewers are given
to solitary pleasures, not the social ones. Children and adolescents frequently revert to thumb-sucking while watching; how much eating and
drinking goes on before the set! The complaint is common enough today
that social visiting has lost its social, conversational, engaged side.

There are two more important aspects of television to consider: its
stimulation and its fantasy. The question can only be asked at this point,
for the television generation is not yet adolescent: what will be the result
of such constant stimulation from such early ages? Will it result in the
need for ever increasing stimulation as the response to the old stimulus
becomes exhausted? In the early 1940s a radio program which created
national interest and caused great excitement was "Take It or Leave It,"
with its climax of the $64.00 Question. This year (1955) television's
greatest success has been the $64,000 Question. Discount the monetary
inflation of the past ten years. What is left is a vivid figure of how much
more it takes to excite. The Lone Ranger served as a radio hero for well
over ten years; Davy Crockett, a hero of almost mythic proportions, lasted
less than one year. What way can stimulation be continuously increased?
As the responses are exhausted, will television move toward increasing
violence, as the movies have? Similarly, it is too soon to know what children so massively exposed to sex on television will consider exciting and
sex-stimulating as adults. A critical question is raised here: is television
ultimately blunting and destructive of sensibility?

Then too, one wonders: Will reality match up to the television fantasies this generation has been nursed on? These children are in a peculiar position; experience is exhausted in advance. There is little they have not seen or done or lived through, and yet this is second-hand experience. When the experience itself comes, it is watered down, for it has already been half lived, but never truly felt. The fate of Emma Bovary may become the common fate. This has always been a "disease" of the literary sensibility and of the romantics, but will this become a mass characteristic?

A word of balance should be put in here. The television generation will not be a completely infantile one, for there are many other forces at work, including the normal growth potentials of the human being. The point here is just to isolate the lines of television's influence. At the same time, equally inherent in its nature, television can be a growth-promoting experience, an enriching force of the most tremendous power.

Horizons have been greatly expanded: millions of people have seen the ballet, have travelled to distant lands, have explored some of the country's best museums; experiences they could never have in their own lifetimes. Television has taken its viewers into the United Nations, into the meetings of Congressional investigating committees. It has led a mass audience into intimate active participation in the political heart of the country in a way never dreamed possible. The range here is without bounds. Television can produce a people wider in knowledge, more alert and aware of the world, prepared to be much more actively interested in the life of their times. Television can be the great destroyer of provincialism. Television can produce a nation of people who really live in the world, not in just their own hamlets. It is here that the great opportunity of educational television lies.

Educational television must be acutely aware of its own nature. By being very conscious of its particular character shaping potential, it can counteract it by extremely careful attention to content. It is always a difficult task for the teacher to liberate his pupil; educational television must remember how many more times difficult it is for it. It must find ways to encourage active audience participation; programs which will not satiate but stimulate its viewers, programs which will leave its audience eager to do and to try. Cooking instruction programs are an example here. Techniques will have to be worked out for educational television for showing, not a baseball game, but how to pitch a curved ball; for sending its audience on nature hunts, into club activity, to the library for books. Being aware of the dependent relationship in its audience, television must look for ways to undo it—the problem of any teacher or parent.

With this orientation, television can overcome the dangers pointed out and find its way to being highly growth-promoting. Otherwise it will find itself degraded into an instrument for the shaping of a group man: dependent, outward seeking, the natural foil of any authoritarianism, be it left or right.

The Nature of Radio and Television

Philip Abrams

Uniquely among the mass media radio and television are given opportunities by time, by the fact that they have the whole day, every day, to dispose of, and that they can break up the day as they please. How do they use these opportunities? We tend to take the existing pattern of programming so much for granted that we do not see the gulf between what could be done in this respect and what actually is done. Time, which might have been used to experiment and innovate, to set contrasting styles and idioms alongside one another and so heighten audience sensibilities, has in fact been used only to reproduce with endless ingenious but minor variations programs built on established formulae of acceptability. With its new lease of time the BBC proposes to fill the night air with "light music"; even the American radio companies are willing to treat the small hours as a time for experiment and for special minority interests. In this country the continuity of broadcasting means that the onslaught on authenticity has become unremitting; there is always something "on"; and the essential nature of what is on is, for almost all of the time, unchanging.

The fact of continuity thus serves to compound the trivializing tendencies of universality. The whole experience of viewing or listening is turned into a glorified version of "Tonight." And the point about a program like "Tonight" is that item follows item too smoothly and rapidly for any one item to engage the attention or grip the imagination for more than the moment of its passage. Comical items and serious items, the calamitous and the diverting parade before us in unending processions. No pause for thought or differentiation is allowed.

The same is true for broadcasting as a whole. Because something must always be on it is virtually impossible to give different weights to different items. Unless one decides to switch off to think or talk in the split second between items or programs one's chance of absorbing or digesting, let alone criticizing, what one sees or hears is lost. It is a standard feature of the reports of people who have "observed" groups watching television that incipient comment or conversation about a program is quashed as attention is drawn back to whatever next appears on the screen. Discussion gives way to asides and appreciative noises. The effect is of a blurring of edges, an ironing-out of differences of stature and scale between items and programs. Individual programs share the fate of the heroes of Webster's play:

> These wretched eminent things
> Leave no more fame behind 'em, than should one
> Fall in a frost, and leave his print in snow—
> As soon as the sun shines it ever melts
> Both form and matter.

In broadcasting the sun of the next program is always shining. Within ten seconds of a tribute to Bertrand Russell there follows a tribute to Ivor Novello. . . .

And these effects are compounded again by another characteristic of broadcasting, its domesticity. It is this characteristic that makes it virtually impossible for radio and television to escape from the tendencies to trivialization which their universality and continuity encourage and permit. Radio and television are provided in the home. And because they are one does not have to make any conscious act of choice in order to be exposed to them. To see a film one has to decide to go to the pictures (not necessarily to see the film one sees, though). Reading a paper or going to a football match or a pub all involve a relatively deliberate effort; one chooses what to do and what should happen to one. None of this is true for watching or listening. These are activities on which one embarks, typically, unthinkingly; they are so easy to embark on. People can and do switch on in a way that is as routine as the way in which they wash and have tea when they come in. These are activities from which the problem of decision has been removed. "Now," as one man put it, "you don't need to worry how you will spend your time."

Ever present, radio and television provide alternatives, not just to other activities, but to the whole problem of thinking what to do. One BBC survey found that the more an individual watched television the less likely he was to describe himself as "choosey" rather than "not choosey" about the programs he watched. And this is not very surprising. Because television is so easily available it is given functions which have nothing to do with conscious choice or cultural discrimination. For people who watch a lot it is not just what they watch but the fact of watching that is important. There seems to be a direct progression in this respect from the "choosey" ten per cent at one end to the ten per cent of "addicts" at the other extreme for whom watching and listening have become rewarding activities in their own right regardless of what is seen or heard. Most people are not in either of these groups of course and do discriminate to a greater or lesser degree. But the domesticity of broadcasting, combining with its universality and continuity, opens a primrose path along which the audience has an open invitation to be led toward addiction.

In one particular way the domesticity of broadcasting furthers the decline of choosiness. Because programs are so easily and constantly available one thing that most members of the audience are likely to ask of the media sooner or later is that they provide a certain minimum of wholly undemanding distraction. Radio and television are asked to do things which other, nondomestic, discontinuous, selective media cannot—to allow listeners and viewers to relax, to provide just the sort of "cushion against reality" that Raymond Williams describes, to create an agreeable background for passing and wasting time. Because they are domestic these media are expected to be unexacting, to provide relief from routine and effort. Nor do I see how this demand, even if we call it a demand for "escape," can be said to be unreasonable or improper. The quality and pace of modern work make it difficult to censure the use of broadcasting for light relief. Broadcasting, in short, through its special character, acquires strictly nonaesthetic, social, and psychological functions which other media do not have (or do not have to nearly the same extent). R. H. S. Crossman, indeed, goes so far as to speak of a "right to triviality." Certainly, a nonstop supply of programs making rigorous demands on the judgment, attention, and imagination would deny to most viewers and listeners an important and proper use of the media. . . .

At the same time, one cannot lead taste if one has no sense of direction; one cannot raise standards unless one will allow that some things are better than others and some worse. And what has happened with these media is that the public service image of their own role has made broadcasters so afraid of imposing that they do seem to have lost all sense of direction. In its place they have set up a largely spurious public service ideal of impartiality. Other mass media may have the wrong values; one's first impression of radio and television is that they have

no values. The press and cinema may glamorize the shoddy and they may
have false, even vicious, priorities. But at least they have priorities; they
do patently select and editorialize; some things are headlined and some
ignored; if a newspaper felt like flaying the government's defense policy
it would do so; it is sensible to talk about the "character" of these media.
Radio and television, on the contrary, have no editors, they do not take
stands, they do not admit to having conscious and consistent principles of
selection—except perhaps the worst of all possible principles, the principle of "news value." The Pilkington Committee had a hard time getting
the controllers of these media to admit that they ever chose or planned
anything. What the broadcasters offered the Committee were the ideas of
neutrality, balance, and the mirroring of society. . . .

Arguments about giving the public what it wants are the over-arching
claims in terms of which all the trivializing tendencies of the media are
drawn together and collectively justified. Like the belief in impartiality
the appeal to what the public wants is spurious through and through.
Just as something has to be selected and something rejected whether the
selecting is done consciously or not, so the highly centralized structure
of broadcasting means that judgments are constantly being made about
the nature of audience wants and that in practice the only test of these
supposed wants is audience size. And I would suggest that to defend
programs that are more "acceptable" than "authentic" on the ground
that such programs have huge audiences and that these huge audiences
show that such programs are what the public "wants" is to ignore the
real relationship that exists between the broadcaster and his public and
to make nonsense of the idea of a want.

Gilbert Seldes, in one of his essays on the mass media, tells a story of
a cinema proprietor in Nigeria who owned, and showed, only two films,
King Kong, and *The Mark of Zorro*. Three days a week he packed the
house with one of these; on the other three he did the same with the
other; on Sunday as a surefire double feature he showed them both. This
went on for years. The story epitomizes the relationship between communicator and public in the mass media. This enterprising man had
fastened on to a *general* demand for entertainment; this he had met in a
somewhat specific way; and he had gone on to work up an audience for
the specific form of entertainment he was able to provide; finally, since
he monopolized the means of entertainment in that region, he had contrived to "prevent an audience for any other sort of entertainment from
coming into existence."

The sorts of demands people actually make are diffuse and unspecific.
If one asks what "want" a particular program is meeting one very rarely

finds that the want is one that could be met *only* by the program in question. Rather, general wants, for amusement, background, excitement, are met in the particular ways the broadcasters find most convenient. The relationship between communicator and public is a manipulative one with the initiative firmly on the side of the communicator. When television provides a glut of Westerns the public selects Westerns as its favorite type of program; when the companies switch to providing hospital dramas the public discovers a want for these. A series of recent studies has shown with growing clarity how far, as Dr. Himmelweit puts it, "taste is the product of the producer, rather than television entertainment the response of the producer to the public's taste." Or as Gilbert Seldes writes:

> Demand is generalized and diffuse—for entertainment, for thrills, for vicarious sadness, for laughs; it can be satisfied by programs of different types and different qualities; and only after these programs have been offered is there any demand (specifically) for them. Supply comes first in this business and creates its own demand.

The nature and working logic of these media tend, in short, "to create those conditions in which the wants that can be most easily satisfied by the communicator take precedence over others." And what this means in practice is that tendencies to trivialization are built into almost everything that the media do. This is the easy and convenient way to operate; to some extent even the unavoidable way.

Trivialization is, at heart, a simple failure to treat the subject one is handling, whatever it may be, with the respect it deserves. A program, as the Pilkington Committee point out in what is perhaps their most important single argument, is not trivial because its matter is light or unimportant; it is trivial if its matter is devalued in the process of communication:

> Triviality resides in the way the subject matter is approached and the manner in which it is presented. A trivial approach can consist in a failure to respect the potentialities of the subject matter no matter what it be, or in a too ready reliance on well-tried themes, or in a habit of conforming to established patterns or in a reluctance to be imaginatively adventurous . . . in a failure to take full and disciplined advantage of the artistic and technical facilities which are relevant to a particular subject, or in an excessive interest in smart packaging at the expense of the contents of the package, or in a reliance on gimmicks so as to give a spurious interest to a program at the cost of its imaginative integrity, or in too great a dependence on hackneyed devices for creating suspense or raising a laugh or evoking tears.

I have quoted this passage at length for it provides the best brief statement I know of the nature of the problem that is built into the organization of television and radio in this country and of the sorts of tests we ought to apply to broadcast material. . . .

The Roles of Radio

Harold Mendelsohn

Generally speaking, radio functions as a diverting "companion," and it helps to fill voids that are created by (1) routine and boring tasks and (2) feelings of social isolation and loneliness.

To the harried mother whose environment is child- and work-centered for the good part of the day, radio introduces an "adult" element that is perceived to be both companionable and diverting.

"I listen to the radio from the time I get up until I go to bed. It regulates my day and it keeps me company. I can do other things at the same time, cook, clean, and still hear it all the time. I do everything with it and because it's in the kitchen I'm in there with it almost all day. Also, when you are home with children, the day seems to have no beginning and no end, and radio really helps to break it up a little."

To the individual who by virtue of either his occupation or incapacity is cut off from much social participation during the normal course of the day, radio serves as a reliable, nonthreatening, pleasant human surrogate that sustains him by keeping him "in touch" with the "realities" of normal social life. A truck driver commented:

"It makes my driving easier. I drive a truck all day and if I didn't have the radio, I'd go batty. I find driving more enjoyable when I hear nice music."

Corollary to radio's major function as a companion is its adaptability to the listener's mood or psychological frame of mind at any given time. The wide variety of radio stations available to the average listener affords him the opportunity to select programs that either (1) correspond to his state of mind or (2) can effect a change of mood in the listener.

"If you are in the house a lot, you can relax. . . . If it's a topic on social affairs it will relax you in that it makes you think more. . . . Also, music is very good, it's relaxing. . . . My first choice is rock-and-roll and then, classics. . . . *It depends on the mood.* . . . There is a time for everything. Rock-and-roll keeps me happy, classical is good to relax with when you are reading."

The two basic mood functions of radio—that of sustaining and creating desired psychological climates—to a great degree affect the listener's choice of kinds of stations and programs. This is particularly true, in regard to music. If the listener is looking for active mood accompaniment, he will seek out music that is in his words "peppy and lively." "I like rock-and-roll. It's lively; it's what keeps you going. It's just what I like; it's good waker-upper music." On the other hand, if the listener desires to eliminate an unpleasant or disagreeable mood tone, he will seek out the "releasing" music that he considers to be "relaxing." "I like to relax with semiclassical music. Actually, I like waltzes best. I just love them. They make me feel so good—particularly when I am overly tired and need a change. Waltzes make me feel as if I am flying or soaring. They do give me a lift."

It is interesting to note that no particular form or style of music is considered to be any more suitable for active moods or for "relaxing" than others. Consequently, classical music, jazz, rock-and-roll, operetta, country music, all are considered to be equally appropriate to the two functions.

Thus far the discussion of the functions radio performs has been in terms of the gratifications to the individual listener. These gratifications are indicative of the *manifest* "entertainment" functions of radio. What qualifications does the conveying of news and information provide?

In times of crises people turn to radio as a source of immediate news in an effort to "keep up" with events as they occur. Thus, for example, 44 percent of the WMCA listeners in the Qualitative Sample reported that they tune in their radios "especially to hear the news."

The possibility of surfeit with the very frequent presentation of news (often the same news) is remote. Listeners simply do not seem to get enough news. Whether the "newscast" is a warmed-over version of what was already heard, whether it adds one or two "new" details, or whether it reports "news"—does not seem to affect the listening habits of the listener. Consequently, 80 of the 100 WMCA listeners who were interviewed intensively claimed they would not switch off a given station's news broadcast—even though they had chosen that station to listen to music and had already heard the news.

"I just leave it on. I may not listen, but I leave it on. I sometimes hear the same news six or seven times a day, and I usually do hear it without making any attempt at listening, unless there is something new; then I perk up my ears. I never get a morning newspaper and I depend on the radio for the news during the day until late afternoon or evening."

In addition to enjoying a sense of being "informed" at all times, radio news and information broadcasts allow the listener to participate vicariously in the great events of the day. In a world of overwhelming complexity where the role of the individual in shaping events is becoming ever more remote, "keeping up" with the news easily becomes a substitute for being actively involved in the issues and events of the day.

On a smaller scale, radio provides information that is of immediate personal utility to the listener, who may be affected by a strictly local event such as an emergent storm, a traffic tie-up, or a strike in the local plant.

"To me, radio gives me the latest happenings. Just what happened at the time it happens. To me news timeliness is very important. At times I am in forefront of news or part of the news. Right now as a police officer, because of my job, I am very interested in the hurricane. I am on alert now so news is very important. As a rule, the radio is on at all times that the TV isn't on."

Just as radio allows the listener to "participate" psychologically in the news events of the day, it also allows him to share with others a wide variety of events of common interest and concern. The listener uses radio to bind him closer to other listeners like himself merely by virtue of having been a witness to the same happenings. To many listeners these shared experiences become foci of attention and conversation.

In this process, much of the "talk" content of radio broadcasts serves as a "social lubricant" by providing listeners with things to talk about. It serves as a rather harmless catalyst in making casual communication between people easier. Consider, for example, the following statement by an adult female listener: "The current events on radio help me to discuss with my husband in the evening."

To the teen-ager who is often particularly in need of approved social cues, radio's role in providing him with such cues is significant. . . .

The Witness Point in the Film

Vernon Young

While the Hollywood motion picture is continually under fire from a variety of fronts for not being sufficiently radical in its social interpretation or for being too radical, for appealing to the twelve-year-old mind or for not appealing to a larger number of twelve-year-old minds, for not filming the classics or for filming too many bad classics (or for filming good ones badly), for being sexually evasive or for being sexually self-conscious, one might well abandon the idea of civic criticism for the amoral and simple question: Just what *is* a movie?

The expense of spirit in a waste of shameful moralizing over content has ignored the fundamental identity of the motion picture as an art—or shall we say as a synthesis of science and of various art forms?—since it is with some such temporization that we must begin. And before we can conclude with high-minded resolutions as to the motion picture's public obligations, we should come to some agreement on its intrinsic endowments. Means determine, or at least qualify, ends; syntax precedes argument.

The instigator of a form should certainly be listened to and remembered when he coins its definition, even if the form thereafter undergoes mutations which modify the original defining. In the late 1870s an American named Edward Muybridge performed an experiment with twelve still cameras in order to record the motions of a trotting horse for Leland Stanford. This is the first known experiment in the development of what later became "moving pictures." Subsequently, Muybridge defined the movie as "an apparatus for synthetically demonstrating movements analytically photographed from life." No purer definition of the movie as a process has been evolved; all extensions of definition derive from this one, since they have had to derive from the nature of the thing in itself.

Later, when the film as a vehicle of aesthetically organized content was being more widely recognized and more intensively urged, Sergei Eisenstein, one of the most voluble theorists working in the film medium, declared that film form was "a question of creating a series of images in such a way that it provokes an effective movement which in turn awakens a series of ideas. From image to sentiment, from sentiment to thesis." Here is a dialectical description rather than a mechanistic analysis. Between Muybridge and Eisenstein we find the essence and the limits of our definition. All elaborations of statement on this subject must assume the premise that the movie begins with *the art of photographed motion.* The movie is the art of making motion meaningful; it is a dynamic of visual relationships, assisted, generally, by the arts of the scenarist and the actor and by the incorporation of selected sound. Within the framework of the pictorialized problem, the director and editor may augment, distill, or diffuse; increase or decrease tempo by mechanical means, compound images after the event and otherwise arbitrarily complicate, simplify, or intensify the continuity originally devised.

Self-evident, it would seem; yet the commercial movie perennially abdicates its own potential in favor of the lazier chronology of the legitimate theater and the novel of the Fielding tradition, using an unimaginative succession of medium, distance, and close shots, little more dynamic than the magic lantern. The great pioneers of the film art, such as Meliès, D. W. Griffith, Abel Gance, and Pudovkin, empirically established the simple fact that a movie *must be kept moving,* and over the years this principle has been fortified by continuing implementations: moving the camera instead of merely moving the object, and moving it from a variety of positions; employing many brief shots to indicate simultaneity or rapid sequence; balancing "dissolves," "irises," and "fade-outs" with direct cuts; flashing rapidly from detail to larger scene and utilizing music in direct or in counterpoint relation with the photographed images. . . .

For the modern sensibility, the moviegoing experience is rightly a manifold one. The agents of a play's action move across one's field of vision at an unvarying distance; those of a movie's travel in a stranger sense. With increased ratio to the degree of directorial sophistication, *you* move into the field of vision. You have the illusion of leaving normal dimensions; you are inescapably involved, mute witness and participator as well; not restricted to a set distance from the drama, you may approach it from in front, from above, even from underneath—see it *in toto, in medias res,* or agonizingly from its peripheral inceptions. The helpless filmgoer is a Gulliver, subject to extraordinary and shaking changes of perspective. More unbearably than Gulliver, he inhabits Lilliput and Brobdingnag simultaneously, or at least within shattering accelerations of time, and may find himself transported in the flutter of an eyelid (a change of lens) from a mountaintop to a dark alleyway, from thence to beneath a table, behind a curtain, or within palpitating distance of the heroine's bosom.

In view (and one means just that) of this superior kaleidoscope of momentum, it is surprising how the inveterate film-goer has taken this wonder for granted, how unaware he is that its artisans have confected an art-science organically expressive of an age that successively finds itself characterized in terms of such process fields as engineering, thermodynamics, psychology, or physics. For the motion picture, so understood, is *the* art of our time analogous with these subjects—mobile, divisive, atomic if you like: a form-breaker, disintegrator, working from specialized and defined mechanical methods toward frequently undetermined ends, incorporating as it goes the ruins of our historical arts of painting, music, and poetry, creating a new whole, plastic, beautiful perhaps, irregularly conditioned by the confused tone of journalism, by the multiple kinesthetic appetites of the driven masses, by our now universal mania for disregarding privacy, for annihilating distance and identity. The movie reflects the inquisitive lust for the panoramic vision indulged by the aviator but present in us all, *malgré nous;* reflects, from each of us, the amateur psychoanalyst, the arrogant sociologist, the latent violator, the cold *voyeur.* (Wouldn't we all rather see Audrey Hepburn than Botticelli's Venus, rising from the foam?) And because it is dedicated to our collateral retinizing, to what Morris Ernst has justly called "the Esperanto of the eye," it is often colossally vulgar. Yet is it more so than Broadway's musical comedies or the average fiction best-seller?

The French, who care pertinently for this subject, have produced, as might be expected, a spokesman with a flair for definition. René Guillère, in an essay primarily concerned with jazz, has provided us with an elegantly exact defense of that world of form in which the cinema finds its justification.

> Formerly the science of aesthetics rested content on the principle of fused elements. In music—on the continuous melodic line threaded through harmonic chords; in literature—on the fusion of a sentence's elements through conjunctions and transitions; in art—on a continuity of plastic forms and structures of combinations of these forms. Modern aesthetics is built upon the disunion of elements, heightening the contrast of each other: repetition of identical elements, which serves to strengthen the identity of contrast. . . .

Allowing with a shrug for M. Guillère's cavalier appropriation of the entire scope of modern art, we must concede that he has herein precisely described the qualitative nature of the motion picture. "The disunion of elements, heightening the contrast of each other" is the basis of film assembly: union through disunion, a somewhat more dynamic modification of terms than Eisenstein's Hegelian "from image to sentiment, from sentiment to thesis."

For all these reasons it is significantly the contemporary world that has, by Hollywood, been most fittingly translated into usable movie terms. We live in a fragmented, motile environment, and in the motion picture the seemingly futile activity of daily American urban life acquires, by reason of its decoction into meaningful rhythms and patterns of sound and image, excitement and acceptability. The modern temper, exasperated and energetic, yet passive under bombardment by accessories to nature, receives, in this visual drama of multiplicity, its most authentic revelation. You may beg this question by supporting Yvor Winters' objection to mimetic poetry as "the fallacy of expressive form," or you may defer to the subtler justice in George Williamson's approval of John Donne: "To be contemporary in the right sense means to find the peculiar emotional tension of the time and to mold language to its expression." In what other medium can one find a language so rhythmically molded to express the peculiar emotional tension of *our* time (no irony avoided) as the language of the movie camera? European moviemakers are not so historically restricted; they have an intimate sense of the past. American producers see the past as no less in mindless frenzy than the present; therefore, the strange hollow sound of our Westerns and our costume epics. During the last decade, certainly, the most expertly made American films have been almost all contemporary in subject matter.

(It is noteworthy to observe, in passing, that largely because the writers are permitted more honesty in this direction, the direct subject has been either the underworld of society or the underside of the mind: cf. *The Strange Love of Martha Ivers, The Killers, The Lady in the Lake, Cross Fire, Act of Violence, Champion, Criss Cross, They Live by Night, Caught, The Sniper.*) . . .

From the literary bias, one could insist that the movie is the art of the novel reduced to absurdity. Like the novel in respect of flexibility, shifts of viewpoint, the ability intimately to dissect or comprehensively to mass, the movie takes the novel one step further, the last, often the disastrous step. It literalizes the novel. (All movie literalism is of course relative; once beyond newsreel immediacy, the artistry is created by a consistent intention and a host of tributary services. And artistry does not necessarily increase with the degree of expressionism, impressionism, surrealism, or plotless vagary the movie may serve. The important fantasists, from Meliès to Cocteau, have sought to transcend all modes of cinematic realism.

Their achivements have often been prodigious. But for purposes of easier reference, I am not attempting, in the ensuing notations, to research the extremist adventure on film.)

On its own naked account, the motion picture cannot take you into the articulated content of thought but it can suggest the content by showing objects so related as to mirror the associations of thought. (Like symbolist poetry it may conceal and delay meaning until its images are completed.) The film version of your literary world banishes ambiguity and alternative renderings. The spectator's private mind is made up for him; the intermediate reaction of the reader is eliminated, his imagination circumscribed, his initiative preempted. There is substituted instead this particular image or sequence, dictatorially composed: not any street lined with poplars, vanishing to a distant sky of one's own impalpable painting but this street, these poplars here, this house-front so, this demarcated horizon with no other arrangement than this embodied-in-Technicolor one, no more, no less, and no time to ask or to wonder what is around this exactly measured corner; not any heroine you might individually have imagined from the subtle clues of a prose writer who would allow you, despite his precise order of coloration and anatomy, freedom to wander by yourself with the creature of your own nocturnal imagination, but *this* actress, vivid and irrevocable, her hairline gliding around the tangible curve of an ear you might never have included, hands scorning the poverty of your tactile invention, mouth promising, perhaps, variations you had not yet arrived at. With a recklessness unavailable to the legitimate theater, the movie teases one into an even greater illusion of spontaneity and volition which is the satisfying and sometimes sinister secret of its power. It is a form of literalism which, if insufficiently transformed, will indeed be "strange to our solid eye." It will stupefy, instead of releasing, the imagination of the spectator. . . .

The Film Generation

Stanley Kauffmann

Some of the following remarks were included, in differing forms, in talks delivered recently at several universities, colleges, and seminars. In one of the audiences were a distinguished poet and a critic of the graphic arts. Afterward, the critic came up to me and said, "You destroyed us. You wiped out our professions. You rendered my friend and me obsolete." I said that I neither believed nor intended that. Then he said wryly, stroking his chin, "On the other hand, if I were twenty years younger, I know I'd go into films."

His dismal reaction had been prompted by my assertion that film is the art for which there is the greatest spontaneous appetite in America at present, and by my reasons for thinking so. I must be clear that this is not to say that it is the art practiced at the highest level in this country; the film public depends more on imports today than does any other art public. But observation and experience, and the experience of others, make me believe that this uniquely responsive audience exists.

Or, in another phrase, there exists a Film Generation: the first generation that has matured in a culture in which the film has been of accepted serious relevance, however that seriousness is defined. Before 1935 films were proportionately more popular than they are now, but for the huge majority of film-goers they represented a regular weekly or semiweekly bath of escapism. Such an escapist audience still exists in large number, but another audience, most of them born since 1935, exists along with it. This group, this Film Generation, is certainly not exclusively grim, but it is essentially serious. Even its appreciations of sheer entertainment films reflect an over-all serious view.

There are a number of reasons, old and new, intrinsic and extrinsic, why this generation has come into being. Here are some of the older, intrinsic reasons.

1. In an age imbued with technological interest, the film art flowers out of technology. Excepting architecture, film is the one art that can capitalize directly and extensively on this century's luxuriance in applied

science. Graphic artists have used mechanical and electronic elements, poets and painters have used computers, composers use electronic tapes. These are matters of choice. The film-maker has no choice: he must use complicated electronic and mechanical equipment. This fact helps to create a strong sense of junction with his society, of membership in the present. American artists have often been ashamed of—sometimes have dreaded—a feeling of difference from the busy "real" American world around them. For the film-maker the very instruments of his art provide communion with the spirit of his age. I think that the audience shares his feeling of union, sometimes consciously (especially when stereophonic sound, special optical effects, or color processes are used). The scientific skills employed are thus in themselves a link between the artist and the audience, and are a further link between them all and the unseen, unheard but apprehended society bustling outside the film theater.

There is a pleasant paradoxical corollary. In an era that is much concerned with the survival of the human being as such, in an increasingly mechanized age, here a complicated technology is used to celebrate the human being.

2. The world of surfaces and physical details has again become material for art. Just as the naturalistic novel seems to be sputtering to a halt, overdescribed down to the last vest button, the film gives some of its virtues new artistic life. A novelist who employs the slow steam-roller apparatus of intense naturalism these days is asking for an extra vote of confidence from the reader, because the method and effects are so familiar that the reader can anticipate by pages. Even when there is the interest of an unusual setting, the reader is conscious that different nouns have been slipped into a worn pattern. The "new" French novel of Robbe-Grillet, Duras, Sarraute attempts to counteract this condition by intensifying it, using surfaces as the last realities, the only dependable objective correlatives. Sometimes, for some readers, this works. But both the old and the latter-day naturalisms must strain in order to connect. Rolf Hochhuth, the author of *The Deputy*, has said:

> When I recently saw Ingmar Bergman's *The Silence*, I left that Hamburg movie house with the question, "What is there left for the novelist today?" Think of what Bergman can do with a single shot of his camera, up a street, down a corridor, into a woman's armpit. Of all he can say with this without saying a word.

Despite Hochhuth's understandable thrill-despair, there is plenty left for the novelist to say, even of armpits, but the essence of his remark rightly strips from fiction the primary function of creating material reality.

The film has not only taken over this function but exalted it: it manages to make poetry out of doorknobs, breakfasts, furniture. Trivial details, of which everyone's universe is made, can once again be transmuted into metaphor, contributing to imaginative act.

A complementary, powerful fact is that this principle operates whether the film-maker is concerned with it or not. In any film except those with fantastic settings, whether the director's aim is naturalistic or romantic or symbolic or anything else, the streets and stairways and cigarette lighters are present, the girl's room is at least as real as the girl—often it bolsters her defective reality. Emphasized or not, invited or not, the physical world through the intensifications of photography never stops insisting on its presence and relevance.

This new life of surfaces gives a discrete verity to many mediocre films and gives great vitality to a film by a good artist. Consciously or not, this vitality reassures the audience, tangentially certifying and commenting on its habitat. Indeed, out of this phenomenon, it can be argued that the film discovered pop art years ago, digested this minor achievement, then continued on its way.

3. The film form seems particularly apt for the treatment of many of the pressing questions of our time: inner states of tension or of doubt or apathy—even (as we shall see) doubts about art itself. The film can externalize some psychical matters that, for example, the theater cannot easily deal with; and it can relate them to physical environment in a manner that the theater cannot contain nor the novel quite duplicate. The film can dramatize post-Freudian man, and his habitat—and the relation between the two. One does not need to believe in the death of the theater or the novel—as I do not—in order to see these special graces in the film.

4. Film is the only art besides music that is available to the whole world at once, exactly as it was first made. With subtitles, it is the only art involving language that can be enjoyed in a language of which one is ignorant. (I except opera, where the language rarely needs to be understood precisely.)

The point is not the spreading of information or amity, as in USIA or UNESCO films, useful though they may be. The point is emotional relationship and debt. If one has been moved by, for instance, Japanese actors in Japanese settings, in actions of Japanese life that have resonated against one's own experience, there is a connection with Japan that is deeper than the benefits of propaganda or travelogue. No one who has been moved by *Ikiru* can think of Japan and the Japanese exactly as he thought before.

Obviously similar experience—emotional and spiritual—is available through other arts, but rarely with the imperial ease of the film. As against foreign literature, foreign films have an advantage besides accessibility in the original language. The Japanese novelist invites us to recreate the scene in imagination. The Japanese film-maker provides the scene for us, with a vividness that our minds cannot equal in a foreign setting. Thus our responses can begin at a more advanced point and can more easily (although not more strongly) be stimulated and heightened.

This universality and this relative simultaneity of artistic experience have made us all members of a much larger empathetic community than has been immediately possible before in history.

5. Film has one great benefit by accident: its youth, which means not only vigor but the reach of possibility. The novel, still very much alive, is conscious of having to remain alive. One of its chief handicaps is its history; the novelist is burdened with the achievements of the past. This is also true of poetry. It flourishes certainly; as with fiction, the state of poetry is far better than is often assumed. But poetry, too, is conscious of a struggle for pertinent survival. In painting and sculpture, the desperation is readily apparent; the new fashion in each new season makes it clear. But the film is an infant, only begun. It has already accomplished miracles. Consider that it was only fifty years from Edison's camera to *Citizen Kane,* which is rather as if Stravinsky had written *Petrouchka* fifty years after Guido d'Arezzo developed musical notation. Nevertheless the film continent has only just been discovered, the boundaries are not remotely in sight. It is this freshness that gives the young generation— what I have called the Film Generation—not only the excitement of its potential but a strong proprietary feeling. The film belongs to them.

These, I think, are some of the reasons for the growth of that new film audience. But they raise a question. As noted, these reasons have been valid to some degree for a long time, yet it is only in about the last twenty years that the Film Generation has emerged. Why didn't this happen sooner? Why have these reasons begun to be strongly operative only since the Second World War?

In that period other elements have risen to galvanize them. Some of these later elements come from outside the film world: the spurt in college education; political and social abrasions and changes; moral, ethical, religious dissolutions and resolutions. All these have made this generation more impatient and more hungry. But, since the Second War, there have also been some important developments within the film world itself.[1] These developments have been in content, not in form. Three elements are especially evident: increased sexuality, an increase in national flavor, and an increased stress on the individual. The latter two are linked.

As for the first, sex has been important currency in the theater since *The Agamemnon,* and with the first films came the first film idols. In fact there are scenes in many silent films that would have censor trouble today. But apart from sexual display or the sex appeal of any actor or actress, there is now—in many foreign films and some American ones—a sexual attitude that can be respected: an attitude closer to the realities of sexual life than the mythology that is preached by clergy of every faith, by mass media, by parents. This relative sexual freedom, long established in fiction and the theater, has been slower to arrive in films because of their wider availability to all ages and mentalities, and the consequent brooding of censors. Now, in a more liberal time, this freedom makes films even more pertinent to this generation. The mythology that still passes for sexual morality is prescriptive, these films are descriptive; but there is more to their merit than verisimilitude. Not by nudity or bedroom calisthenics nor frank language but by fidelity to the complexities of sexual behavior, these films provide more than recognition. By accepting and exploring complexities, they provide confidence in the fundamental beauty of those complexities, in the desirability of being human, even with all the trouble it involves.

The second element, national flavor, has been described by the English critic Penelope Houston in *The Contemporary Cinema* (1963):

> However partial or distorted an image one gets of a society through its cinema, it is still possible to discern the national face behind the screen. It is difficult to conceive of a neorealist idealism [in Italy] without the jubilant preface of the liberation of Rome; or to look at Britain's films of the past few years without reference to our redbrick radicalism; or to ignore the effect of the political climate on a French cinema which declares its awareness of

[1] These do not include linguistic developments. Nothing has changed the language of film as, for example, electronics has changed music or abstract expressionism has altered the vision of painting. There have been many technical film developments—wide screens, stereophonic sound, color refinements—but so far they have largely been peripheral to the art itself. They, and the improved hand-held camera and recorder, may affect the basic language of film in future; they have not yet markedly done so. This fact can be taken as an implied strength. Experiments in artistic technique are usually a sign that a boundary has been reached with old techniques. In film there is no hint of exhaustion in the techniques that were known to Griffith and Eisenstein forty years ago.

strain in the very insistence with which it puts private before public life and creation for creation's sake before either.

It would be easy to add a similar sentence for almost every major film-producing country. Japanese films are concerned with contemporary unrest, directly and indirectly. Many of their costume pictures about samurai swordsmen are set in the 1860s when the feudal system was crumbling and immense social metamorphosis was taking place. The Soviet film has deepened in lethargy as revolutionary fervor wore off, as Stalinist despotism made it nervous, as some subsequent economic and scientific successes made it smug. It has become, with a few exceptions, either war glory or the ideologic equivalent of the petty bourgeois confection. As for America, the poor boy and rich girl story (or rich boy and poor girl) which was the staple of the popular film before the Second War has disappeared. Money as romance, the Gatsby dream, has receded, not because everyone is now rich but because the middle-class image has replaced both the poor image and the rich image. What American would now relish the ancient compliment "poor but honest"? And what is the difference *in appearance* between the clerk's car and the boss's? The much-mooted ascendancy of the middle class has reached the point where it is strong enough to control cultural forms, to magnify its own image in art.

With this ascendancy we have seen the emergence of a new romantic hero, posed against this bourgeois background, since all such heroes must contrast with their societies. The new romantic is the liberated prole, with a motorcycle or a Texas Cadillac, seeking his life by assaulting convention and morality, rather than by striving for success in accepted modes, either with money or with women. This hero scoffs at ideals of excellence and aspiration at the same time that he wants to dominate. There are signs that this hero may have run his course, but in the last twenty years or so he was pre-eminent.

A lesser companion of his still continues: the Frank Sinatra-Dean Martin figure, the smart, cool operator just inside the law, a philanderer righteously resentful of any claims on him by women. His casual *persona* derives in part from the night-club microphone, which was first a necessity, then became a prop, then a source of power and ease for those who had little power and could achieve nothing but ease. The invisible hand-held microphone accompanies the crooner-as-hero wherever he goes. His oblique, slithering solipsism seems likely to persist after the Brando figure, more directly descended from the proletarian rebel and Byronic individualist, has passed. Mere "coolness" persists; purposeful rebellion fades.

All the national colors described above apply both to popular and serious films. If we concentrate on serious film—film made primarily as personal expression, not as contractual job or money-spinner—then we often find, besides intensified national color, an intensified introspection. This is the third of our elements: a concern with the exploration of the individual as a universe. It is not a novelty in films. No more introspective films have ever been made than Wiene's *The Cabinet of Dr. Caligari* (1919) or Pabst's *Secrets of a Soul* (1926). But merely to mention such names as Bergman, Antonioni, Fellini, Ozu, Torre Nilsson, Olmi, Truffaut is to see that, for many outstanding directors, there has lately been more reliance on inner conflict than on classic confrontation of antagonists. These men and others, including some Americans, have been extending the film into the vast areas of innermost privacy, even of the unconscious, that have been the province of the novel and of metaphysical poetry. Saul Bellow has complained that the modern novelist doesn't tell us what a human being *is* today. Bellow is a notable exception to his own complaint; but whether we agree or not, we can see that many contemporary film-makers have tried to answer that question, with a more consistent application than ever before in the history of the art.

These two elements—national color and the exploration of the individual—are obviously inseparable. Society and the man affect each other, even if it is in the man's withdrawal. These elements are further linked in a curious contradictory motion against our time. In an age when internationalism is promulgated as a solution to political difficulties, national colors have become more evident in films. In an age when social philosophers have begun to question the durability of individualism—which is, after all, a fairly recent concept in history and almost exclusive to the West—the film is tending to cherish the individual. Does this indicate a time lag between the film and the advances of political and social philosophy? On the contrary, I believe it indicates a perverse penetration to truth. The truth of art sometimes runs counter to what seems politically and intellectually desirable; that is always a risk of art. I think the film is showing us that nationalism, in the purely cultural sense, is becoming more necessary to us as jet plane and Telstar threaten to make us one world. I think that just at the time when technological and power structures challenge individualism, our own minds and souls have become more interesting to us. Up to now, technology has outraced self-discovery. Only now—in this postreligious, self-dependent age—are we beginning to appreciate how rich and dangerous each one of us is.

These elements have led, directly and by implication, to the phenomenon we are examining; the historical moment for the rise of the Film Generation, a surge of somewhat nostalgic revolution; a reluctance to lose what seems to be disappearing, accompanied by an impulse to dis-affection, an insistence on an amorphous cosmos. ("Stay loose." "Swing.") Doubtless that nostalgia is sentimental, an unwillingness to be banned from an Eden of individualism that in fact never existed. But much of the revolution is clearheaded; not so much an attempt to halt change as to influence it; a natural and valuable impulse to scratch on the chromium fronts of the advancing tanks of factory-society "Kilroy was here."

The divided attitude toward social change leads to another, crucial polarity. This generation has an ambivalent view of cultural tradition. On the one hand there is a great desire for such tradition, admitted or not. Everyone wants to know that he came from somewhere; it's less lonely. But this desire is often accompanied by a mirror attitude that looks on the past as failure and betrayal. It is of course a familiar indict-ment, the young accusing the old of having made a mess, but now the accusation is more stringent and more general because of the acceleration of change and the diminutions of choice.

This ambivalence toward tradition—this polarity that both wants and rejects it—has created a hunger for art as assurance of origins together with a preference for art forms that are relatively free of the past. Out-standing among these is film. Even though it has been on hand for sixty-five years or so, the film seems much more of the present and future than other forms. It has its roots—of content and method—in older arts: drama, literature, dance, painting; yet it is very much less entailed by the past than these arts. It satisfies this generation's ambivalent need in tradition. . . .

The Road Beyond Neorealism

Federico Fellini
(as interviewed by Gideon Bachmann)

BACHMANN: Your serious film career, then, began during the period of the flowering of Italian neorealism. The relation between your films

Excerpt from "The Road Beyond Neorealism" by Federico Fellini and Gideon Bachmann, in *Film: Book One*, edited by Robert Hughes, Grove Press, 1959. Reprinted with the permission of Gideon Bachmann.

and "classical" neorealism has been much debated by the critics. Do you feel that your work in any way derives from, or was influenced by the neorealist directors with whom you have worked, like de Sica, Rossellini, Lattuada, etc.?

FELLINI: Well, I was one of the first to write scripts for neorealist films. I think all my work is definitely in the neorealist style, even if in Italy today some people don't think so. But this is a long story. For me, neorealism is a way of seeing reality without prejudice, without the interference of conventions—just parking yourself in front of reality without any preconceived ideas.

BACHMANN: You don't mean simply to put the camera in front of "life" and photograph what's there?

FELLINI: No, it's a question of having the feeling for reality. Naturally, there is always the need for an interpretation. What has happened in Italy is that after the war everything for us was completely new. Italy was in ruins; you could say everything you felt by just looking around. Later, the leftist press capitalized on this inadvertent one-sidedness by saying that the only valid thing to do in films is to show what happens around you. But this has no value from an artistic point of view, because always the important thing is to know *who* sees the reality. Then it becomes a question of the power to condense, to show the essence of things. After all, why are the films we make so much better than newsreels?

BACHMANN: Though, of course, even newsreels are already one step removed from reality, through the selectivity of the cameraman who took them.

FELLINI: Right. . . . But why should people go to the movies, if films show reality only through a very cold, objective eye? It would be much better just to walk around in the street. For me, neorealism means looking at reality with an honest eye—but any kind of reality: not just social reality, but also spiritual reality, metaphysical reality, anything man has inside him.

BACHMANN: You mean anything that has reality for the director?

FELLINI: Yes.

BACHMANN: Then the completed film is really *two* steps removed from nature: first the personal *view* of it by the director, and then his *interpretation* of that personal view.

FELLINI: Yes, yes. For me, neorealism is not a question of *what* you show—its real spirit is in *how* you show it. It's just a way of looking around, without convention or prejudice. Certain people still think neorealism is fit to show only certain kinds of reality; and they insist that this is social reality. But in this way, it becomes mere propaganda. It is a program; to show only certain aspects of life. People have written that I am a traitor to the cause of neorealism, that I am too much of an individualist, too much of an individual. My own personal conviction, however, is that the films I have done so far are in the same style as the first neorealist films, simply telling the story of people. And always, in telling the story of some people, I try to show some truth.

BACHMANN: Is there any underlying philosophy in your films? I mean besides the depiction of what is truth for you.

FELLINI: Well, I could tell you what for me is one of the most pressing problems, one which provides part of the theme for all my films. It's the terrible difficulty people have in talking to each other—the old problem of communication, the desperate anguish to be *with*, the desire to have a real, authentic relationship with another person. You'll find this in *I Vitelloni,* in *La Strada,* in *Il Bidone,* and also in *Notti di Cabiria.* It may be that I'll change, but for now I'm completely absorbed in this problem—maybe because I have not yet solved it in my private life.

BACHMANN: Do you feel that the reason for this difficulty in interpersonal communication is that we have created a kind of society which makes it hard for people to have true relationships?

FELLINI: It is the fault of society only because society is made up of men. I believe that everyone has to find truth by himself. It is completely useless to prepare a statement for a crowd, or make a film with a message for everyone. I don't believe in talking to a crowd. Because what is a crowd? It is a collection of many individuals, each with his own reality. That is also the reason why my pictures never end. They never have a simple solution. I think it is immoral (in the true sense of the word) to tell a story that has a conclusion. Because you cut out your audience the moment you present a solution on the screen. Because there are no "solutions" in their lives. I think it is more moral—and more important—to show, let's say, the story of one man. Then everyone, with his own sensibility and on the basis of his own inner development, can try to find his own solution.

BACHMANN: You mean to say that by "ending" a problem, the filmmaker takes away from the audience the feeling that what they are seeing is the truth?

FELLINI: Yes, or even worse. For when you show a true problem and then resolve it, the spectator is beguiled into feeling that the problems in his own life, too, will solve themselves, and he can stop working on them for himself. By giving happy endings to films, you goad your audience into going on living in a trite, bland manner, because they are now sure that sometime, somewhere, something happy is going to happen to them, too, and without their having to do anything about it. Conversely, by not serving them the happy ending on a platter, you can make them think; you can remove some of that smug security. Then they'll *have* to find their own answers.

BACHMANN: This would seem to indicate that you're not just making pictures to make pictures, but because there are certain things you want to say.

FELLINI: Well, I don't start that way. What usually starts me on a film idea is that something happens to me which I think has some bearing on other people's experiences. And the feeling is usually the same: to try, first of all, to tell something about myself; and in doing so, to try to find a salvation, to try to find a road toward some meaning, some truth, something that will be important to others, too. And when, as often happens, people who have seen my films come to visit me—not to discuss my films, but to talk to me about their personal problems—I feel I have achieved something. It is always a great satisfaction for me. Of course, I can't help them clarify their problems, but it means the picture has done some good.

BACHMANN: When you say you don't start that way, do you mean to say that the real "message" of your films develops out of the material?

FELLINI: Well, a picture is a mixture of things. It changes. That is one of the reasons why making films is such a wonderful thing.

BACHMANN: Could you tell me about the process in your film work? A kind of step-by-step description of your work on any given film?

FELLINI: First, I have to be moved by a feeling. I have to be interested in one character or one problem. Once I have that, I don't really need a very well-written story or a very detailed script. I need to begin without knowing that everything is in perfect order; otherwise I lose all the fun of it. If I knew everything from the start, I would no longer be interested in doing it. So that when I begin a picture, I am not yet sure of the location or the actors. Because for me, to make a picture is like leaving for a trip. And the most interesting part of a trip is what you discover on the way. I am very open to suggestions when I start a film. I am not rigid about what I do. I like the people with me on the film to share this new adventure. Certainly, I do remember that I am shooting, sometimes.

When the picture is finished, I would, if possible, like not to see it. I often say to my producer, joking: "Let's not cut this one; let's make a new one instead." But I cut all my own films. Cutting is one of the most emotional aspects of film-making. It is the most exciting thing to see the picture begin to breathe; it is like seeing your child grow up. The

rhythm is not yet well identified, the sequence not established. But I
never reshoot. I believe that a good picture has to have defects. It has
to have mistakes in it, like life, like people. I don't believe that beauty,
in the sense of perfection, exists—except maybe for the angels. A beautiful woman is attractive only if she is not perfect. The most important
thing is to see to it that the picture is alive. This is the most rewarding
moment in making films: when the picture begins to live. And I never
go back to look at what I have already done—I edit the whole film right
through. When it's finished, and I go into the projection room to see
it for the first time, I like to be alone. I can express exactly what happens. I look at the picture; the picture looks at me. A lot of things happen. Some ideas are born; some die. Later I begin to "clean" the picture.
In Italy we do not use the sound we shoot on location, but redo the
whole track in the studio. But the first answer print still has the location
sound on it. Once that is removed, something happens again. The answer
print still has the flavor of the adventure of making the film—a train
that passed, a baby that cried, a window that opened. I remember the
people who were with me on location. I remember the trip. I would
like to retain these memories. Once they put the clean, new track on it,
it's like a father seeing his little girl wear lipstick for the first time. You
have to get to know this new creature that is emerging; you have to try
to like it. Then when you add the music, again something is added and
something is lost. Every time you see it again, there is some new feeling.
When it is completely finished, you have lost the objective point of view.
Then, when others see it, I react personally—I feel they have no right
to say anything about *my* picture. But I listen carefully, nevertheless—
I am trying to find out whether for them the picture is alive.

BACHMANN: Do you feel that in all the films you have made you have
always remained faithful to what you were trying to say when you started
the picture?

FELLINI: Yes, I do.

BACHMANN: Do you feel there is a relation between your work and
that of the current crop of Italian writers, like, for example, Carlo Levi
and Ennio Flaiano?

FELLINI: Yes, I think this core of neorealism in films has influenced
all the arts.

BACHMANN: Have you, yourself, done any writing except scripts?

FELLINI: No. Just some short stories when I worked for newspapers.
But not since I've worked in films. It's a different medium. A writer
can do everything by himself—but he needs discipline. He has to get up
at seven in the morning, and be alone in a room with a white sheet of

paper. I am too much of a *vitellone* to do that. I think I have chosen the best medium of expression for myself. I love the very precious combination of work and of living together that film-making offers. I approach film-making in a very personal way. That's why I consider myself a neorealist. Any research that a man does about himself, about his relationships with others and with the mystery of life, is a spiritual and—in the true sense—religious search. I suppose that is the extent of my formal philosophy. I make movies in the same way that I talk to people —whether it's a friend, a girl, a priest, or anyone: to seek some clarification. That is what neorealism means to me, in the original, pure sense. A search into oneself, and into others. In any direction, any direction where there is life. All the formal philosophy you could possibly apply to my work is that there is no formal philosophy. In film-making, as in living, you must take the experiences that life presents, those which apply to yourself and to others. Except that in film-making only the absolute truth will work. In life I may be a swindler or a crook, but that wouldn't work in a film. A man's film is like a naked man—nothing can be hidden. I must be truthful in my films.

III · Critiques and Cases

THE CRITICISM of individual works produced in the various media can take many forms which go beyond the usual kind of snap value judgments of newspaper and magazine reviewers. The selections in this section illustrate several of these forms.

The approach to a genre or general type of program or a film—such as a musical, detective story, or tough-guy film—is a frequent one; and of these genres the Western has been the subject of more discussion than any of the others. In his selection, T. J. Ross focuses on the genre of the Western as it has developed in television form. Delineating the sociological implications that are common in treatment of the Western, he finds the new form unsettling.

Similarly, Glenn E. Reddick examines the television situation comedy via one of its basic plot patterns and devices—deception—and draws some disturbing moral and sociological conclusions about them.

Leslie A. Fiedler takes a medium that is often the target of criticism, the comics, and uses them as a starting point for a complex analysis of why critics attack the comics as well as other forms of the mass media.

The genre approach is again illustrated by Susan Sontag's discussion of science fiction films as she places them in the current cultural and historical context and defines the kinds of hopes and tensions that they embody.

This kind of examination of the latent or underlying meaning that audiences derive, consciously and unconsciously, from the mass media is also found in the selection by Parker Tyler, who was one of the first critics to approach the film from a psychological perspective. Tyler applies this psychological method to the discussion of a single film, Marlon Brando's *One-Eyed Jacks*.

In the final pair of selections, Pauline Kael and Alan Casty explicate and defend the artistry of two different kinds of films—the new type of European film and the American realist film at its best. The two films discussed were the subject of adverse criticism, and in both selections the authors attempt to counter the opposing views and to approach the films from a more valid perspective.

The TV Western:
Debasement of a Tradition

T. J. Ross

Among the staple TV Westerns is one called *Colt .45*. Its hero, as in most of these shows, is a cowboy-cop. The paces he was put through in an episode of a few months back—something entitled "Gallows at Granite Gap"—exemplify the moral slant of all the TV action shows, a slant worth remarking on not only for its own grotesque sake, but also as a depressing reminder of how the tradition of the old-fashioned Hollywood action movie (before cinemascope) has been turned inside out by TV.

The *Colt .45* skit went this way: A criminal known as the Comanche Kid is about to be hanged. A matron seeks out the Kid's captors, Special Agent Colt and the neighborhood sheriff, to inquire about the prisoner's true ancestry, for she suspects the Kid may be her long-lost son. He had been kidnapped by the Indians in his infancy, but the mother hopes to ascertain his identity by means of a telltale scar on his chest. In a state of dramatic turmoil, she begs to be allowed to make this examination. Should the criminal prove to be her son, her joy of discovery will be scarred by the ghastly knowledge that she had given birth to a criminal-type. Since she herself is an innocent-mother-type, both Colt and the Sheriff feel for her and wish they could Do Something.

We have here an interesting and starkly simple situation, one which approximates to the primitively horrific and simple dilemmas of ancient tragedy, and which, in consequence, might have led (all within the half hour's format) to the moment of recognition and then perhaps to a resounding speech by Mother as she reproached the dooming paradoxes of fate, her eyes fixed all the while on her flesh-and-blood being marched off to his death. Or she might have risen to the more complex action of Choice and committed herself to death by her son's side as she attempted vainly to help him escape. Remaining, therefore, within the Code, the action might still have played itself out to a dignified and rousing conclusion. But what happens?

Sheriff leads Mother to the outlaw's cell. The Kid lurks in the shadows, a jauntily tilted sombrero covering half his face. He bares his chest, and it proves to be unscarred. Mother is so relieved that she explodes with a

From "Debasement of a Tradition" by T. J. Ross, in *Dissent*, Autumn 1960, 395–399. Reprinted by permission of the publisher.

109

holier-than-thou crack at the Kid's expense: "I feel sorry for you"—then
hastens away to catch the next coach back home, safe in the shelter of her
stance as the wide-eyed, innocent-mother type.

But when the cell's incumbent removes his sombrero he proves to be
—you guessed it—none other than the Special Agent, his vapid face con-
torted in a big "sheepish grin." The End.

The point of the trick ending, however, contains a grim message of
its own: that the Man with the Badge Knows What's Good For You
even to the extent of being allowed *carte blanche* to poke his finger in
the familial pie. The Man with the Badge now enjoys this freedom on all
the action shows, Western or plainclothes; generally, his role, as in the
skit just described, is to free a wholesome, adjusted type from guilt
feelings aroused by a sudden sense of connection to a shady, failure-type
(the failure-type is quickly recognizable as the character who is or is
about to become a criminal).

Take this skit from a Western called *Lawman:* A vicious badman
comes to town. The Lawman-hero is a mature, hard-bitten type; his
deputy is an apple-cheeked young sourpuss named Johnny. Of mysterious origins, Johnny has been adopted, and deputized, by the Lawman.
But badman tauntingly reports that he is Johnny's dad. His morale upset,
Johnny offers to resign his deputyship, for if badman is his dad then he
himself is probably no good (a simplified point of view which none of the
characters ever thinks to pause over). In the showdown badman is fatally
shot by Lawman after drawing on both him and Johnny. Badman makes
a death-bed clean-breast-of-it, exonerating Johnny of any blood-guilt.
The hint is that the villain is kidding and engaging in a last minute,
beau geste for the sake of his boy's peace of mind. We gather that a pep
talk, and mauling about, given him by the Lawman before the showdown
influenced his final testimony. By means, this time, of exacting false con-
fessions the Lawman fulfills his role as tight-lipped smooth manipulator
of peaceful states of mind.

But what if the action is such that a dread truth, or fact, cannot be
avoided; how then does the Lawman help a hapless type adjust? Here is
a *Gunsmoke* skit which offers the purest example of what the message,
in such instances, always adds up to: A girl is raped, beaten, and enslaved
by a gang of bad guys; they kill her dad, too. That most elephantine of
all TV Big Dads—Marshal Dillon—effects her rescue only after shooting, clobbering, and pitchforking to death the desperate gang. Just before
the fadeout the victimized woman stares up at the hero for the Word.

Standing ready to depart from the shack of horrors he says, with a throaty, hard-bitten sincerity: "Don't be bitter."

And this is precisely why Special Agent Colt hid the truth from mother. He didn't want her to become bitter. For think where bitterness may lead to. Mother might have become Belle Star, or Florence Nightingale, or Stella Dallas; that is, she might have been transformed from an anonymous, lovable Type to a being with a singular, problematic, personal history. In a well-earned bitterness, after all, lurks sometimes the beginnings of idea or desire.

II

Resistance on a TV character's part to a given culture or situation is allowed only when it is asserted with the connivance of the law officer. Thus the cards of the plot are so heavily stacked that the action skits must be pointlessly simple or, in the "adult" Westerns, inhumanly grotesque and archaic in situation and treatment. In each case, the point of resistance involves a betrayal of a member of a family, or a friend, or lover. This act of betrayal signifies a "weak" character's moment of self-assertion, of growth to manhood. After the moment of betrayal, the character is shown collapsing limply and gratefully into the arms of the Lawman; this gesture marks the acceptance of a character's validity by the State.

Gunsmoke, for example, is supposed to be the classiest of the Western shows. It deals with characters so "colorful," quaint and sturdy that their shenanigans are supposed to represent a "realistic" slice of Old West life. One skit had to do with a brace of sons tyrannized by a dad who was a religious hophead. The hobby of this colorful trio was to waylay ungodly-seeming wayfarers and beat them up. In between-times, Dad beats the sons for the slightest defection from his holy orders. One day this team (about as "realistic" a crew as will be found this side of Charles Addams) waylays Chester Goode, the Marshal's crippled assistant; to punish Chester for his frivolous attitudes, the father decides to chop off his arm. But the Younger Son, feeling some qualms over such extremism, hastens to summon the Marshal. Dad raises his axe to clobber Chester; the Younger Son and the Marshal burst through the clearing in the nick of time. It is the son who fires, killing Dad. He asserts his manhood by destroying his father in such a way as to win special approval from the representative of the State.

Here is an even less charming example taken from a show titled, *Detectives.* The detectives are sure that a certain racketeer is guilty of mur-

der; the racketeer's alibi depends on the testimony of his mistress, a jolly
night club "entertainer."

The cops go to work on the mistress. She is shown as being in a perfectly cozy relation with her lover; entertaining no illusions about her
set-up, she is nonetheless as faithful to her "friend" as she is vulnerable
to society. The cops first attempt to sneak a cop-gigolo-spy (unmarried,
we are assured) into her confidence. When this fails, the cops tighten the
screws by exposing to her the two-timing activities of her lover. They
next employ keen psychology by taunting her with the difference in age
between herself and her younger rival. The mistress still refuses to be-
tray her lover. Finally, the cops terrify her by staging a mock attempt
on her life. She begs for police protection; it is refused unless she squeals.
So she squeals, collapsing hysterically into the paws of the square-faced
gigolo-cop.

III

In its heyday, the Hollywood action movie—pirate, gangster, or Western—did contain, among its gross and silly aspects, some qualities of wit
and emotion. Its sources and conventions made for such qualities even as
the TV action shows destroy them. In contrast to TV's cowboy-cop, for
example, the traditional Western hero was a Lone Rider, something of
an ur-Hipster of the Plains. His origins, like those of the TV deputy,
were mysterious, but unlike the deputy's, his code was neither formed
nor approved by the State; nor was his style that of a trained seal. He was
self-taught, autonomous, and, like Hemingway's types, a "hurt" man. His
enemy was the gang in the backroom of the saloon, led by the com-
pulsively competitive capitalist, who owned the town. The villain's
henchmen were outlaws of the sort our hero understood well, for he was
usually an ex-outlaw himself, haunted by his romantic past. As a classless
hero, he was more graceful than the plebeian homesteaders, more vulnerable and isolated than the bourgeois ranchers; and he threw in his lot
with one or another side on the personal basis of friendship, or love for
the girl in one of the camps, or, as Robert Warshow has observed,
through the romantic need to assert the inviolability of his style, that is,
of his private attitudes.

Rather than manipulate situations himself, he usually acted on the
spur of situations arranged by the ever-plotting bad guys. Because his
was not the holier-than-thou code of the insider to the inside born; because he tended to resist organized power rather than reinforce it, he
was the recognizable stranger in town, the Outsider whose key strength

lay in his fancy style, a *shaneh bochur* whose name, in the most well-known depiction of this type, is, sure enough, Shane.

In the peppiest and purest types of action movie the hero's personal choice was spiced frequently by a revenge-motif, the imperative to square accounts for an outrage perpetrated on a member of his family, or a friend. The revenge-motif from Seneca through the Renaissance to Dumas has been a constant in the tradition of the thriller in its liveliest and most free-wheeling aspects. The motif had carried over into the movies, from the earliest silents on up to a stray underground film or two of the fifties, like Randolph Scott's *Seven Men From Now*. So long as the action movie was anchored in what we may call, by comparison, this Grand Tradition (grand signifying a free-wheeling, sentimental, flamboyant, romantic-decadent mode not devoid of humanitarian meanings), it remained anchored to history, its convention and mood rooted in popular forms of the past. It served thus to assuage the aggressions and aches and pains of the populace in a traditional mode: a mode, that is, allied to the more vulgar aspects of humanism.

But the present efforts of movie and TV are empty of emotionality, wit, or fanfare. "Commercial" entertainment has become a form in a void; repressive rather than expressive, it is an entertainment which, like an iron curtain, separates the populace from its past moods. So, like the mother on the *Colt .45* show, the populace is being reduced to a *thing* without a personal history. It remains wide-eyed and genial-seeming, unaware of its true, wild blood relations.

For now it is the "hero" who sits in the front room of the jailhouse, surrounded by his coffee *klatsch,* waiting to be roused to action against some maladjusted lout. As a true-blue cop, he is the agent of the public attitude; his style is plain, *heimisch,* and threatening. When not perched in the front office of the jailhouse, he may be seen like Dale Robertson in the front office of his Organization, serving to untangle personnel problems and to test those characters with suspicious pasts who may deserve a chance to fit-in to the Organization once they have passed a loyalty test arranged by the agent.

The TV cop incarnates Function. He is of necessity a wise-cracking bore, using the wisecrack (or slogan) as a bludgeon to destroy the implications of thought or emotion. His very tautness stems entirely from the imperatives of function and evasiveness. He is indeed a creature of the post-McCarthy period.

Gathered in the TV room, family and friends nightly watch such a character operate to put strangers and family black sheep in their place. The audience stares at an "entertainment" which neither soothes nor teases it, but solemnly and religiously reduces it to the sum of its lowest common fears and pins it back on the sources of its own intellectual and emotional inarticulateness.

Deception as a TV Comedy Tool

Glenn E. Reddick

When television quiz game "fixes" were exposed some years ago Britisher John Ridley, who had been a big winner on "Dotto" but had received no help in answering questions, was not in the least surprised. What did surprise him was that Americans should have been so shocked at the revelations. The *Chicago Daily News* quoted him:

> Isn't this the land of the fix? Don't you take pride in knowing shortcuts, in getting merchandise at wholesale rates, in bribing your policemen? You sneer at eggheads, you sneer at the starry-eyed people. You ask, "Look, what's in it for me?" You do misuse your television terribly, you know. You lack spontaneity. You lack immediacy. Your people put on programs only to sell merchandise. I'm puzzled that you don't realize that. Why do you expect anything else?

Quiz game fixes are apparently a thing of the past. But that deception is still a handy television tool became apparent to me after I made a study of the "situation comedies" presented on the Chicago outlets of the three major networks, ABC, CBS and NBC, from November 1964 to March 1965. My evaluation was based on personal viewing and on the plots as summarized in the weekly program guide put out by the *Chicago Daily News*. I set certain limitations: to be considered, a show had to carry a story with comedy intent through an entire half-hour period; no variety programs or programs featuring skits (the Red Skelton and Danny Kaye shows, for instance) were included; the deception involved had to be deliberate (lying, spying, masquerading), but mistaken identity was ruled out; the deception could constitute either a minor or major part of the plot; only two cartoon series were included.

We find deception in situation comedies appearing in at least four general areas: keeping a person's identity secret, covering mistakes or weaknesses, interesting someone of the opposite sex or keeping romance going, and outwitting an "authority" figure.

Some shows are built entirely around keeping a person's identity secret; for instance, "My Favorite Martian," "Bewitched" and "My Living Doll" —all extremely fanciful in character and incident.

The simplest form of deception employed is that whose purpose is to cover mistakes or weaknesses. A woman schemes to make an expensive watch appear inexpensive (the "Cara Williams Show"); in order to impress her home economics teacher, a girl who can't cook tries to pass off as her own creation food she has obtained from a restaurant ("Donna Reed"). Under the romantic category we find a boy feigning illness to gain the attention of a girl ("Dobie Gillis"); a man pretending to be engaged to one girl in order to escape another ("Love That Bob"); a handsome boy substituting for an "ordinary" pen pal when the partner arrives in town ("Ozzie and Harriet"); a woman masquerading as a 12-year-old to advance her teen-age house guest's romance ("Wendy and Me"); a man donning a general's uniform to gain entrance to an army camp so he can try to patch up a romance ("Many Happy Returns").

Fashions in "authority" figures as protagonists in "deception" situations change. Just now the most popular seem to be the employer, the commanding officer and the father—with the deceiver deciding that the victim deserves to be outwitted because he is ignorant, unfair, pompous, inefficient or hypocritical. Mothers are definitely out, as are physicians, scientists, political figures and clergymen, while policemen, teachers and school principles are less frequently used in this manner than formerly.

Deception of or by the employer is a standard formula in shows with business settings. For instance, on the "Cara Williams Show" we find employees agreeing to keep an office mistake secret, but when the boss fires one of the employees she threatens to tell his secretary of the mistake and as a result is rehired at once. In this case we have intimidation by both employee and employer—with everyone happy in the end.

A favorite field for deception as a plot tool is the enlisted military personnel—military superior conflict. Week in and week out "Broadside" was loaded with deception as the commander tried to induce the Waves under his command to leave against their will. The plots proceeded through such devices as placing a loudspeaker and flame thrower outside the commander's sleeping quarters to persuade him that he was under a spell that could be lifted only if the Waves stayed on the base. The assumption seems to be that enlisted personnel are justified in taking advantage of the hobbies or interests or weaknesses of officers; the commander's cook, for instance, got away with insubordination (including addressing his superior as "Fatso") by playing up to his love for certain foods.

Generally speaking, in situation comedies the father as authority figure is a comic soul whose authority is not acknowledged; mother and children find some way to dupe the poor fellow into thinking he is the one who decides a question, whereas as a matter of fact they had it planned that way in the beginning. Mother is right in there with the kids, speaking their language, but father is so out of touch there is not much reason to take him seriously. When the children have problems it is mother's task to explain to father how they are straightened out.

On the basis of the situation comedies I examined during that five-month period I would estimate that 25 per cent of the situations presented involve deception as a major or minor part of the plot. Here is the lesson those comedies are giving viewers: Deception is a proper device to use when you make a mistake, want to interest or hold the interest of a member of the opposite sex, try to improve your working conditions or your family situation or change the rules of the game, hope to exercise more influence over your employees—or help someone else achieve any of these goals. Furthermore, by employing deception you will have a lot of fun, often achieve your goal even if your deception is discovered, no hard feelings or evil consequences will follow—in fact, the victim is so happy in the end that you can feel free to resort to deception the next time the opportunity arises. If the victim is disturbed, reach for one of his weaknesses (keep them filed for ready use) and use it to intimidate him; he will laugh and the two of you will remain on good terms.

How seriously should such findings be taken? Do they offer implications for religious education?

At the outset it must be acknowledged that there are valid arguments for not taking the matter too seriously. For one thing, deception is not new in comedy; it has been employed by such masters of the art as Shakespeare, Molière, Wilde and Shaw, and it is the stock in trade of many musical comedies. Disguise, in particular, offers opportunity for double meanings, exaggeration, fanciful costuming and lampooning of stuffed shirts. A major defense offered by the writers and producers of the situation comedies is that no one is shown to be harmed, that the characters remain friends and everything ends happily. True—because deceiver and deceived agree that the goal justified the attempt. It is also true that not all situation comedies rely on deception as a major device; such "monster" shows as "The Addams Family" and "The Munsters," for instance, reverse the normal and abnormal and require their characters to be very frank. Others, particularly those that keep the identity secret, are so bizarre that it is very unlikely anyone will identify himself with the characters.

As to possible effects on child viewers, I have found from questioning a number of bright children aware of standards of honesty that they can easily spot deception and apparently do not associate it with real life. Mary Ann Callan of the *Los Angeles Times* interviewed children aged eight to twelve at an elementary school and got such comments as these on television's portrayal of fathers: "It's not my family they show; I know the difference." "TV has nothing to do with what really happens." "Television is over-exaggerated. Dads are dads, not nitwits." There is something to the argument, too, that there is in broadcasting considerable antidote in the form of educational and religious programs that, often successfully, promote honesty and respect.

All arguments aside, however, there remain definite reasons for concern about the acceptance of deception as a major tool in television's situation comedies.

Consider how extensive is the proportion of such comedies in the total television picture. Last season we had 33 in prime evening hours (7:30 to 11 P.M., E.S.T.) and 43—a 30 per cent increase—are projected for the coming months. In a typical week last season Chicago viewers had access to 76 comedy episodes in 37 programs. It is estimated that 18 of the programs are reaching more than 10 million households; another eight or ten, over 7 million. A Senate committee has reported that 17 million children under 12 are watching television at 8 P.M. on any given evening; in Chicago, children of that age watching television from 6:30 to 8:30 had one or two situation comedies from which to choose every evening.

Studies conducted by Paul Witty of Northwestern University indicate that children's viewing habits are coming increasingly to approximate those of their elders, which means that their favorites are the prime-time programs among which situation comedies—always found among any "top ten" listings—are well represented. When sold as daytime reruns, these shows are often placed in viewing periods when many children are watching. That the owners of one show—"Phil Silvers"—consciously try to sell their product on the basis of its appeal to children is indicated by their ad in *Broadcasting*. It notes that a 25-city survey taken during the show's 1963–64 run in prime time showed that 39.3 per cent of its audience was under 18. Hence their claim: "Kids love—the—Fun!—Fun!—Fun!"

We are told that children identify most readily with characters in life situations similar to their own. Thus it is significant that the majority of the situation comedies to be seen in Chicago last season had a "home" setting. Alert children may be able to differentiate intellectually between television and real-life situations, but is that recognition also present at the suggestion level? What of the vast audience of children who are not intellectually alert or who have not been exposed to examples of honesty and respect? A fifth-grade teacher in a Chicago suburb reported recently that she has in her class pupils who tell of their parents' boast of how they have avoided customs duties by hiding merchandise when they cross the border, of their fathers' outwitting the boss by padding expense accounts. One can only conclude that such children are quite able to identify with television characters who engage in deception that is apparently fun, that achieves desired goals. Certainly this is an area in which careful studies need to be made.

We know enough about suggestion to recognize that two conditions for high suggestibility are present in situation comedies depicting family life: repetition and passivity. The plots are variations on a basic formula, varying just enough to provide some stimulation. Further, the programs die slowly; some enjoy as many as six reruns. It is probable that for the most part viewers watch the programs not out of active interest but because there is nothing better to do at the moment. They very well may be bored, but the passivity that accompanies their boredom strengthens rather than weakens suggestibility.

A major matter for concern is, of course, the fact that the situation comedies involving deception end happily—even though intimidation may be necessary to ensure that outcome. The incautious viewer may very well conclude that deception has no evil consequences, or at any rate none that cannot easily be overcome. Some writers even laugh off the deception with a wisecrack; thus in "Gilligan's Island" we have the millionaire and one of his fellow castaways reprimanded for stealing water from the others. "Aren't you sorry?" he is asked. And when he replies, "Sorry that we got caught" the laughter from the soundtrack soars in volume. Again, deception sometimes comes close to being rewarded. For instance, when the girl confesses that she has tried to pass off restaurant food as her own creation her teacher tells her: "There is more to homemaking than cooking; it also involves quick thinking and you have shown that, so you get an A."

The highly respectable place in the community the characters in situation comedies occupy would lead one to assume that many of them must be church members and that religion would have some effect on their concepts of right and wrong. But if that is so there is no evidence of it in the interpretations offered; references to religion seldom appear.

Potentially the greatest danger in television's use of deception as a comedy device lies in the portrayal of authority figures. What might be justifiable satire when well motivated and presented occasionally becomes incentive to disrespect when motivation is automatic and portrayals are repetitive. Such examples as the cook's addressing the commander as "Fatso" and the boy's calling his father a "creep" may be extreme, but they reflect the general tone of disrespect permeating many of the situation comedies. Of "Hank," a new NBC offering this fall, an ad in *Broadcasting* tells us: "[Hank is] an unmatriculated (and undiscovered) undergraduate at Western State . . . who manages to attend classes under an ingenious and delightful assortment of aliases. . . . There's never been a campus hero quite as funny as Hank." Nor, apparently, as deceitful, or as disrespectful of an entire university.

Television, as our British critic reminded us in the opening paragraph above, supplies whatever sells. And today deception as comedy sells. The remedy, obviously, is to stop buying. There is no doubt that the ultimate check on content is audience rejection either through individual or group action—by selective viewing, by boycott of products, by letters to sponsors —or through political measures. Of these means, only selective viewing seems to me to be a long-range answer; the others would be effective only if employed on a scale almost impossible to achieve. Television has such a good thing going that it would take an overwhelming volume of mail and a product boycott of unprecedented proportions to effect more than temporary relief. And there is little hope in legislation. True, initiation of pay TV would undoubtedly result in improved fare—but only for those viewing it; the many who would profit most from higher standards would probably shun the kind of programs it would provide. Competition from pay TV would lead to improvement in commercial fare only if enough viewers switched to it to make that fare unprofitable—an unlikely outcome.

So we return to selective viewing, with its corollary: guidance in such selection. What is needed from schools, churches and other agencies to which we can expect to turn for help is not guidance of censorial nature but a program that will explain the role of mass media, particularly television, in American life. We do have something of this sort now, but it is confined to higher education. Analytical study of the role played by mass media, particularly in the light of ethical and religious considerations, should have a place at all levels of education, certainly of religious education. In such study I would suggest that high priority be given examination of television's currently successful comedy formula: Deception = Fun. A good text would be Sir Walter Scott's wise words from "Marmion":

> O what a tangled web we weave
> When first we practice to deceive.

The Comics: Middle Against Both Ends

Leslie A. Fiedler

I am surely one of the few people pretending to intellectual repectability who can boast that he has read more comic books than attacks on comic books. I do not mean that I have consulted or studied the comics—I have read them, often with some pleasure. Nephews and nieces, my own children, and the children of neighbors have brought them to me to share their enjoyment. An old lady on a ferry boat in Puget Sound once dropped two in my lap in wordless sympathy: I was wearing, at the time, a sailor's uniform. . . .

In none of the books on comics I have looked into, and in none of the reports of ladies' clubs, protests of legislators, or statements of moral indignation by pastors, have I come on any real attempt to understand comic books: to define the form, midway between icon and story; to distinguish the sub-types: animal, adolescent, crime, western, etc.; or even to separate out, from the deadpan varieties, tongue-in-cheek sports like *Pogo*, frank satire like *Mad*, or semi-surrealist variations like *Plastic Man*. It would not take someone with the talents of an Aristotle, but merely with his method, to ask the rewarding questions about this kind of literature that he asked once about an equally popular and bloody genre: what are its causes and its natural form?

From "The Comics: Middle Against Both Ends" by Leslie A. Fiedler, in *Encounter*, Vol. 5 (1955), pp. 16–23. Reprinted by permission of the author.

A cursory examination would show that the super-hero comic (*Superman, Captain Marvel, Wonder Woman,* etc.) is the final form; it is statistically the most popular with the most avid readers, as well as providing the only new legendary material invented along with the form rather than adapted to it.

Next, one would have to abstract the most general pattern of the myth of the super-hero and deduce its significance: the urban setting, the threatened universal catastrophe, the hero who never uses arms, who returns to weakness and obscurity, who must keep his identity secret, who is impotent, etc. Not until then could one ask with any hope of an answer: what end do the comics serve? Why have they gained an immense body of readers precisely in the past fifteen or twenty years? Why must they be disguised as children's literature though read by men and women of all ages? And having answered these, one could pose the most dangerous question of all: why the constant, virulent attacks on the comics, and, indeed, on the whole of popular culture of which they are especially flagrant examples?

Strategically, if not logically, the last question should be asked first. Why the attacks? Such assaults by scientists and laymen are as characteristic of our age as puritanic diatribes against the stage of the Elizabethan Era, and pious protests against novel-reading in the later eighteenth century. I suspect that a study of such conventional reactions reveals at least as much about the nature of a period as an examination of the forms to which they respond. The most fascinating and suspicious aspect of the opposition to popular narrative is its unanimity; everyone from the members of the Montana State Legislature to the ladies of the Parent Teachers' Association of Boston, Massachusetts, from British M.P.s to the wilder post-Freudians of two continents agree on this, though they may agree on nothing else. What they have in common is, I am afraid, the sense that they are all, according to their lights, righteous. And their protests represent only one more example (though an unlikely one) of the notorious failure of righteousness in matters involving art.

Just what is it with which vulgar literature is charged by various guardians of morality or sanity? With everything: encouraging crime, destroying literacy, expressing sexual frustration, unleashing sadism, spreading anti-democratic ideas, and, of course, corrupting youth. To understand the grounds of such charges, their justification and their bias, we must understand something of the nature of the sub-art with which we are dealing.

Perhaps it is most illuminating to begin by saying that it is a peculiarly

American phenomenon, an unexpected by-product of an attempt, not only to extend literacy universally, but to delegate taste to majority suffrage. I do not mean, of course, that it is found only in the United States, but that wherever it is found, it comes first from us, and is still to be discovered in fully-developed form only among us. Our experience along these lines is, in this sense, a preview for the rest of the world of what must follow the inevitable dissolution of the older aristocratic cultures.

One has only to examine certain Continental imitations of picture magazines like *Look* or *Life* or Disney-inspired cartoon books to be aware at once of the debt to American examples and of the failure of the imitations. For a true "popular literature" demands a more than ordinary slickness, the sort of high finish possible only to a machine-produced commodity in an economy of maximum prosperity. Contemporary popular culture, which is a function in an industrialized society, is distinguished from older folk art by its refusal to be shabby or second-rate in appearance, by a refusal to know its place. It is a product of the same impulse which has made available the sort of ready-made clothing which aims at destroying the possibility of knowing a lady by her dress.

Yet the articles of popular culture are made, not to be treasured, but to be thrown away; a paperback book is like a disposable diaper or a paper milk-container. For all its competent finish, it cannot be preserved on dusty shelves like the calf-bound volumes of another day; indeed, its very mode of existence challenges the concept of a library, private or public. The sort of conspicuous waste once reserved for an *élite* is now available to anyone; and this is inconceivable without an absurdly high standard of living, just as it is unimaginable without a degree of mechanical efficiency that permits industry to replace nature, and invents— among other disposable synthetics—one for literature.

Just as the production of popular narrative demands industrial conditions most favorably developed in the United States, its distribution requires the peculiar conditions of our market places: the mass or democratized market. Sub-books and sub-arts are not distributed primarily through the traditional institutions: museums, libraries, and schools, which remain firmly in the hands of those who deplore mass culture. It is in drugstores and supermarkets and airline terminals that this kind of literature mingles without condescension with chocolate bars and soap-flakes. . . .

Those who cry out now that the work of a Mickey Spillane or *The Adventures of Superman* travesty the novel, forget that the novel was long accused of travestying literature. What seems to offend us most is not the further downgrading of literacy standards so much as the fact that the medium, the very notion and shape of a book, is being parodied by the comics. . . .

It is the final, though camouflaged, rejection of literacy implicit in this new form which is the most legitimate source of distress, but all arts so universally consumed have been for illiterates, even stained glass windows and the plays of Shakespeare. What is new in our present situation, and hence especially upsetting, is that this is the first art for *post*-literates, i.e. for those who have refused the benefit for which they were presumed to have sighed in their long exclusion. Besides, modern popular narrative is disconcertingly not oral; it will not surrender the benefits of the printing press as a machine, however indifferent it may be to that press as the perpetuator of techniques devised first for pen or quill. Everything that the press can provide—except matter to be really read—is demanded: picture, typography, even in many cases the illusion of reading along with the relaxed pleasure of illiteracy. Yet the new popular forms remain somehow prose narrative or pictographic substitutes for the novel; even the cognate form of the movies is notoriously more like a novel than a play in its handling of time, space and narrative progression.

From the folk literature of the past, which ever since the triumph of the machine we have been trying sentimentally to recapture, popular literature differs in its rejection of the picturesque. Rooted in prose rather than verse, secular rather than religious in origin, defining itself against the city rather than the world of outdoor nature, a by-product of the factory rather than agriculture, present-day popular literature defeats romantic expectations of peasants in their embroidered blouses chanting or plucking balalaikas for the approval of their betters. The haters of our own popular art love to condescend to the folk; and on records or in fashionable nightclubs in recent years, we have had entertainers who have earned enviable livings producing commercial imitations of folk songs. But contemporary vulgar culture is brutal and disturbing: the quasi-spontaneous expression of the uprooted and culturally dispossessed inhabitants of anonymous cities, contriving mythologies which reduce to manageable form the threat of science, the horror of unlimited war, the general spread of corruption in a world where the social bases of old loyalties and heroisms have long been destroyed. That such an art is exploited for profit in a commercial society, mass-produced by nameless collaborators, standardized and debased, is of secondary importance. It is the patented nightmare of us all, a packaged way of coming to terms with one's environment sold for a dime to all those who have rejected the unasked-for gift of literacy.

Thought of in this light, the comic books with their legends of the eternally threatened metropolis eternally protected by immaculate and modest heroes (who shrink back after each exploit into the image of the crippled newsboy, the impotent and cowardly reporter) are seen as inheritors, for all their superficial differences, of the *inner* impulses of traditional folk art. Their gross drawing, their poverty of language cannot disguise their heritage of aboriginal violence, their exploitation of the ancient conflict of black magic and white. Beneath their journalistic commentary on A-bomb and Communism, they touch archetypal material: those shared figures of our lower minds more like the patterns of dream than fact. In a world where men threaten to dissolve into their most superficial and mechanical techniques, to become their borrowed newspaper platitudes, they remain close to the impulsive, subliminal life. They are our not quite machine-subdued Grimm, though the Black Forest has become, as it must, the City; the Wizard, the Scientist; and Simple Hans, Captain Marvel. In a society which thinks of itself as "scientific"—and of the Marvelous as childish—such a literature must seem primarily children's literature, though, of course, it is read by people of all ages.

We are now in a position to begin to answer the question: what do the righteous really have against comic books? In some parts of the world, simply the fact that they are American is sufficient, and certain home-grown self-contemners follow this line even in the United States. But it is really a minor argument, lent a certain temporary importance by passing political exigencies. To declare oneself against "the Americanization of culture" is meaningless unless one is set resolutely against industrialization and mass education.

More to the point is the attack on mass culture for its betrayal of literacy itself. In a very few cases, this charge is made seriously and with full realization of its import; but most often it amounts to nothing but an accusation of "bad grammar" or "slang" on the part of some school marm to whom the spread of "different than" seems to threaten the future of civilized discourse. What should set us on guard in this case is that it is not the fully literate, the intellectuals and serious writers who lead the attack, but the insecure semi-literate. In America, there is something a little absurd about the indignant delegation from the Parent Teachers' Association (themselves clutching the latest issue of *Life*) crying out in defence of literature. Asked for suggestions, such critics are likely to propose *The Reader's Digest* as required reading in high school—or to urge more comic book versions of the "classics"; emasculated Melville, expurgated Hawthorne, or a child's version of something "uplifting" like

"The Fall of the House of Usher." In other countries, corresponding counterparts are not hard to find.

As a matter of fact, this charge is scarcely ever urged with much conviction. It is really the portrayal of crime and horror (and less usually sex) that the enlightened censors deplore. It has been charged against vulgar art that it is sadistic, brutal, full of terror; that it pictures women with exaggeratedly full breasts and rumps, portrays death on the printed page, is often covertly homosexual, etc., etc. About these charges, there are two obvious things to say. First, by and large, they are true. Second, they are also true about much of the most serious art of our time, especially that produced in America.

There is no count of sadism and brutality which could not be equally proved against Hemingway or Faulkner or Paul Bowles—or, for that matter, Edgar Allan Poe. . . . You cannot condemn *Superman* for the exploitation of violence, and praise the existentialist-homosexual-sadist shockers of Paul Bowles. It is possible to murmur by way of explanation something vague about art of catharsis; but no one is ready to advocate the suppression of anything merely because it is aesthetically bad. In this age of conflicting standards, we would all soon suppress each other.

An occasional Savonarola is, of course, ready to make the total rejection; and secretly or openly, the run-of-the-mill condemner of mass culture does condemn, on precisely the same grounds, most contemporary literature of distinction. Historically, one can make quite a convincing case to prove that our highest and lowest arts come from a common anti-bourgeois source. Edgar Allan Poe, who lived the image of the dandy that has been haunting high art ever since, also, one remembers, invented the popular detective story; and there is a direct line from Hemingway to O'Hara to Dashiell Hammett to Raymond Chandler to Mickey Spillane.

Of both lines of descent from Poe, one can say that they tell a black and distressing truth (we are creatures of dark impulse in a threatened and guilty world), and that they challenge the more genteel versions of "good taste." . . . I should hate my argument to be understood as a defence of what is banal and mechanical and dull (there is, of course, a great deal!) in mass culture; it is merely a counter-attack against those who are aiming through that banality and dullness at what moves all literature of worth. Anyone at all sensitive to the life of the imagination would surely prefer the kids to read the coarsest fables of Black and White contending for the City of Man, rather than have them spell out, "Oh, see Jane. Funny, funny Jane," or read to themselves hygienic accounts of the operation of supermarkets or manureless farms. Yet most school-

board members are on the side of mental hygiene; and it is they who lead
the charge against mass culture.

Anyone old enough to have seen, say *Rain,* is on guard against those
who in the guise of wanting to destroy savagery and ignorance wage war
on spontaneity and richness. But we are likely to think of such possibilities purely in sexual terms; the new righteous themselves have been
touched lightly by Freud and are firm believers in frankness and "sex
education." But in the very midst of their self-congratulation at their
emancipation, they have become victims of a new and ferocious prudery.
One who would be ashamed to lecture his masturbating son on the
dangers of insanity, is quite prepared . . . to predict the electric chair for
the young scoundrel caught with a bootlegged comic. Superman is our
Sadie Thompson. We live in an age when the child who is exposed to
the "facts of life" is protected from "the facts of death." In the United
States, for instance, a certain Doctor Spock has produced an enlightened
guide to childcare for modern mothers—a paperback book which sold,
I would guess, millions of copies. Tell the child all about sex, the good
doctor advises, but on the subject of death—hush!

By more "advanced" consultants, the taboo is advanced further towards absurdity: no bloodsoaked Grimm, no terrifying Andersen, no
childhood verses about cradles that fall—for fear breeds insecurity;
insecurity, aggression; aggression, war. There is even a "happy," that is to
say, expurgated, Mother Goose in which the three blind mice have become "kind mice"—and the farmer's wife no longer hacks off their tails,
but "cuts them some cheese with a carving knife." Everywhere the fear of
fear is endemic, the fear of the very names of fear; those who have most
ardently desired to end warfare and personal cruelty in the world
around them, and are therefore most frustrated by their persistence, con-
spire to stamp out violence on the nursery bookshelf. This much they
can do anyhow. If they can't hold up the weather, at least they can break
the bloody glass.

This same fear of the instinctual and the dark, this denial of death
and guilt by the enlightened genteel, motivates their distrust of serious
literature, too. Faulkner is snubbed and the comic books are banned, not
in the interests of the classics or even of Robert Louis Stevenson, as the
attackers claim, but in the name of a literature of the middle ground
which finds its fictitious vision of a kindly and congenial world attacked
from above and below. I speak now not of the few intellectual converts
to the cause of censorship, but of the main body of genteel book-banners,
whose idol is Lloyd Douglas or even A. J. Cronin. . . .

This "trend" is nothing more than the standard attitude of a standard kind of literature, the literature of slick-paper ladies' magazines, which prefers the stereotype to the archetype, loves poetic justice, sentimentality, and gentility, and is peopled by characters who bathe frequently, live in the suburbs, and are professionals. Such literature circles mindlessly inside the trap of its two themes: unconsummated adultery and the consummated pure romance. There can be little doubt about which kind of persons and which sort of fables best typify our plight, which tell the truth—or better: a truth in the language of those to whom they speak.

In the last phrase, there is a rub. The notion that there is more than one language of art, or rather, that there is something not quite art, which performs art's function for most men in our society, is disquieting enough for anyone, and completely unacceptable to the sentimental egalitarian, who had dreamed of universal literacy leading directly to a universal culture. It is here that we begin to see that there is a politics as well as pathology involved in the bourgeois hostility to popular culture. I do not refer only to the explicit political ideas embodied in the comics or in the literature of the cultural *élite;* but certainly each of these arts has a characteristic attitude: populist-authoritarian on the one hand, and aristocratic-authoritarian on the other.

It is notorious how few of the eminent novelists or poets of our time have shared the political ideals we . . . would agree are the most noble available to us. The flirtations of Yeats and Lawrence with fascism, Pound's weird amalgam of Confucianism, Jeffersonianism, and social credit, the modified Dixiecrat principles of Faulkner—all make the point with terrible reiteration. Between the best art and poetry of our age and the critical liberal reader there can be no bond of shared belief; at best we have the ironic confrontation of the sceptical mind and the believing imagination. It is this division which has, I suppose, led us to define more and more narrowly the "aesthetic experience," to attempt to isolate a quality of seeing and saying that has a moral value quite independent of *what* is seen or heard.

> Time that with this strange excuse
> Pardoned Kipling and his views,
> And will pardon Paul Claudel,
> Pardons him for writing well.

But the genteel middling mind which turns to art for entertainment and uplift, finds this point of view reprehensible; and cries out in rage against those who give Ezra Pound a prize and who claim that "to permit other considerations than that of poetic achievement to sway the decision would . . . deny the validity of that objective perception of value on which any civilized society must rest." We live in the midst of a strange two-front class war: the readers of the slicks battling the subscribers to the "little reviews" and the consumers of pulps; the sentimental-egalitarian conscience against the ironical-aristocratic sensibility on the one hand and the brutal-populist mentality on the other. The joke, of course, is that it is the "democratic" center which calls here and now for suppression of its rivals; while the *élite* advocate a condescending tolerance, and the vulgar ask only to be let alone.

It is disconcerting to find cultural repression flourishing at the point where middling culture meets a kindly, if not vigorously thought-out, liberalism. The sort of right-thinking citizen who subsidizes trips to America for Japanese girls scarred by the Hiroshima bombing, and deplores McCarthy in the public press, also deplores, and would censor, the comics. In one sense, this is fair enough; for beneath the veneer of slogans that "crime doesn't pay" and the superficial praise of law and order, the comics do reflect that dark populist faith which Senator McCarthy has exploited. There is a kind of "black socialism" of the American masses which underlies formal allegiances to one party or another: the sense that there is always a conspiracy at the centers of political and financial power; the notion that the official defenders of the commonwealth are "bought" more often than not; an impatience with moral scruples and a distrust of intelligence, especially in the expert and scientist; a willingness to identify the enemy, the dark projection of everything most feared in the self, on to some journalistically-defined political opponent of the moment.

This is not quite the "fascism" it is sometimes called. There is, for instance, no European anti-Semitism involved, despite the conventional hooked nose of the scientist-villain. (The inventors and chief producers of comic books have been, as it happens, Jews.) There is also no adulation of a dictator-figure on the model of Hitler or Stalin; though one of the archetypes of the Deliverer in the comics is called Superman, he is quite unlike the Nietzschean figure—it is the image of Cincinnatus which persists in him, an archetype that has possessed the American imagination since the time of Washington: the leader who enlists for the duration and retires unrewarded to obscurity.

It would be absurd to ask the consumer of such art to admire in the place of images that project his own impotence and longing for civil peace some hero of middling culture—say, the good boy of Arthur Miller's *Death of a Salesman,* who, because he has studied hard in school, has become a lawyer who argues cases before the Supreme Court and his friends who own their own tennis courts. As absurd as to ask the general populace to worship Stephen Dedalus or Captain Ahab! But the high-minded petty-bourgeois cannot understand or forgive the rejection of his own dream, which he considers as nothing less than the final dream of humanity. The very existence of a kind of art based on allegiances and values other than his challenges an article of his political faith; and when such an art is "popular," that is, more read, more liked, more bought than his own, he feels his basic life-defense imperiled. The failure of the petty-bourgeoisie to achieve cultural hegemony threatens their dream of a truly classless society; for they believe, with some justification, that such a society can afford only a single culture. And they see, in the persistence of a high art and a low art on either side of their average own, symptoms of the re-emergence of classes in a quarter where no one had troubled to stand guard.

The problem posed by popular culture is finally, then, a problem of class distinction in a democratic society. What is at stake is the refusal of cultural equality by a large part of the population. It is misleading to think of popular culture as the product of a conspiracy of profiteers against the rest of us. This venerable notion of an eternally oppressed and deprived but innocent people is precisely what the rise of mass culture challenges. Much of what upper-class egalitarians dreamed for him, the ordinary man does not want—especially literacy. The situation is bewildering and complex, for the people have not rejected completely the notion of cultural equality; rather, they desire its symbol but not its fact. At the very moment when half of the population of the United States reads no *hard-covered* book in a year, more than half of all high-school graduates are entering universities and colleges; in twenty-five years almost all Americans will at least begin a higher education. It is clear that what is demanded is a B.A. for everyone, with the stipulation that no one be forced to read to get it. And this the colleges, with "objective tests" and "visual aids," are doing their reluctant best to satisfy.

One of the more exasperating aspects of the cultural defeat of the egalitarians is that it followed a seeming victory. For a while (in the Anglo-Saxon world at least) it appeared as if the spread of literacy, the rise of the bourgeoisie, and the emergence of the novel as a reigning form would succeed in destroying both traditional folk art and an aristocratic literature still pledged to epic, ode, and verse tragedy. But the novel itself (in the hands of Lawrence, Proust, Kafka, etc.) soon passed beyond the comprehension of those for whom it was originally contrived; and the retrograde derivations from it—various steps in a retreat towards wordless narrative: digests, pulp fiction, movies, picture magazines—revealed that middling literature was not in fact the legitimate heir of either folk art or high art, much less the successor of both, but a *tertium quid* of uncertain status and value.

The middlebrow reacts with equal fury to an art that baffles his understanding and to one which refuses to aspire to his level. The first reminds him that he has not yet, after all, *arrived* (and, indeed, may never make it); the second suggests to him a condition to which he might easily relapse, one perhaps that might have made him happier with less effort (and here exacerbated puritanism is joined to baffled egalitarianism)— even suggests what his state may appear like to those a notch above. Since he cannot on his own terms explain to himself why anyone should choose any level but the highest (that is, his own), the failure of the vulgar seems to him the product of mere ignorance and laziness—a crime! And the rejection by the advanced artist of his canons strikes him as a finicking excess, a pointless and unforgivable snobbism. Both, that is, suggest the intolerable notion of a hierarchy of taste, a hierarchy of values, the possibility of cultural classes in a democratic state; and before this, puzzled and enraged, he can only call a cop. The fear of the vulgar is the obverse of the fear of excellence, and both are aspects of the fear of difference: symptoms of a drive for conformity on the level of the timid, sentimental, mindless-bodiless genteel.

AUTHOR's NOTE: Rereading this essay after eleven years, I am astonished and pleased at how prophetic it seems in retrospect. Certainly we have lived into a moment when the comic book is having a double renaissance: reinvented by the Marvel Comic group (*The Fantastic Four* etc.), it is anthologized and analyzed and revived on TV. But most important of all, it has become a standard mythology referred to by writers under 35, as once only Homer and the Bible were referred to. Images of Batman and Superman and Captain Marvel live in the deep minds of urbanites in an electronic age as, say, Oedipus does not, unless some learned book suggests it. Now certain novels evoke their scarcely believed-in archetypal presences for richness and resonance and a kind of humor (self-mocking without bitterness or embarrassment) which begins to seem the hallmark of the age.

Science Fiction Films:
The Imagination of Disaster

Susan Sontag

Science fiction films are not about science. They are about disaster, which is one of the oldest subjects of art. In science fiction films disaster is rarely viewed intensively; it is always extensive. It is a matter of quantity and ingenuity. If you will, it is a question of scale. But the scale, particularly in the wide-screen Technicolor films (of which the ones by the Japanese director Inoshiro Honda and the American director George Pal are technically the most convincing and visually the most exciting), does raise the matter to another level.

Thus, the science fiction film (like that of a very different contemporary genre, the Happening) is concerned with the aesthetics of destruction, with the peculiar beauties to be found in wreaking havoc, making a mess. And it is in the imagery of destruction that the core of a good science fiction film lies. Hence, the disadvantage of the cheap film—in which the monster appears or the rocket lands in a small dull-looking town. (Hollywood budget needs usually dictate that the town be in the Arizona or California desert. In *The Thing From Another World* [1951] the rather sleazy and confined set is supposed to be an encampment near the North Pole.) Still, good black-and-white science fiction films have been made. But a bigger budget, which usually means Technicolor, allows a much greater play back and forth among several model environments. There is the populous city. There is the lavish but ascetic interior of the spaceship—either the invaders' or ours—replete with streamlined chromium fixtures and dials and machines whose complexity is indicated by the number of colored lights they flash and strange noises they emit. There is the laboratory crowded with formidable boxes and scientific apparatus. There is a comparatively old-fashioned-looking conference room, where the scientists unfurl charts to explain the desperate state of things to the military. And each of these standard locales or backgrounds is subject to two modalities—intact and destroyed. We may, if we are lucky, be treated to a panorama of melting tanks, flying bodies, crashing walls,

awesome craters and fissures in the earth, plummeting spacecraft, colorful deadly rays; and to a symphony of screams, weird electronic signals,
the noisiest military hardware going, and the leaden tones of the laconic
denizens of alien planets and their subjugated earthlings.

Certain of the primitive gratifications of science fiction films—for instance, the depiction of urban disaster on a colossally magnified scale—
are shared with other types of films. Visually there is little difference between mass havoc as represented in the old horror and monster films and
what we find in science fiction films, except (again) scale. In the old
monster films, the monster always headed for the great city, where he
had to do a fair bit of rampaging, hurling busses off bridges, crumpling
trains in his bare hands, toppling buildings, and so forth. The archetype
is King Kong, in Schoedsack's great film of 1933, running amok, first in
the African village (trampling babies, a bit of footage excised from most
prints), then in New York. This is really no different in spirit from the
scene in Inoshiro Honda's *Rodan* (1957) in which two giant reptiles—
with a wingspan of 500 feet and supersonic speeds—by flapping their
wings whip up a cyclone that blows most of Tokyo to smithereens. Or
the destruction of half of Japan by the gigantic robot with the great
incinerating ray that shoots forth from his eyes, at the beginning of
Honda's *The Mysterians* (1959). Or, the devastation by the rays from a
fleet of flying saucers of New York, Paris, and Tokyo, in *Battle in Outer
Space* (1960). Or, the inundation of New York in *When Worlds Collide*
(1951). Or, the end of London in 1966 depicted in George Pal's *The Time
Machine* (1960). Neither do these sequences differ in aesthetic intention
from the destruction scenes in the big sword, sandal, and orgy color
spectaculars set in Biblical and Roman times—the end of Sodom in
Aldrich's *Sodom and Gomorrah,* of Gaza in De Mille's *Samson and
Delilah,* of Rhodes in *The Colossus of Rhodes,* and of Rome in a dozen
Nero movies. Griffith began it with the Babylon sequence in *Intolerance,*
and to this day there is nothing like the thrill of watching all those
expensive sets come tumbling down.

In other respects as well, the science fiction films of the 1950s take up
familiar themes. The famous 1930s movie serials and comics of the
adventures of Flash Gordon and Buck Rogers, as well as the more recent
spate of comic book super-heroes with extraterrestrial origins (the most
famous is Superman, a foundling from the planet Krypton, currently
described as having been exploded by a nuclear blast), share motifs with
more recent science fiction movies. But there is an important difference.
The old science fiction films, and most of the comics, still have an essentially innocent relation to disaster. Mainly they offer new versions of

the oldest romance of all—of the strong invulnerable hero with a mysterious lineage come to do battle on behalf of good and against evil. Recent science fiction films have a decided grimness, bolstered by their much greater degree of visual credibility, which contrasts strongly with the older films. Modern historical reality has greatly enlarged the imagination of disaster, and the protagonists—perhaps by the very nature of what is visited upon them—no longer seem wholly innocent.

The lure of such generalized disaster as a fantasy is that it releases one from normal obligations. The trump card of the end-of-the-world movies —like *The Day the Earth Caught Fire* (1962)—is that great scene with New York or London or Tokyo discovered empty, its entire population annihilated. Or, as in *The World, The Flesh, and The Devil* (1957), the whole movie can be devoted to the fantasy of occupying the deserted metropolis and starting all over again, a world Robinson Cruso.

Another kind of satisfaction these films supply is extreme moral simplification—that is to say, a morally acceptable fantasy where one can give outlet to cruel or at least amoral feelings. In this respect, science fiction films partly overlap with horror films. This is the undeniable pleasure we derive from looking at freaks, beings excluded from the category of the human. The sense of superiority over the freak conjoined in varying proportions with the titillation of fear and aversion makes it possible for moral scruples to be lifted, for cruelty to be enjoyed. The same thing happens in science fiction films. In the figure of the monster from outer space, the freakish, the ugly, and the predatory all converge—and provide a fantasy target for righteous bellicosity to discharge itself, and for the aesthetic enjoyment of suffering and disaster. Science fiction films are one of the purest forms of spectacle; that is, we are rarely inside anyone's feelings. (An exception is Jack Arnold's *The Incredible Shrinking Man* [1957].) We are merely spectators; we watch.

But in science fiction films, unlike horror films, there is not much horror. Suspense, shocks, surprises are mostly abjured in favor of a steady, inexorable plot. Science fiction films invite a dispassionate, aesthetic view of destruction and violence—a *technological* view. Things, objects, machinery play a major role in these films. A greater range of ethical values is embodied in the décor of these films than in the people. Things, rather than the helpless humans, are the locus of values because we experience them, rather than people, as the sources of power. According to science fiction films, man is naked without his artifacts. *They* stand for different values, they are potent, they are what get destroyed, and they are the indispensable tools for the repulse of the alien invaders or the repair of the damaged environment.

The science fiction films are strongly moralistic. The standard message is the one about the proper, or humane, use of science, versus the mad, obsessional use of science. This message the science fiction films share in common with the classic horror films of the 1930's like *Frankenstein, The Mummy, Island of Lost Souls, Dr. Jekyll and Mr. Hyde.* (George Franju's brilliant *Les Yeux Sans Visage* [1959], called here *The Horror Chamber of Doctor Faustus,* is a more recent example.) In the horror films, we have the mad or obsessed or misguided scientist who pursues his experiments against good advice to the contrary, creates a monster or monsters, and is himself destroyed—often recognizing his folly himself, and dying in the successful effort to destroy his own creation. One science fiction equivalent of this is the scientist, usually a member of a team, who defects to the planetary invaders because "their" science is more advanced than "ours."

This is the case in *The Mysterians,* and, true to form, the renegade sees his error in the end, and from within the Mysterian spaceship destroys it and himself. In *This Island Earth* (1955), the inhabitants of the beleaguered planet Metaluna propose to conquer earth, but their project is foiled by a Metalunan scientist named Exeter who, having lived on earth a while and learned to love Mozart, cannot abide such viciousness. Exeter plunges his spaceship into the ocean after returning a glamorous pair (male and female) of American physicists to earth. Metaluna dies. In *The Fly* (1958), the hero, engrossed in his basement-laboratory experiments on a matter-transmitting machine, uses himself as a subject, exchanges head and one arm with a housefly which had accidentally gotten into the machine, becomes a monster, and with his last shred of human will destroys his laboratory and orders his wife to kill him. His discovery, for the good of mankind, is lost.

Being a clearly labeled species of intellectual, scientists in science fiction films are always liable to crack up or go off the deep end. In *Conquest of Space* (1955), the scientist-commander of an international expedition to Mars suddenly acquires scruples about the blasphemy involved in the undertaking, and begins reading the Bible mid-journey instead of attending to his duties. The commander's son, who is his junior officer and always addresses his father as "General," is forced to kill the old man when he tries to prevent the ship from landing on Mars. In this film, both sides of the ambivalence toward scientists are given voice. Generally, for a scientific enterprise to be treated entirely sympathetically in these films, it needs the certificate of utility. Science, viewed without ambivalence, means an efficacious response to danger. Disinterested intellectual curiosity rarely appears in any form other than caricature, as a maniacal dementia that cuts one off from normal human relations. But this suspicion is usually directed at the scientist rather than his work. The creative scientist may become a martyr to his own discovery, through an accident or by pushing things too far. But the implication remains that other men, less imaginative—in short, technicians—could have administered the same discovery better and more safely. The most ingrained contemporary mistrust of the intellect is visited, in these movies, upon the scientist-as-intellectual.

The message that the scientist is one who releases forces which, if not controlled for good, could destroy man himself seems innocuous enough. One of the oldest images of the scientist is Shakespeare's Prospero, the overdetached scholar forcibly retired from society to a desert island, only partly in control of the magic forces in which he dabbles. Equally classic is the figure of the scientist as satanist (*Doctor Faustus,* and stories of Poe and Hawthorne). Science is magic, and man has always known that there is black magic as well as white. But it is not enough to remark that contemporary attitudes—as reflected in science fiction films—remain ambivalent, that the scientist is treated as both satanist and savior. The proportions have changed, because of the new context in which the old admiration and fear of the scientist are located. For his sphere of influence is no longer local, himself or his immediate community. It is planetary, cosmic.

One gets the feeling, particularly in the Japanese films but not only there, that a mass trauma exists over the use of nuclear weapons and the possibility of future nuclear wars. Most of the science fiction films bear witness to this trauma, and, in a way, attempt to exorcise it.

The accidental awakening of the super-destructive monster who has slept in the earth since prehistory is, often, an obvious metaphor for the Bomb. But there are many explicit references as well. In *The Mysterians,* a probe ship from the planet Mysteroid has landed on earth, near Tokyo. Nuclear warfare having been practiced on Mysteroid for centuries (their civilization is "more advanced than ours"), ninety percent of those now born on the planet have to be destroyed at birth, because of defects caused by the huge amounts of Strontium 90 in their diet. The Mysterians have come to earth to marry earth women, and possibly to take over our relatively uncontaminated planet. . . . In *The Incredible Shrinking Man,* the John Doe hero is the victim of a gust of radiation which blows over the water, while he is out boating with his wife; the radiation causes him to grow smaller and smaller, until at the end of the movie he steps through the fine mesh of a window screen to become "the

infinitely small." . . . In *Rodan,* a horde of monstrous carnivorous prehistoric insects, and finally a pair of giant flying reptiles (the prehistoric
Archeopteryx), are hatched from dormant eggs in the depths of a mine
shaft by the impact of nuclear test explosions, and go on to destroy a
good part of the world before they are felled by the molten lava of a
volcanic eruption. . . . In the English film, *The Day the Earth Caught Fire,*
two simultaneous hydrogen bomb tests by the United States and Russia
change by 11 degrees the tilt of the earth on its axis and alter the
earth's orbit so that it begins to approach the sun.

Radiation casualties—ultimately, the conception of the whole world
as a casualty of nuclear testing and nuclear warfare—is the most ominous
of all the notions with which science fiction films deal. Universes become
expendable. Worlds become contaminated, burnt out, exhausted, obsolete.
In *Rocketship X-M* (1950) explorers from the earth land on Mars, where
they learn that atomic warfare has destroyed Martian civilization. In
George Pal's *The War of the Worlds* (1953), reddish spindly alligator-
skinned creatures from Mars invade the earth because their planet is
becoming too cold to be inhabitable. In *This Island Earth,* also American, the planet Metaluna, whose population has long ago been driven
underground by warfare, is dying under the missile attacks of an enemy
planet. Stocks of uranium, which power the force field shielding
Metaluna, have been used up; and an unsuccessful expedition is sent to
earth to enlist earth scientists to devise new sources for nuclear power.
In Joseph Losey's *The Damned* (1961), nine icy-cold radioactive children
are being reared by a fanatical scientist in a dark cave on the English
coast to be the only survivors of the inevitable nuclear Armageddon.

There is a vast amount of wishful thinking in science fiction films, some
of it touching, some of it depressing. Again and again, one detects the
hunger for a "good war," which poses no moral problems, admits of no
moral qualifications. The imagery of science fiction films will satisfy the
most bellicose addict of war films, for a lot of the satisfactions of war
films pass, untransformed, into science fiction films. Examples: the dog-
fights between earth "fighter rockets" and alien spacecraft in the *Battle of
Outer Space* (1959); the escalating firepower in the successive assaults
upon the invaders in *The Mysterians,* which Dan Talbot correctly described as a non-stop holocaust; the spectacular bombardment of the underground fortress of Metaluna in *This Island Earth.*

Yet at the same time the bellicosity of science fiction films is neatly
channeled into the yearning for peace, or for at least peaceful coexistence.
Some scientist generally takes sententious note of the fact that it took the

planetary invasion to make the warring nations of the earth come to their senses and suspend their own conflicts. One of the main themes of many science fiction films—the color ones usually, because they have the budget and resources to develop the military spectacle—is this UN fantasy, a fantasy of united warfare. (The same wishful UN theme cropped up in a recent spectacular which is not science fiction, *Fifty-Five Days in Peking* [1963]. There, topically enough, the Chinese, the Boxers, play the role of Martian invaders who unite the earthmen, in this case the United States, England, Russia, France, Germany, Italy, and Japan.) A great enough disaster cancels all enmities and calls upon the utmost concentration of earth resources.

Science—technology—is conceived of as the great unifier. Thus the science fiction films also project a Utopian fantasy. In the classic models of Utopian thinking—Plato's Republic, Campanella's City of the Sun, More's Utopia, Swift's land of the Houyhnhnms, Voltaire's Eldorado— society had worked out a perfect consensus. In these societies reasonable- ness had achieved an unbreakable supremacy over the emotions. Since no disagreement or social conflict was intellectually plausible, none was possible. As in Melville's *Typee,* "they all think the same." The universal rule of reason meant universal agreement. It is interesting, too, that societies in which reason was pictured as totally ascendant were also traditionally pictured as having an ascetic or materially frugal and eco- nomically simple mode of life. But in the Utopian world community projected by science fiction films, totally pacified and ruled by scientific consensus, the demand for simplicity of material existence would be absurd.

Yet alongside the hopeful fantasy of moral simplification and inter- national unity embodied in the science fiction films lurk the deepest anxieties about contemporary existence. I don't mean only the very real trauma of the Bomb—that it has been used, that there are enough now to kill everyone on earth many times over, that those new bombs may very well be used. Besides these new anxieties about physical disaster, the prospect of universal mutilation and even annihilation, the science fiction films reflect powerful anxieties about the condition of the individual psyche.

For science fiction films may also be described as a popular mythology for the contemporary *negative* imagination about the impersonal. The other-world creatures that seek to take "us" over are an "it," not a "they." The planetary invaders are usually zombie-like. Their movements are either cool, mechanical, or lumbering, blobby. But it amounts to the same thing. If they are non-human in form, they proceed with an absolutely regular, unalterable movement (unalterable save by destruction). If they are human in form—dressed in space suits, etc.—then they obey the most rigid military discipline, and display no personal characteristics whatsoever. And it is this regime of emotionlessness, of impersonality, of regimentation, which they will impose on the earth if they are successful. "No more love, no more beauty, no more pain," boasts a converted earthling in *The Invasion of the Body Snatchers* (1956). The half-earthling, half-alien children in *The Children of the Damned* (1960) are absolutely emotionless, move as a group and understand each others' thoughts, and are all prodigious intellects. They are the wave of the future, man in his next stage of development.

These alien invaders practice a crime which is worse than murder. They do not simply kill the person. They obliterate him. In *The War of the Worlds*, the ray which issues from the rocket ship disintegrates all persons and objects in its path, leaving no trace of them but a light ash. In Honda's *The H-Man* (1959), the creeping blob melts all flesh with which it comes in contact. If the blob, which looks like a huge hunk of red Jello and can crawl across floors and up and down walls, so much as touches your bare foot, all that is left of you is a heap of clothes on the floor. (A more articulated, size-multiplying blob is the villain in the English film *The Creeping Unknown* [1956].) In another version of this fantasy, the body is preserved but the person is entirely reconstituted as the automatized servant or agent of the alien powers. This is, of course, the vampire fantasy in new dress. The person is really dead, but he doesn't know it. He is "undead," he has become an "unperson." It happens to a whole California town in *The Invasion of the Body Snatchers,* to several earth scientists in *This Island Earth,* and to assorted innocents in *It Came From Outer Space, Attack of the Puppet People* (1958), and *The Brain Eaters* (1958). As the victim always backs away from the vampire's horrifying embrace, so in science fiction films the person always fights being "taken over"; he wants to retain his humanity. But once the deed has been done, the victim is eminently satisfied with his condition. He has not been converted from human amiability to monstrous "animal" bloodlust (a metaphoric exaggeration of sexual desire), as in the old vampire fantasy. No, he has simply become far more efficient—the very model of technocratic man, purged of emotions, volitionless, tranquil, obedient to all orders. (The dark secret behind human nature used to be the upsurge of the animal—as in *King Kong*. The threat to man, his availability to dehumanization, lay in his own animality. Now the danger is understood as residing in man's ability to be turned into a machine.)

The rule, of course, is that this horrible and irremediable form of murder can strike anyone in the film except the hero. The hero and his family, while greatly threatened, always escape this fate and by the end of the film the invaders have been repulsed or destroyed. I know of only one exception, *The Day That Mars Invaded Earth* (1963), in which after all the standard struggles the scientist-hero, his wife, and their two children are "taken over" by the alien invaders—and that's that. (The last minutes of the film show them being incinerated by the Martians' rays and their ash silhouettes flushed down their empty swimming pool, while their simulacra drive off in the family car.) Another variant but upbeat switch on the rule occurs in *The Creation of the Humanoids* (1964), where the hero discovers at the end of the film that he, too, has been turned into a metal robot, complete with highly efficient and virtually indestructible mechanical insides, although he didn't know it and detected no difference in himself. He learns, however, that he will shortly be upgraded into a "humanoid" having all the properties of a real man.

Of all the standard motifs of science fiction films, this theme of dehumanization is perhaps the most fascinating. For, as I have indicated, it is scarcely a black-and-white situation, as in the old vampire films. The attitude of the science fiction films toward depersonalization is mixed. On the one hand, they deplore it as the ultimate horror. On the other hand, certain characteristics of the dehumanized invaders, modulated and disguised—such as the ascendancy of reason over feelings, the idealization of teamwork and the consensus-creating activities of science, a marked degree of moral simplification—are precisely traits of the savior-scientist. It is interesting that when the scientist in these films is treated negatively, it is usually done through the portrayal of an individual scientist who holes up in his laboratory and neglects his fiancée or his loving wife and children, obsessed by his daring and dangerous experiments. The scientist as a loyal member of a team, and therefore considerably less individualized, is treated quite respectfully.

There is absolutely no social criticism, of even the most implicit kind, in science fiction films. No criticism, for example, of the conditions of our society which create the impersonality and dehumanization which science fiction fantasies displace onto the influence of an alien It. Also, the notion of science as a social activity, interlocking with social and political interests, is unacknowledged. Science is simply either adventure (for good or evil) or a technical response to danger. And, typically, when the fear of science is paramount—when science is conceived of as black magic rather than white—the evil has not attribution beyond that of the perverse will of an individual scientist. In science fiction films the antithesis of black magic and white is drawn as a split between technology, which is beneficent, and the errant individual will of a lone intellectual.

Thus, science fiction films can be looked at as thematically central allegory, replete with standard modern attitudes. The theme of depersonalization (being "taken over") which I have been talking about is a new allegory reflecting the age-old awareness of man that, sane, he is always perilously close to insanity and unreason. But there is something more here than just a recent, popular image which expresses man's perennial, but largely unconscious, anxiety about his sanity. The image derives most of its power from a supplementary and historical anxiety, also not experienced *consciously* by most people, about the depersonalizing conditions of modern urban life. Similarly, it is not enough to note that science fiction allegories are one of the new myths about—that is, one of the ways of accommodating to and negating—the perennial human anxiety about death. (Myths of heaven and hell, and of ghosts, had the same function.) For, again, there is a historically specifiable twist which intensifies the anxiety. I mean, the trauma suffered by everyone in the middle of the 20th century when it became clear that, from now on to the end of human history, every person would spend his individual life under the threat not only of individual death, which is certain, but of something almost insupportable psychologically—collective incineration and extinction which could come at any time, virtually without warning.

From a psychological point of view, the imagination of disaster does not greatly differ from one period in history to another. But from a political and moral point of view, it does. The expectation of the apocalypse may be the occasion for a radical disaffiliation from society, as when thousands of Eastern European Jews in the 17th century, hearing that Sabbatai Zevi had been proclaimed the Messiah and that the end of the world was imminent, gave up their homes and businesses and began the trek to Palestine. But people take the news of their doom in diverse ways. It is reported that in 1945 the populace of Berlin received without great agitation the news that Hitler had decided to kill them all, before the Allies arrived, because they had not been worthy enough to win the war. We are, alas, more in the position of the Berliners of 1945 than of the Jews of 17th century Eastern Europe; and our response is closer to theirs, too. What I am suggesting is that the imagery of disaster in science fiction is above all the emblem of an *inadequate response*. I don't mean to bear down on the films for this. They themselves are only a sampling, stripped of sophistication, of the inadequacy of most people's response to the unassimilable terrors that infect their consciousness. The interest of the films, aside from their considerable amount of cinematic charm, consists in this intersection between a naïve and largely debased commercial art product and the most profound dilemmas of the contemporary situation.

Ours is indeed an age of extremity. For we live under continual threat of two equally fearful, but seemingly opposed, destinies: unremitting banality and inconceivable terror. It is fantasy, served out in large rations by the popular arts, which allows most people to cope with these twin specters. For one job that fantasy can do is to lift us out of the unbearably humdrum and to distract us from terrors—real or anticipated—by an escape into exotic, dangerous situations which have last-minute happy endings. But another of the things that fantasy can do is to normalize what is psychologically unbearable, thereby inuring us to it. In one case, fantasy beautifies the world. In the other, it neutralizes it.

The fantasy in science fiction films does both jobs. The films reflect world-wide anxieties, and they serve to allay them. They inculcate a strange apathy concerning the processes of radiation, contamination, and destruction which I for one find haunting and depressing. The naïve level of the films neatly tempers the sense of otherness, of alien-ness, with the grossly familiar. In particular, the dialogue of most science fiction films, which is of a monumental but often touching banality, makes them wonderfully, unintentionally funny. Lines like "Come quickly, there's a monster in my bathtub," "We must do something about this," "Wait, Professor. There's someone on the telephone," "But that's incredible," and the old American stand-by, "I hope it works!" are hilarious in the context of picturesque and deafening holocaust. Yet the films also contain something that is painful and in deadly earnest.

There is a sense in which all these movies are in complicity with the abhorrent. They neutralize it, as I have said. It is no more, perhaps, than the way all art draws its audience into a circle of complicity with the thing represented. But in these films we have to do with things which are (quite literally) unthinkable. Here, "thinking about the unthinkable"—not in the way of Herman Kahn, as a subject for calculation, but as a subject for fantasy—becomes, however inadvertently, itself a somewhat questionable act from a moral point of view. The films perpetuate clichés about identity, volition, power, knowledge, happiness, social consensus, guilt, responsibility which are, to say the least, not

serviceable in our present extremity. But collective nightmares cannot be
banished by demonstrating that they are, intellectually and morally,
fallacious. This nightmare—the one reflected, in various registers, in
the science fiction films—is too close to our reality.

[*1965*]

One-Eyed Jacks and Psychodrama

Parker Tyler

The Psychodrama, which I capitalize gratuitously, is a distinctly minor
form of clinical practice. But I think its moral motivation and express
theatrical pattern far more significant in American culture than its
psychiatric limits technically suggest. Actually, it is the private therapy
of the mentally and emotionally handicapped individual turned into a
collective enterprise. In what may be termed the ritual of the Psychodrama, the individual patient tries to explicate his dilemma in terms of
pantomime, possibly words too, before a small audience of others like
himself: those with similar difficulties. The psychiatrist functions as a
stage-manager director without script, more like the moderator of a discussion panel than like a stage director. Group therapy is but a less the-
atricalized version of the Psychodramatic session, which may take place
on an actual stage or platform. In group therapy, a round robin of story-
tellers (groping autobiographers) replaces the actor-patient in the spot-
light.

However fragmentary, even chaotic, a session of either sort of therapy
may be, its social implications are fairly obvious and simple. It is a form
of communication among individuals, each of whom has the right to be
both hero and critic—critic of another as well as himself. Historically, in
terms of drama as an art form, the monologue may well come to mind
here. Because the subject matter of *Hamlet,* for instance, is deeply involved with psychological mysteries, that play's soliloquist may spring up

Excerpts from "An American Theater Motif: The Psychodrama" by Parker
Tyler, in *American Quarterly*, XV, Summer 1963. Reprinted with the permission
of the author and the University of Pennsylvania. Copyright 1963, Trustees of
the University of Pennsylvania.

in the same thought. Is not Hamlet acting out a sort of Psychodrama for an uninitiated audience, the court of Denmark, and is not the Ghost, to this audience, an express element of Hamlet's imagination? Many features of this hero's fame attest to the conclusion that he is a prophetic "Psychodramatist." In this century, however, the uniqueness of his historic enigma has been permanently altered by Pirandello's plays.

Pirandello's *Six Characters in Search of an Author* are members of one family, ordinary people with ordinary problems, who feel the strange need of acting out their difficulties before a public audience. Like the people who used to expose their private lives in the former American radio program, "Court of Human Relations," they wish to be judged by something beyond the moral standards prevailing among them as a family because their domestic conflicts have balked, defeated and sundered them. If they cannot be put together again, they at least wish to define themselves as individuals, so they can be free to act, to begin their lives anew. But even this, in the case of Pirandello's "six characters," is in doubt owing to the power of the family idea that has such a grip on them. . . .

The Method, derived from the Stanislawski Method, is an institution in the American theater: the Actors' Studio in New York. Many directors and actors of stage and screen are its successful graduates, and at least two great stars, Marlon Brando and the late Marilyn Monroe, are widely thought to have been "made" by it. One may observe of these two popular actors that their private difficulties in past years have received some very open publicity. In the case of Miss Monroe, her private life and her professional life overlapped at a truly Pirandellian angle inasmuch as the star's relations with her husband, Arthur Miller, came to a crisis in Reno while she was making there *The Misfits,* a film about a neurotic woman's divorce.

What is proudly termed The Method runs into some trouble with veteran actors as well as, allegedly, into some trouble with itself. Ingrid Bergman, after playing in television with a new American "Method" actor, Rip Torn, told a newspaper reporter that she thought Mr. Torn's acting very good but that, nevertheless, a Method actor seemed to make "trouble for himself." It was widely reported by the press that John Huston, who directed *The Misfits,* had some difficulty with the star, who at one point abruptly absented herself from work on the film. Anna Magnani, of all actresses, cannot be called hardened in the mold of the professional tradition. Yet, according to Tennessee Williams, it was Miss Magnani who (rather unfamiliar with English, the language she was using) became flustered during scenes in *The Fugitive Kind* by Marlon Brando's habit of being behind her cues and even inventing lines she had not heard before. This was how Mr. Williams accounted for his view that, in this film, Miss Magnani gave a performance below her usual level.

All this may be somewhat mysterious to those uninformed of the nature of The Method. The Method initiates the actor into a strong rapport with the role being played so that the edges between life and artifice, the private individual and the actor, necessarily become fluid and vague. This means that the given script, as such, is subject to change. In *One-Eyed Jacks,* a film which Brando directed and whose lead he played, he was reported by *Life* to have instructed his actors (in scenes re-shot and re-shot) to make up their own lines with only the gloss of the plot to guide them. He coached them by showing them how well *he* could get along without memorized lines. Surely, in a film molded by the classic saga of the good-bad outlaw of the Old West, one can appreciate the worth of something intending to make it look fresh. But the hero-myths of nineteenth-century fiction—such as, for example, Natty Bumppo's—are so archaic that The Method, as a form of resuscitation, looks touchingly naïve. . . .

What has Brando been able to do with the old-fashioned Western of vintage period (1880–85) through The Method? He has logically touched the spirit of the Psychodrama. The Psychodrama is, so to speak, a one-man theater with an audience of potential actors under the charge of a new-fashioned psychiatrist. The Psychodramatist's own unconscious helps and so does the "coaching" of the psychiatrist; so does the spectacle of other Psychodramatists engaged, it is likely, with very similar "scripts." Let us consider in passing the professional one-man theater, whose American exponents have been monologists such as Ruth Draper and Cornelia Otis Skinner. Of course, they adhered to given scripts. But sometimes these were written by themselves; moreover, their "theater" was a succession of imaginary selves so that their art was limited to ever renewed effort to be "somebody else." The abstraction from drama as a collective form of expression is the same as in the Psychodrama. But according to The Method, this abstraction is the actor's *normal* way of *participating in* a play. He makes up his own speeches in given situations *as though* he were playing "himself," *as though* he were living "life."

A professional phenomenon that helps us comprehend the Method actor's viewpoint is the existence in popular art of performers who always "play themselves" anyway. This is true of most film comedians; one need mention only W. C. Fields and Charlie Chaplin as men whose personalities (and this was even true of Chaplin when he invented a double) were the public images of their private temperaments. Mae West is, and was, simply Mae West, and so was Mary Pickford till she had to mature. Then there was Garbo. Her public had been so much in love with her romantic mystery, abysmal voice and eyes haunted by a past and shaded by sinister black eyelashes, that both she and her public became confused when she tried to be "somebody else." Marlon Brando, because of distinct personal traits, has come to be in much the same position as Garbo. For him to "act roles" in the sense that Laurence Olivier does would not only be intolerable; it would seem unnatural.

Brando's personality fits so well into his role as Rio the Kid in *One-Eyed Jacks* because he plays a grown-up, permanently rebellious child, strangely isolated in a brooding privacy, perhaps nursing some profound, elusive hurt, beautiful physically, and as tender as he is tough. To some extent, all these qualities are familiar as those of the American "criminal hero." But Brando is supercharged with them. He is a criminal in this film and a quasi or potential criminal in past films; he simply carries the atmosphere of the "innocent sinister" like Mark Antony's mantle. There have been lots of Western heroes, with the seamy side plainly written on their faces, who have had to be reformed in their maturity or have carried their lonely good-bad ambiguity into the distance with them. Brando's image, on the other hand, is that of the juvenile delinquent whose rebellion has survived; the grown-up "boy" still mystified by his responsibilities as an adult.

Brando is instinctively right to coach himself in the stance of the Method actor, for in this way he stays closest to the personality-type I have indicated. He is quite old enough to have seams in his face (as candid shots of him prove) but in *One-Eyed Jacks,* excellently photographed in color, he wears a seam-suppressing make-up, dramatically lit and registered by a cameraman who knows how to bring out the actor's ideal qualities. Hence, the truth is that Brando's face and his person are seen with the maximum of artifice. He is so graceful that at moments he looks balletic without losing virility: the male dancer's ideal achievement. He even has the lightninglike rapidity that defines the brilliant balletic style when reaching its climaxes. This accomplishment is the more remarkable in that it is precisely when Brando shows sudden violence, indeed explosive *savagery,* that his stylish brilliance, in *One-Eyed Jacks,* comes to the fore.

In his case, The Method provides that tension of inner alertness that projects character spontaneously, with *inspiration,* to the audience. "Living one's role" has long been a part of the theatrical idiom. But an extra dimension is given it by The Method. Both in psychology and fiction, modern researches in personality and behavior have revealed the presence of the involuntary act arising from the unconscious and completed without the consent of the conscious. Albert Camus, in *The Stranger,* created a hero whose personality and fate are entirely governed by such an act. The pattern of the "involuntary" act can easily be seen in *One-Eyed Jacks* in those cases where Brando, after a period of more or less conscious brooding, uncontrollably explodes into action—always wreaking destruction. This pattern, of course, has many ancestors in the repertory of romantic fiction. Here it has a special, very channelized function.

It is a "sign" which an initiated audience perfectly understands both because of Brando and the thinking customs of our time. Event by event, Rio's conduct becomes increasingly the result of being more "put upon" than "putting upon." He has learned all he knows as the result of bitter experience, the experience of outraged "innocence," and his character is simply a carefully coached reflex-action to the aggression of others. There is no secret made of the fact, from the film's very beginning, that Rio the Kid is a bank robber who often shoots to kill. Then he is betrayed by a close confederate, and starts out (according to the Western stereotype) on his revenge-mission after suffering enough in prison to lend this mission the color of righteousness.

No mature movie-goer can complain that there is anything unorthodox about the plot and look of *One-Eyed Jacks.* The plot could not be more type-tailored; we have seen it literally thousands of times and its settings here are simply glorious. Yet its manipulation is subtly marked with still further novelty by The Method. In the dialogue, a great deal is made of the fact that people *lie.* The original betrayal of Rio is the withdrawal of a promise to rescue him from capture. Even before that, Rio is portrayed as a fraudulent love-maker who tells a woman he is giving her a ring worn by his mother when he has just stolen the said ring. Later, when inevitably he meets his true love, a really pure girl, he proceeds to seduce her by a similar deception in which a necklace he has just bought plays the same role. This time the seduction is successful and the girl conceives an illegitimate baby. But she lies to her stepfather (the object of Rio's revenge), and though she confesses to her mother, her mother in turn lies to her husband. This world of fraud, this round-robin of lies, is familiar in crime films; it is *supposed* to be there. But no one is prepared to deny its moral viciousness, or the moral viciousness of bloody cruelty which may go hand in hand with it.

I maintain that The Method has done a great deal to make this familiar world of fraud more acceptable without changing it a jot. Rio is duly dissuaded from his revenge by the love of the girl he has seduced, eventually wins the underdog's smashing triumph—and tantalizingly departs at the end on his perpetual flight from the Law, promising the girl that he may turn up again some day. Why should this incredibly tarnished stereo-type deserve all the "trouble" taken by Method acting? One reason I have already given: the hero is Brando's one-man part. He played it in *The Fugitive Kind* with a guitar instead of a six-shooter; if the role was different, the person and his moral reflexes were the same. These moral reflexes, as I have noted, are communicated through the graces of The Method. But inevitably, roles in films are self-chosen when a great star plays them. Rio the Kid is played to the hilt with innocence aforethought. He is made to live (and speak) in that quasi-Pirandellian climate where the "plot," by its nature, is a suspect quantity (perhaps even a "pack of lies") and its true usefulness is the simple test of one's private integrity. If the style is the man, so, in Method acting and the Psychodrama, is the plot.

One must note the significance of the title in *One-Eyed Jacks*. The slang epithet is spoken by Brando to characterize duplicity, being based indirectly on the proverb that, if a man's eyes are too close together, he is not to be trusted. Rio's betraying confederate has become a flourishing town's sheriff, hence a model of virtue whose criminal past is unknown. Both men, meeting again at last, deceive one another by pretending to be friendly; actually, they remain enemies. If Rio, too, is duplicit because he has a grudge-mission, one senses (for reasons already given) that he alone rebels against the world of fraud to which the plot has condemned him. Isn't he oddly like Hamlet in this respect? It is the world of fraud, which hides a crime, against which Hamlet rebels. Moreover, we sense in Hamlet his rebellion against the very revenge-mission to which he has dedicated himself.

Bluntly speaking, Hamlet's world, too, is full of "one-eyed Jacks." The term comes from the profile of the black Jacks on playing cards, who keep the other sides of their faces hidden, and in this way establish a plastic relation with the man whose eyes "are too close together." Symbolically, a liar's true face is the motive which is hidden behind his visible face. Rio himself must be a one-eyed Jack, but he is a one-eyed Jack "with a difference." What is the difference? The difference is that self-promoted "innocence" of the plot which a Method actor *pretends to have,* and which a Psychodramatist, at least according to theory, *really has.* The world as a fraudulent plot is imposed on Rio no less than it is on Hamlet. The substance of their similar protests against it is consciousness of an original innocence, which has been tricked into being a medium of violence and bloodshed. The whole theory of the Psychodrama is that its uncertain, confused protagonist has also been imposed on by a plot he never made, and thus his chief business is to free himself from its entanglements. To do this, both the Psychodramatist and the clinical patient have to invent words and acts. Each invents them as he goes along. In being an "antagonist" of himself, he is an antagonist of a certain plot, a given plot. . . . The Psychodramatist of clinic or theater starts out with the idea he can turn this allergy into its own antidote: he can discover the new world of his own truth. The Method actor is debonair about the plots in which he finds himself; they are all external artifices in which the lie is basically the lie of the actor's pretense; therefore stage characters who lie offer the same problem as stage characters who tell the truth. For the Method actor draws only upon the hidden truth of *himself.*

If the sources of this contemporary American "Method," as a theater motif, are Russian and otherwise European, this is only what is true of American social origins. It is perfectly apt that, to intellectual Europe, our nation traditionally should be Cowboy-and-Indian country. The gangster was simply an urban version of a world picaresque hero who was revived here. In England, Robin Hood became a scholar's archaism after being enshrined as a romantic legend; over here, he raised fresh dust as the Lone Ranger and the fleeing gangster. Such lively vestiges as he now shows seem oddly alien in this global, and notably psychiatric, era. Yet these vestiges, via The Method, have sneaked back into the Psychodrama's clinical stage, where the "lost" individual attempts to reintegrate with the group.

Robin Hood was a mythical gangster who might have chosen (as even the Knight Errant) to go "on his own." As a sheriff, he was put on his own, in a sociological sense, in *High Noon,* when a whole town denied him co-operation. In *One-Eyed Jacks,* he rejoins society as a cousin of the audacious district attorney of another urban myth: the hero (maybe tainted himself) who tackles, alone, organized political corruption. What survives as the moral emblem of this hero-type? His magic individualism as one who wishes (like a Huey Long) to lead and reform the group: one who has renounced it out of moral disgust, out of his own inherent virtue. The mount he always rides is our country's undying cult of personality. This cult is the Psychodrama's "ghost horse." . . .

Jules and Jim

Pauline Kael

When the Legion of Decency condemned *Jules and Jim,* the statement read: the story has been developed "in a context alien to Christian and traditional natural morality." It certainly has. The Legion went on to say: "If the director has a definite moral viewpoint to express, it is so obscure that the visual amorality and immorality of the film are predominant and consequently pose a serious problem for a mass medium of entertainment." It would be possible to make a fraudulent case for the film's morality by pointing out that the adulterous individuals suffer and die, but this is so specious and so irrelevant to the meanings and qualities of the work that surely the Legion, expert in these matters, would recognize that it was casuistry. The Legion isn't wrong about the visual amorality either, and yet, *Jules and Jim* is not only one of the most beautiful films ever made, and the greatest motion picture of recent years, it is also, viewed as a work of art, exquisitely and impeccably *moral.* Truffaut does not have "a definite moral viewpoint to express" and he does not use the screen for messages or special pleading or to sell sex for money; he uses the film medium to express his love and knowledge of life as completely as he can.

The film is adapted from Henri-Pierre Roche's autobiographical novel, written when he was seventy-four, with some additional material from his even later work, *Deux Anglaises et le Continent.* If some of us have heard of Roche, it's probably just the scrap of information that he was the man who introduced Gertrude Stein to Picasso—but this scrap shouldn't be discarded, because both Stein and Picasso are relevant to the characters and period of *Jules and Jim.* Roche is now dead, but the model for Catherine, the Jeanne Moreau role, is a German literary woman who is still alive: it was she who translated *Lolita* into German. Truffaut has indicated, also, that some of the material which he improvised on location was suggested by Apollinaire's letters to Madeleine—a girl whom he had met for a half-hour on a train.

The film begins in Paris before the First World War. Jules the Austrian (Oskar Werner) and Jim the Frenchman (Henri Serre) are Mutt and Jeff,

From *I Lost It at the Movies* by Pauline Kael, by permission of Atlantic–Little, Brown and Co. Copyright 1954, © 1955, 1961, 1962, 1963, 1964, 1965, by Pauline Kael.

149

Sancho Panza and Don Quixote, devoted friends, contentedly arguing about life and letters. Catherine enters their lives, and Jules and Jim try to have both the calm of their friendship and the excitement of her imperious, magical presence. She marries Jules who can't hold her, and in despair he encourages Jim's interest in her—"That way she'll still be *ours*." But Catherine can't subjugate Jim: he is too independent to be dominated by her whims. Not completely captivated, Jim fails to believe in her love when she most desperately offers it. She kills herself and him.

The music, the camera and editing movement, the rhythm of the film carry us along without pauses for reflection. Truffaut doesn't linger; nothing is held too long, nothing is overstated or even *stated*. Perhaps that's why others besides the Legion of Decency have complained: Stanley Kauffmann in the *New Republic* says that *Jules and Jim* "loses sight of purposes. . . . It is a confusion of the sheer happiness of being in the studio . . . with the reason for being there." Truffaut, the most youthfully alive and abundant of all the major film directors, needs a *reason* for making movies about as much as Picasso needs a reason for picking up a brush or a lump of clay. And of what film maker could a reference to a *studio* be less apt? He works everywhere and with anything at hand. Kauffmann says of *Jules and Jim*, "There is a lot less here than meets the eye," and Dwight MacDonald, who considers Kauffmann his only peer, is reassured: "one doesn't want to be the only square," he writes. If it gives him comfort to know there are two of them . . .

What is the film about? It's a celebration of life in a great historical period, a period of ferment and extraordinary achievement in painting and music and literature. Together Jules and Jim have a peaceful friendship (and Jim has a quiet love affair with Gilberte) but when Jules and Jim are with Catherine they feel alive. Anything may happen—she's the catalyst, the troublemaker, the source of despair as well as the source of joy. She is the enchantress who makes art out of life.

At the end, Jules, who has always given in to everything in order to keep Catherine, experiences relief at her death, although he has always delighted in the splendor she conferred on his existence. (Don't we all experience this sort of relief when we say goodbye to a particularly brilliant house-guest?) The dullness in Jules, the bourgeois under the Bohemian, the passivity is made clear from the outset: it is why the girls don't fall in love with him. At the end, the excitements and the humiliations are over. He will have peace, and after a lifetime with Catherine he has earned it.

Catherine is, of course, a little crazy, but that's not too surprising. Pioneers can easily become fanatics, maniacs. And Catherine is part of a

new breed—the independent, intellectual modern woman, so determined
to live as freely as a man that while claiming equality she uses every
feminine wile to gain extra advantages, to demonstrate her superiority,
and to increase her power position. She is the emerging twentieth-century
woman satirized by Strindberg, who also adored her; she is the woman
with rights and responsibilities who entered Western literature after the
turn of the century and has almost always been seen by the male authors
as demanding the rights but refusing the responsibilities. This is the
traditional male view of the feminist, and the film's view is not different.
Don't we now hear complaints that Negroes are so sensitive about their
rights that you can't treat them casually and equally as you would
anybody else, you can't disagree on a job or question their judgment, you
have to defer to their sensitivities and treat them as if they were super-
whites—always in the right? So it is with Catherine.

Catherine, in her way, compensates for the homage she demands. She
has, despite her need to intrude and to dominate, the gift for life. She
holds nothing in reserve; she lives out her desires; when she can't control
the situation, she destroys it. Catherine may be wrong-headed, as those
who aspire to be free spirits often are (and they make this wrongness
more visible than pliable, amiable people do), but she is devoid of
hypocrisy and she doesn't lie. In one of the most upsetting and odd
little scenes in the film she takes out a bottle which she says is "vitriol
for lying eyes"—and Jim doesn't react any more than if it were aspirin.
Catherine the free spirit has the insanity of many free spirits—she believes that she knows truth from lies, right from wrong. Her absolutism
is fascinating, but it is also rather clearly *morally insane*. She punishes
Jim because he has not broken with Gilberte, though she has not broken
with Jules. Only the relationships *she* sets and dominates are *right*.
Catherine suffers from the fatal ambivalence of the "free and equal"
woman toward sex: she can leave men, but if they leave her, she is as
abandoned and desolate, as destroyed and helpless as any clinging vine
(perhaps *more* destroyed—she cannot even ask for sympathy). *Jules and
Jim* is about the impossibility of freedom, as it is about the many losses of
innocence.

All these elements are elliptical in the film—you catch them out of the
corner of your eye and mind. So much happens in the span of an hour
and three quarters that even if you don't take more than a fraction of
the possible meanings from the material, you still get far more than if
you examined almost any other current film, frame by frame, under
a microscope. *Jules and Jim* is as full of character and wit and radiance
as *Marienbad* is empty, and the performance by Jeanne Moreau is so

vivid that the bored, alienated wife of *La Notte* is a faded monochrome. In *Jules and Jim* alienation is just one aspect of her character and we see how Catherine got there: she *becomes* alienated when she can't get her own way, when she is blocked. It is not a universal condition as in *La Notte* (neither Jules nor Jim shares in it): it is her developing insanity as she is cut off from what she wants and no longer takes pleasure in life.

Jules and Jim are portraits of artists as young men, but they are the kind of artists who grow up into something else—they become specialists in some field, or journalists; and the dedication to art of their youth becomes the *civilizing* influence in their lives. The war blasts the images of Bohemian life; both Jules and Jim are changed, but not Catherine. She is the unreconstructed Bohemian who does *not* settle down. She needed more strength, more will than they to live the artist's life—and this determination is the *un*civilizing factor. Bohemianism has made her, underneath all the graces, a moral barbarian: freedom has come to mean whatever she says it is. And when she loses what she believes to be freedom—when she can no longer dictate the terms on which Jim will live— she is lost, isolated. She no longer makes art out of life: she makes life hell.

She chooses death, and she calls on Jules to observe her choice, the last demonstration of her power over life and death, because Jules by a lifetime of yielding his own freedom to her has become, to her, a witness. He can only observe grand gestures; he cannot *make* them. In the last moment in the car, when self-destruction is completely determined, she smiles the smile of the statue: this was the mystery that drew them to her —the smile that looks so easy and natural but which is self-contained and impenetrable.

Jules and Jim ends after the burning of the books in Germany, the end of an epoch, as Truffaut has said, for intellectual Bohemians like Jules and Jim. The film is, in a way, a tribute to the books that were burned; I can't think of another movie so full of books, and of references to books and of writing and translating books. Books were the blood of these characters: they took their ideas of life from books, and writing books was their idea of living.

Jules and Jim is, among other things, the best movie ever made about what I guess most of us think of as the Scott Fitzgerald period (though it begins much earlier). Catherine jumping into the waters of the Seine to demonstrate her supremacy over Jules and Jim, who are discussing the weaknesses of women, is not unlike Zelda jumping over that balustrade. This film treatment of the period is a work of lyric poetry and a fable of the world as playground, a work of art as complex and suggestive in its way as the paintings and poetry and novels and music of the period that it is based on. It is a tribute to the school of Paris when art and Paris were synonymous; filmically it is a new school of Paris—and the new school of Paris is cinema. You go to movies, you talk movies, and you make movies. The young French painters don't compare with the Americans, and French literature is in a fancy trance, but oh, how the young French artists can make movies!

Several of the critics, among them Kauffmann, have complained that the song Jeanne Moreau sings is irrelevant to the action of the film. It's embarrassing to have to point out the obvious, that the song is the theme and the spirit of the film: Jules and Jim and Catherine are the ones who "make their way in life's whirlpool of days—round and round together bound." And, in the film, the song is an epiphany: when Catherine sings, the story is crystallized, and the song, like Jim and the child rolling on the hill, seems to belong to memory almost before it is over. In the same way, the still shots catch for us, as for the characters, the distillation, the beauty of the moment. Throughout the film, Georges Delerue's exquisite music—simple and fragrant, popular without being banal—is part of the atmosphere; it is so evocative that if you put the music on the phonograph, like the little phrase from Vinteuil's sonata, it brings back the images, the emotions, the experience. Though emotionally in the tradition of Jean Renoir, as a work of film craftsmanship *Jules and Jim* is an homage to D. W. Griffith. Truffaut explores the medium, plays with it, overlaps scenes, uses fast cutting in the manner of *Breathless* and leaping continuity in the manner of *Zero for Conduct,* changes the size and shape of the images as Griffith did, and in one glorious act of homage he recreates a frame out of *Intolerance,* the greatest movie ever made. *Jules and Jim* is the most exciting movie made in the West since *L'Avventura* and *Breathless* and Truffaut's earlier *Shoot the Piano Player;* because of the beauty and warmth of its images, it is a richer, a more satisfying film than any of them. I think it will rank among the great lyric achievements of the screen, right up there with the work of Griffith and Renoir.

Robert Rossen's *The Hustler*

Alan Casty

The familiarity of the materials and the preconceptions of the critics kept most from seeing Robert Rossen's *The Hustler* for what it was: a breakthrough on Rossen's part into the techniques and insights needed for the dramatic fulfillment of his deeper understanding and sympathy. This breakthrough was achieved not by applying extraneous conventions to his core concerns, but by extending the range and limits of the kind of social realism with which he had begun. At this point, realism had become for him (as he told *Cahiers du Cinema*):

> not a matter of a servile reproduction of reality. Rather it will be necessary to capture things as they are and modify them so as to give them a poetic significance. Furthermore, it matters little whether you call it poetic or not; what matters is that in this way something situated beyond and above life be delivered, and that, thus, one should feel what one deeply thinks. To reach, if you will, through the objective become universal.

When *The Hustler* was released in 1961, the American critics were not interested in approaching it on these terms. Henry Hart in *Films in Review* emphasized its "low life subject matter," which Hart felt was limiting. Most reviews of the film were favorable (it received the New York Film Critics' Award for Best Direction); but of these reviews Brendan Gill's in *The New Yorker* was typical. While he liked it, he complained that Rossen had become "over-ambitious"; he worried about "the marvelous picture it might have been if it hadn't got so big and diffuse." Gill wanted the film to stay within the realistic depiction of the tricks of the trade of the pool hall, and within the conventional conflict between the aging champion and the young, brash challenger. For him, the complex character of Bert Gordon was just another "tough gangster-gambler."

Rossen produced and directed the film and, along with Sidney Carroll, wrote the screenplay from the Walter Tevis novel. Rossen had had a hard time convincing 20th Century Fox about the property, but the studio was pleasantly surprised when it became one of their most successful products of the period.

The studio's synopsis of the film is a striking and unusual indication

Excerpt from "The Films of Robert Rossen," by Alan Casty. © 1966 by The Regents of the University of California. Reprinted in revised form from *Film Quarterly*, Vol. XX, No. 2, pp. 3–12, by permission of The Regents.

of their lack of understanding of the project, and an indication, as well, of the way in which the materials were strengthened and deepened by Rossen as he worked with them and discovered their significance. The studio synopsis, apparently based on an early treatment of the story by Carroll, has little relationship to the finished film. According to the synopsis, the theme of the picture is that a young pool "shark" loses his head while playing the champ and loses the game, but he is then "taken in hand by a manager who teaches him the psychology of being a winner. He then plays a return match with the Chicago man and wins." That is all, and the plot summary involves nothing more: Eddie arrives and loses. He is taken under the wing of the amateur psychologist, Bert, and then refuses to go to Louisville for a match when Bert demands seventy-five percent of the take. In a cheap pool hall his thumbs are broken, and while he recovers he meets the girl, Sarah. He then goes to Louisville with Bert. He is taken aback when the game is billiards instead of pool, he wins anyway, and returns to Chicago to reject Sarah whom he recognizes is a born loser, and beats Fats for the championship.

That is not, of course, a synopsis of the film Rossen actually made. By the film's completion Rossen saw it this way: "The game represents a form of creative expression. My protagonist, Fast Eddie, wants to become a great pool player, but the film is really about the obstacles he encounters in attempting to fulfill himself as a human being. He attains self-awareness only after a terrible personal tragedy which he has caused —and then he wins his pool game." As Rossen later told *Cahiers*: "He [Eddie] needs to win before everything else; that is his tragedy."

Fast Eddie, the hustler, is, then, one of Rossen's vital young seekers. He has the élan, he has the craft, he has the need and drive for success and power that twists his potential, and pulls him from the other pole of his being, self-fulfillment, and love. In its surface terms the film has much the same patterns as Rossen's earlier boxing film, *Body and Soul;* it depicts the struggle between the gambler and the girl for the unshaped energies of the young American, the wanderer, who is skilled but isolated, without clear purpose, mission, or connection. But while the triangle of conflict is much the same, this time it has been made much more complex, more meaningful, more fully human. Rossen has pushed beyond the usual classifications of his and other American films, the usual neatly patterned boundaries for the audience's response, and the pat socioeconomic allegory of his earlier films.

Certainly, the picture is still about the corrupting influences of money, but even on that level it has greater complexity. We no longer have the empty symbol of the corruption of capitalism in the gambler-promoter.

In Bert Gordon (George C. Scott) we have a man of both satanic power and human weakness. His lust for money is only a part of a syndrome of illusory symbols of identity. There is in him a lust for power and possession of more than money—the need for possession and violation of another human being as an object of one's ego. This drive for power rises from an ego that is paradoxically both strong and uncertain. It is reflected as well in sexual lust shaped into the same terms of domination and destruction, a sexual lust that is sadistic and perverse, twisted by sexual insecurity and ending in sexual failure.

In the same way, Eddie is a more completely realized version of Rossen's young seeker. His sense of the fulfilling potential of his skill is damagingly intertwined with his own need for the power of success and money. His own sense of love is warped by the same kind of aggression. This drive for power—and its undercurrent of insecurity—results in the misuse of his talents and the misuse of the object of his attempted love.

The girl, too, is more fully developed than any of Rossen's previous female characters. She is a potential artist, a writer; she is sensitive to the possibilities of love. But there is in her a despair and a resignation to failure that is finally self-destructive. It is true that she is physically crippled (lame) while the others are emotionally crippled, but she too does not escape the psychic crippling. When Rossen was asked about his tendency to speak of disability in his last films, he replied:

> It is because if I look at the world in which we live, if I think about this world of today, I cannot keep from seeing in it a great number of cripples, and I cannot speak of them as if it were a matter of contemptibly depraved beings. I want to speak of them with sympathy, to try to understand them.

The network of ambiguous emotions and relations of these characters is only partly revealed in the direct actions of the plot; it is there as well in the suggestions of the visual images, and in the disquieting emotional aura that surrounds all but is never fully defined. As Claude Ollier noted in the French film journal, *N.R.F.*:

> One has the constant impression that something else is happening that is escaping, being only briefly suggested by acting and dialogues with two meanings. . . . A sense of indecision hovers permanently over this strange film; and the final explanations are not enough to dispel it.

When Eddie (Paul Newman) first arrives in the pool hall—brash, eager, yet beneath the surface uncertain, even sensitive—Bert Gordon recognizes that Eddie can be the kind of winner that he needs as a gambler, and also the kind of loser that he needs as a man. Eddie establishes an early lead over the self-contained, placid Minnesota Fats, but he presses too hard; the game outlasts his endurance. He drinks, weakens; Fats resiliently endures and wins all. Bert begins his slow conquest of Eddie.

Broke and broken emotionally, Eddie finds in Sarah not only a soothing tenderness, but also an alluring weakness. In the hemmed-in, trapped tightness of her small apartment cluttered with her papers, her whiskey bottles, her groceries, and dirty dishes, they are thrown together in a relationship of growing tenderness and intensifying violence. She is demanding, and he rebels—his anxiety before the demands of the girl and love itself is especially conveyed in the scenes in which his hands (after his beating) are awkwardly encased in plaster casts. He is dominating and she succumbs, even though they both seem to know that at the lowest ebb of his self-esteem there is a twisted use that is being made of their relationship.

Yet, on occasion, there is a deepening of love and understanding. In one scene Rossen uses the wide screen to set up the striking contrast between the outdoors (and the openness and possibilities it suggests) and the confining destructiveness of the life in the apartment. Eddie reclines, full length across the screen, on a sloping hill of grass and here he can verbalize his sense of his skill as more than a tool of conquest—as, rather, a creative and fulfilling personal artistry—and his sense of love as more than a battle for victory of the self.

But the lures of Bert are too strong, and the defenses of the others are too weak and traitorous. Eddie agrees to go to Louisville. Sarah, knowing the meaning of her rivalry with Bert, goes along with them—as much out of fear of loneliness and out of need for defeat, as out of any last hope of victory.

Derby Week at Louisville—gambling, money-making, and spending, and their attendant pleasures—is the background for the final power struggle. The girl's isolation and inevitable doom is captured strikingly (again taking full advantage of the wide screen) in a long, dollying shot that follows her uneven, unnoticed path down a stairway and through a lobby and bar crowded mainly with men who pay no attention to her until she stops at a doorway at the screen's right and is eyed, briefly but completely, by an objectifying glance of disinterested lust.

A bright, hot, and cloistered downstairs billiards room (an expensive, sophisticated hell) is the final battlefield. The hustler's broken thumbs have healed, but not his spirit. He needs more than money now from the gambler; he needs an almost sexual reflection of fulfillment from the gambler's taunting eyes—an assurance that will prove his manhood even as he is destroying it, even as he turns from the girl and thus seals her destruction. The game's "sucker" is obviously a homosexual, and no mean player himself. His excitement builds with the budding sweat on their faces as he struggles expertly and daringly before succumbing, with obvious masochistic pleasure in his inevitable submission before the hustler and the power of men. But who is the "sucker"; who is the half-man who submits because it appears he might (and in Eddie's case does) win? Eddie can only flee from this twisted triumph, and return too late to prevent the gambler's final twisted triumph over Sarah.

At the reception Bert whispers in her ear and Sarah then slaps him and breaks down and cries. It is a moment that sums up his insight into her torments, his challenge to her own self-awareness of what she wants and what she is willing to do, and his final control over her. Back at the hotel, unable to bear any further the kind of mysteries suggested by that whisper and the kind of defeats she is undergoing, she scrawls "twisted," "crippled," "perverted" on the mirror, and in a final gesture of tormented self-destruction gives herself to Bert and then kills herself.

As for Bert, he seems honestly shaken by himself and his results; it has been more than even he has bargained for. But he is himself again, dour, controlled, cynical, at the resolution, as Eddie defeats Fats and regains himself. Although it is certainly likely that Eddie would have learned something from the girl's death, the details of the phoenix-like regeneration of his spirit do not (as Ollier has noted) carry the authority and credibility of the earlier scenes. In his *Cahiers* interview, Rossen defended the ending; but in its stereotype of winning the game, this time in the right way and with the right attitude, there is perhaps too much of the cowboys and Indians that he had earlier referred to in conversation with Robert Penn Warren during the shooting of *All the King's Men*. Warren has related that when they were discussing several alternative endings to the film, Rossen told him: "Son, when you are dealing with American movies you can forget, when you get to the end, anything like what you call irony—then it's cops and robbers, cowboys and Indians."

PART TWO

THE MASS MEDIA
AND
INFORMATION

I · Backgrounds and Perspectives

THE MASS MEDIA affect more than our cultural lives. The pictures of the world that we hold in our minds (and the ideas we have about those pictures) are the result not only of personal experience, but also of what might be called audience experience. In our personal worlds, the data of our experience is often present in random, fluctuating forms; it may take the patterns we have read or heard or seen in the media to shape this data into meaningful patterns of our own. In the public worlds of science, economics, law, government, diplomacy, and war, the effect of the media is even stronger; for here it is the media that supply the data, the information, and the patterns that give life meaning for us. We are not necessarily victims or targets; but we are members of the audience while witnessing events, reports of events, discussion about events, and discussion about the reports of events.

How the media work in shaping this world of information for us and how they should and should not work are approached from four differing perspectives in this section.

In a selection from a larger work, Bernard Berelson, one of the pioneers of this type of analysis, examines the factors which influence the way the media affect their audience. He depicts situations where the media achieve more or less influence on audiences.

Wilbur Schramm, who has probably done more than any other single writer to further the analytical approach to the mass media of information, here studies the nature of news in terms of the two basic types of rewards it offers its audience and the psychological implications of those rewards.

Theodore Peterson's piece (a part of a larger study on four theories of the press; see the bibliography under Siebert) defines the theory underlying the media of information that is subscribed to by most people in the field today. It is a theory that goes beyond the concept of freedom of the press to that of the responsibility of the press to society.

In contrast, in his own lively and colorful style, Tom Wolfe examines and condemns a prevalent situation in which freedom is not hedged in by a corresponding sense of responsibility—the treatment of violence in the media.

The Variable Influence of Communication

Bernard Berelson

The effectiveness of communications as an influence upon public opinion varies with the nature of the communication.

First let us deal with the effect of certain media characteristics. The more personal the media, the more effective it is in converting opinions. This means (other things being equal) that personal conversation is more effective than a radio speech, and that a radio speech is more effective than a newspaper account of it. The greater the amount of "personalism" the communication act contains, the more effective it presumably is. Recent analyses have confirmed the critical importance in opinion formation of personal contact between the individual and his fellows. The individual's opinions are formed in the context of his formal and informal group associations. College students become more liberal in political opinion over the period of their college attendance largely through the influence of the liberality of the college community, that is, the older students and the instructional staff.[1] Intensive case studies of current opinion toward the USSR held by adult men reveal the powerful influence of personal contacts: "The need to conform in one's opinion to the opinions of one's associates and of members of favored groups is an important motivational factor."[2] This effect operated in two ways: directly through the process of conformity as such and indirectly through the sharing of common values and information. The formation of political opinion during a presidential campaign was dependent upon personal influence to a large extent; the political homogeneity of social groups was strikingly high. "In comparison with the formal media of communication, personal relationships are potentially more influential for two reasons: their coverage is greater and they have certain psychological advantages over the formal media."[3] Personal contacts are more

Excerpts from "Communications and Public Opinion" by Bernard Berelson, in *Communication in Modern Society,* edited by Wilbur Schramm. Copyright 1948. Reprinted by permission of the University of Illinois Press.

[1] Theodore M. Newcomb, *Personality and Social Change: Attitude Formation in a Student Community,* Holt, Rinehart and Winston, Inc., 1943.

[2] Mahlon Brewster Smith, *Functional and Descriptive Analysis of Public Opinion.* Doctoral dissertation, Harvard University, 1947, p. 500.

[3] Paul Lazarsfeld, Bernard Berelson, and Hazel Gaudet, *The People's Choice: How the Voter Makes up His Mind in a Presidential Campaign,* Duell, Sloan and Pearce-Meredith Press, New York, 1944, p. 150.

casual and nonpurposive than the formal media, they are more flexible in countering resistance, they can provide more desirable rewards for compliance, they offer reliance and trust in an intimate source, and they can persuade without convincing.[4]

The greater effectiveness of radio over newspapers derives to some extent from its greater "personalism." The radio speaks "to you" more than the newspaper does; it more closely approximates a personal conversation and can thus be more persuasive. The listener can "get a feel" of the speaker's personality, and this is often more effective a factor making for conversion of opinion than the content of the argument itself. The dominant characteristic which enabled Kate Smith to sell nearly $40,000,000 worth of war bonds in one day was the listener's image and evaluation of her personality established over a period of time.[5] In other areas, too, the (radio) personality of such influencers of public opinion as Raymond Gram Swing or Gabriel Heatter or Franklin Delano Roosevelt contributes to their influence.

This discussion of the role of personal contact in opinion formation would not be complete without mention of the relationship between personal conversation and the formal media of communication. This relationship introduces the notion of the "opinion leader" or "opinion transmitter" who takes material from the formal media and passes it on, with or without distortion or effect, to associates who do not use the formal media so frequently in the particular area of concern. There are such people in all social groups and for all social topics, from politics to sports and fashions. This "two-step flow of communication" has been identified and is currently being studied intensively.[6] The concept is of central importance for the formation of a general theory of communication and public opinion.

Within a medium of communication, the particular channels specialized to the subject's predispositions are more effective in converting his opinion than the generalized channels. "The specialized magazine already has a foot in the door, so to speak, because it is accepted by the reader as a reliable spokesman for some cause or group in which he is greatly interested and with which he identifies himself. The general magazine

[4] For a full discussion of these factors, see Chapter 16 of *The People's Choice*.

[5] Robert K. Merton with the assistance of Marjorie Fiske and Alberta Curtis, *Mass Persuasion: The Social Psychology of a War Bond Drive*. Harper & Row, Publishers, New York, 1946.

[6] See *The People's Choice*, pp. 49–51 and pp. 151–52; and the . . . study of the flow of influence among women in a midwestern community by Paul Lazarsfeld and C. Wright Mills.

tries to speak to everyone at once and as a result is less able to aim its shots directly at a particular target. . . . In Erie County in 1940, the *Farm Journal* was mentioned as a concrete influence upon changes in vote intention as frequently as *Collier's,* despite their great difference in circulation, and the Townsend publication as frequently as *Life* or the *Saturday Evening Post.*"[7] Similarly farm programs on the air are probably more effective in influencing farmers' opinions than general radio programs dealing with the same issues.[8] Although there is little direct evidence on this point, it is at least a plausible hypothesis that the specialized communication, per unit of exposure, is more effective in promoting opinion changes than the generalized communication. In a sense, then, this is an obstacle to the homogenizing influence of the mass channels in the mass media.

These are a few ways in which distinctions among the media themselves are involved in the effect of communication upon opinion. What about communication content? Obviously it has a central position in this process. Perhaps the primary distinction in communication content as a factor affecting public opinion is the most primitive, namely, the distinction between the reportorial content and the editorial or interpretive content. Too often discussions of the general problem of the effect of communications upon public opinion is restricted to the latter kind of content. Yet the former is probably more effective in converting opinion. The events reported through the media presumably change more minds—or solidify more—than the comments of editorial writers, columnists, and commentators. "It was Sherman and Sheridan, and not Greeley and Raymond, who had elected him (Lincoln in 1864)."[9] And again, "Opinion is generally determined more by events than by words—unless those words are themselves interpreted as an 'event.' "[10] In addition events tend to solidify opinion changes produced by words, changes which otherwise would be short-lived; and the *fait accompli* crystallizes opinion in favor of the event even though words had not previously been able to do so.[11] Thus the reportorial content of the media is probably more influential than the interpretive.

[7] Lazarsfeld, Berelson, and Gaudet, *The People's Choice,* pp. 135–36.

[8] Some indirect evidence for this is available in William S. Robinson, "Radio Comes to the Farmer" in Lazarsfeld and Stanton, editors, *Radio Research, 1941,* Duell, Sloan and Pearce-Meredith Press, New York, 1941, pp. 224–94.

[9] Frank Luther Mott, "Newspapers in Presidential Campaigns," *Public Opinion Quarterly,* Vol. VIII, 1944, p. 354.

[10] Hadley Cantril, "The Use of Trends," in Cantril, editor, *Gauging Public Opinion,* Princeton, 1944, p. 226.

[11] See *ibid.,* pp. 227–28, for examples.

However, it is necessary to make two remarks here. First, the distinction between "events" and "words" is not easy to make. Is a major speech by the President of the United States an "event" or just "propaganda"? Or a report issued by a pressure group? Or an investigation by a congressional committee? Or a tour of inspection? What about "propaganda of the deed"? Although the distinction is useful, the borderline is not always crystal clear. And secondly, many events exercise influence not in and of themselves, but with active assistance from "words." Thus, for example, the relatively sharp changes in opinion on the interventionist-isolationist issue which occurred at the time of the fall of France in June, 1940, are often attributed to the event itself. However, it must be recognized that this event was strongly interpreted in one way (i.e., pro-interventionism) by most newspapers and radio commentators and by the pronouncements of the national administration. What if most communication channels and the official administration had taken another view of the event? At the least one might suppose that the effect of "the event" would have been different. More recently, the event represented by people's experience in the meat crisis in the fall of 1946 was sometimes credited with the Republican congressional victory at that time. Yet it must be remembered that the communication media gave that event a dominant interpretation (i.e., anti-administration) even though another was possible. In short, the interrelationship of "events" and "words" must be recognized in this connection. The fact is that the communication media are most effective when their reportorial and interpretive contents are in congruence.

Finally, to illustrate this aspect of the process, there is the hypothesis that emotional content of the media is more effective in converting opinions than rational content. There is some evidence for this. Votes for a Socialist candidate were increased more by "emotional" leaflets than by "rational" ones. The highly effective bond broadcasts by Kate Smith even omitted two "rational" themes in favor of emphasis upon various "emotional" ones. In the case of this distinction, of course, the need is not so much to test the finding as to refine it, especially, for different population groups. . . .

Finally, the media of communication have different kinds of effects upon public opinion.

First, a distinction should be made between the effect of the media upon the holding of certain opinions rather than others and their effect upon the holding of political opinions at all. Most attention has been given to the former problem, but the latter—the problem of the creation and maintenance of political interest or political apathy—is of considerable importance. The media have a major influence in producing an interest in public affairs by constantly bringing them to people's attention in a context of presumed citizenly concern. The more the media stress a political issue, the less indecision there is on the issue among the general public.[12] At the same time, however, the communication media may also be promoting in actuality, but without intention, a sense of political apathy among some of its audience. This can occur in at least two ways.

In the first place, it is at least a plausible hypothesis that the attractive substance and easy accessibility of the entertainment or recreational or diversionary content of the mass media operate to minimize political interest for some groups in the population. Comedians, dramatic sketches, and popular music on the air; light fiction of the adventure, mystery, or romantic variety in magazines and books; comics and comic strips; feature films of "straight entertainment"—such "non-serious" content of the media may well serve to divert attention from political affairs directly and also to recreate the audience so that it is under less compulsion to "face up" to the general political problems which confront it and which shape its life. This is said with complete recognition of the psychological relief provided by such communication materials for many people; at the same time, their effect in lowering political interest and attention seems equally clear.

Secondly, the media may increase political apathy simply through presentation of the magnitude, the diversity, and the complexity of the political issues on which the responsible citizen is supposed to be informed. Some readers and listeners, conscious of their inability to become informed rather than superficially on more than a few public problems, retreat from the whole area. How can one know what should be done about the Palestine partition, about inflation, about the Greek guerrillas and the Chinese communists, about race relations in the United States, about the cold war with the USSR, about labor-management relations generally or the latest strike specifically, about "free enterprise" or "planning," about the atom—all at the same time? The media atmosphere of public responsibility for public actions may thus become a boomerang: the more the public is enjoined to exercise its duty to become an "informed citizenry," the less it feels able to do so. And, overwhelmed by the presentation of issues and problems of a public nature, part of the audience may withdraw into the relative security of their private problems and their private lives.

[12] Bernard Berelson, "The Effects of Print upon Public Opinion," in Waples, editor, *Print, Radio, and Film in a Democracy,* University of Chicago Press, 1942, p. 53.

In any discussion of the effect of the media upon the *kinds* of political opinions held by people, an initial distinction should be made between long-run and short-run effects. The importance of the former is inversely related to the research attention which has been given them. The fact that it is easier to study short-run changes in attitudes produced by the communication media—not that that is easy!—should not divert attention from the pervasive, subtle, and durable effects of the media over long periods of time. For example, motion pictures undoubtedly affect the political attention of their audiences over the long run by strengthening certain "basic" values in terms of which political issues are later decided. The influence is remote and indirect, but it is nonetheless present and active. Or again, the communication media affect public opinion over the long run by providing a set of definitions for key political terms (of an affective nature) which come to be accepted through lack of adequate challenge. Thus, "freedom" in this country has mainly been defined in the media in terms of the absence of governmental intervention; and when the value of "freedom" is invoked in a political argument, it usually carries this meaning into the attitudinal battle. Other definitions are possible, but not so current. When it is suggested that "freedom of the press" be defined in terms of the ability of various population groups to secure the kind of communication they want (or someone thinks they should have) rather than in terms of governmental control, the proposal is confronted by the established definition—established through repetition over a long period of time.

Now for the short-run effects of the media upon opinion. Most is known about this area of the general problem, but not much is known. At the least, distinction should be made among the various kinds of effects which the communication media can have upon public opinion. Usually the term "effect" includes only the conversion of opinions (i.e., changes away from a predispositional position or prior attitudes), but the (more frequent) reinforcement and activation effects should not be overlooked. The media are extremely effective in providing partisans with the deference and the rationalizations needed to maintain their position (i.e., reinforcement): "If the press follows a tenacious policy during an economic crisis, it may be able to retard or prevent shifts from one major party to another."[13] And they are also effective in bringing to visibility people's latent attitudes (i.e., activation).[14]

More than that, the media are effective in structuring political issues

[13] Harold F. Gosnell, *Machine Politics: Chicago Model,* University of Chicago Press, 1937, p. 181.
[14] For a fuller description of these effects, see Lazarsfeld, Berelson, and Gaudet, *op. cit.,* Chapters VIII–X.

for their audiences. For example, there is a tendency for partisans on each side of a controversial matter to agree with their own side's argument in the order in which those arguments are emphasized in mass communications. Thus, the media set the political stage, so to speak, for the ensuing debate. In addition, there is some evidence that private discussions of political matters take their cue from the media's presentation of the issues; people talk politics along the lines laid down in the media.[15]

Finally, one thing must be made quite clear in this discussion of the effects of the media upon public opinion. That is that effects upon the audience do not follow directly from and in correspondence with the intent of the communicator or the content of the communication. The predispositions of the reader or listener are deeply involved in the situation, and may operate to block or modify the intended effect or even to set up a boomerang effect. This has been found time and again in studies of the effectiveness of materials promoting tolerance toward ethnic groups, on which topic predispositions run strong.[16] In another context —and under relatively favorable conditions—Communist propaganda provided a catharsis for its subjects, inefficiently for its own objectives, because its themes directly countered strong feelings of individualism and nationalism held by the audience.[17] . . .

[15] For documentation of these points, see Berelson, *op. cit.*

[16] For example, see Eunice Cooper and Marie Jahoda, "The Evasion of Propaganda," *Journal of Psychology*, Vol. XXIII, 1947, pp. 15–25.

[17] Harold D. Lasswell and Dorothy Blumenstock, *World Revolutionary Propaganda: A Chicago Study*, Knopf, 1939. Section V: "The Influence of Propaganda," pp. 247–358.

The Nature of News

Wilbur Schramm

I think it is self-evident that a person selects news in expectation of a reward.

This reward may be either of two kinds. One is related to what Freud calls the Pleasure Principle, the other to what he calls the Reality Prin-

Excerpt from "The Nature of News" by Wilbur Schramm, in *Journalism Quarterly*, September 1949. Reprinted with the permission of the author and *Journalism Quarterly*.

ciple. For want of better names, we shall call these two classes *immediate reward* and *delayed reward.*

In general, the kind of news which may be expected to furnish immediate reward are news of crime and corruption, accidents and disasters, sports and recreation, social events, and human interest.

Delayed reward may be expected from news of public affairs, economic matters, social problems, science, education, and health.

News of the first kind pays its rewards at once. A reader can enjoy a vicarious experience without any of the dangers or stresses involved. He can shiver luxuriously at an axe-murder, shake his head sympathetically and safely at a tornado, identify himself with the winning team or (herself) with the society lady who wore a well-described gown at the reception for Lady Morganbilt, laugh understandingly (and from superior knowledge) at a warm little story of children or dogs. News of the second kind, however, pays its rewards later. It sometimes requires the reader to endure unpleasantness or annoyance—as, for example, when he reads of the ominous foreign situation, the mounting national debt, rising taxes, falling market, scarce housing, cancer, epidemics, farm blights. It has a kind of "threat value." It is read so that the reader may be informed and prepared. When a reader selects delayed reward news, he jerks himself into the world of surrounding reality to which he can adapt himself only by hard work. When he selects news of the other kind, he retreats usually from the world of threatening reality toward the dream world.

For any individual, of course, the boundaries of these two classes are not stable. For example, a sociologist may read news of crime as a social problem, rather than for its immediate reward. A coach may read a sports story for its threat value: he may have to play that team next week. A politician may read an account of his latest successful rally, not for its delayed reward, but very much as his wife reads an account of a party. In any given story of corruption or disaster, a thoughtful reader may receive not only the immediate reward of vicarious experience, but also the delayed reward of information and preparedness. Therefore, while the division of categories holds in general, the predispositions of the individual may transfer any story from one kind of reading to another, or divide the experience between the two kinds of reward.

But what is going on psychologically beneath these two kinds of choice of news?

The kind of choice which we have called immediate reward is simple associational learning, or problem solving. A stimulus is presented; a response is made; the response is rewarded. When the stimulus is again presented, there is a tendency to make the same response. If it is again rewarded, the tendency to make that same response is progressively reinforced. If it is not rewarded, the tendency is progressively extinguished. The stimulus in this case, of course, is the news item. The response is the decision to read or listen to the item. The reward may be either a reduction of tension or discomfort (e.g., curiosity, worry) or an increase in satisfaction (e.g., from a vicarious enjoyment of the achievements of the winning team).

But what is the process which leads a reader or listener to select a news item even though he knows it may not reduce tension, but actually *increase* tension; not relieve discomfort, but actually *increase* discomfort; not bring satisfaction, but actually bring dissatisfaction and worry? We have already suggested that these two kinds of reading are related to what Freud called the two principles of mental functioning, the Pleasure Principle and the Reality Principle. That is, the immediate reward choice is learned through trial and error, because it succeeds in reducing drives and tensions. The delayed reward choice, on the other hand, is made not because it is pleasant, but because it is realistic. It is not pleasant to be afraid or to anticipate danger; but it is necessary, if one is to avert harm and avoid danger.

O. H. Mowrer, in his reinterpretation of conditioning and problem solving, has advanced a concept of learning which is extremely suggestive to any student of the process of communication. He points out that there are really two aspects of learning, related respectively to the two nervous systems. The central nervous system is the one chiefly through which we affect society; the autonomic nervous system is the one chiefly through which society affects us. The central system is the one through which habits—that is, learned responses of the skeletal musculature—are formed. The autonomous system is the one through which attitudes or emotions —that is, learned responses of glands, smooth muscle, and vasomotor tissue—are formed. Habits, of course, come into being to reduce drives and solve problems. Attitudes and emotions, on the other hand, are themselves drives or problems, and call forth skeletal reactions on the basis of which the central nervous system may go into action and develop habits.

Therefore, responses to the two kinds of news correspond to what Sherrington calls *anticipatory* and *consummatory* responses. One is made as the consummation of a drive and with the expectation of immediate reward. The other is made to set up a drive, and in expectation of danger or delayed reward. One reduces a drive and is therefore pleasant; the other sets up a drive and may be painful. The two responses are not always cleanly differentiated. For example, the dramatic quality in a foreign news story may give an immediate reward, while the content arouses only fear or anticipation of danger. But learning may take place through either method. Gordon Allport gives an example of learning through the anticipatory response: "Suppose I mispronounce a word in a public speech . . . and suffer mounting shame and discomfort. Tension has been *created,* not reduced; *dissatisfaction* and not satisfaction has resulted; but in this sequence of events I shall surely learn."

When a child starts to read a newspaper, he usually begins with the comics and the pictures. He proceeds to the sports news, the human interest stories, and sensational stories of crime and disaster, all before he makes much use of public affairs news. It is interesting to conjecture how a child begins to read public affairs news. Perhaps he has an experience in which he is able to make not-too-long-delayed use of something he has read in the paper. Perhaps it helps him to answer a question at school, or to take his raincoat and avoid a soaking, or to avoid a street which is closed for repairs—in other words, to avoid trouble by being informed. He looks at the paper with new respect. If reading that particular item was of benefit to him, would it not be well for him to read other items also? As his understanding broadens, he perceives more of the causative and repetitive relation of events in society. And thus he substitutes other stimuli for the stimulus which has had a proved reward, and as his horizon broadens comes to see more and more reason for reading news of public affairs.

Thus the time when he comes to read public affairs news is an important point in his socialization. Most of the news in the immediate reward group is important to him individually because of the individual satisfaction and drive-reduction it accomplishes. But the news in the delayed reward group is important to him because it arouses the tensions and anticipation that are necessary for survival and development, that help him to be more effective, better prepared, *socially.* . . .

The Social Responsibility Theory
of the Press

Theodore Peterson

Down one turning goes a theory of social responsibility as it is being evolved by the most articulate spokesmen for the press itself; down the other goes the theory as it has been formulated in its most coherent elaboration by the Commission on Freedom of the Press. Both roads head away from traditional libertarian theory, and they parallel one another for various distances at various places. Although the press was generally hostile to the report of the Commission, its criticisms were not directed to several of the primary assumptions of the report. Evidently few if any of the media took issue with the Commission on the fundamental point that the press has a social responsibility, for example, or even on the function of the press in contemporary democratic society. Indeed, many spokesmen for the press have views coinciding with those of the Commission on those very points, and the Commission has said that it took most of its ideas from the professions of the communications industry itself. What the press did criticize were the Commission's evaluation of press performance, which the press thought was not as bad as the Commission depicted; the Commission's assertion that concentration in the media has endangered the free flow of ideas, to which the press replied that the nature of competition has changed; and, above all, the Commission's suggestion that the power of the government over the media be extended, even cautiously. . . .

The Commission has listed five things which contemporary society requires of its press, and together they provide a measure of press performance. The standards were not original with the Commission; as the Commission notes, they were drawn largely from the professions and practices of those who operate the media.

The first requirement of the press in contemporary society, according to the Commission, is to provide "a truthful, comprehensive, and intelligent account of the day's events in a context which gives them meaning." This requirement demands that the press be accurate; it must not lie. It means, also, the Commission says, that the press must identify fact as fact and opinion as opinion.

The press itself seems to be in substantial agreement with the Commission that the media should be accurate and should separate news and opinion. There is perhaps no better evidence of this agreement, no better evidence of a growing fidelity to the public interest, than the development of objective reporting, which Herbert Brucker has included among the outstanding achievements of the American newspaper. In the early years of the nineteenth century, papers used the news as a political weapon; it was distorted, biased, and suppressed to meet the needs of the moment. Later in the century newspapers began to confine their opinions to the editorial page; they strove to record the news objectively, without personal intrusion and comment, and to present not just one side but all sides. True, there were economic reasons for the development of objective reporting, apart from a growing sense of professionalism. But there was a philosophical foundation as well. For by separating news and comment, by presenting more than one side, the press was expediting the self-righting process; it was making it easier for the rational reader to discover truth. By the time that the Commission issued its report in 1947, objectivity was no longer a goal of the press; it was a fetish.

But a truthful, comprehensive account of the news is not enough, says the Commission. "It is no longer enough to report the *fact* truthfully. It is now necessary to report *the truth about the fact*." Here then is the suggestion that the press has developed a curious sort of objectivity—a spurious objectivity which results in half-truths, incompleteness, incomprehensibility. In adhering to objective reporting, the press has tried to present more than one side to a story; but in doing so, the suggestion is, the media have not bothered to evaluate for the reader the trustworthiness of conflicting sources, nor have they supplied the perspective essential to a complete understanding of a given situation. Instead of assuming that two half-truths make a truth, the Commission says in effect, the press should seek "the whole truth." . . .

A second requirement of the press, according to the Commission, is that it serve as "a forum for the exchange of comment and criticism." This requirement means that the great agencies of mass communications should regard themselves as common carriers of public discussion, although it does not mean that laws should compel them to accept all applicants for space or that the government should regulate their rates or even that one can demand, as a right, that the media disseminate his ideas. In simple terms, it means that the giants of the press should carry views contrary to their own without abdicating their own right of advocacy. The press should try to represent all important viewpoints, not merely those with which the publisher or operator agrees; and in doing so, it should carefully identify all sources of news. The reason for this requirement is that control of the press has become vested in fewer and fewer hands. No longer can the individual with something to say reach the necessary audience with the unaided human voice, no longer can he found a newspaper or magazine, no longer can he issue his ideas in pamphlets which will have the prestige that the mass media confer upon their contents.

On this point, too, the media operators seem to concur in large measure with the Commission. Thus Norman Isaacs, managing editor of the Louisville *Times* and 1952–53 president of the Associated Press Managing Editors Association, has stated: "The one function we have that supersedes everything is to convey information. We are common carriers. The freedom of the press was given for that purpose—and that purpose alone. Freedom of the press cannot mean the license to keep people from knowing. And we keep them from knowing whenever we are backward and arrogant in operating our papers." Editors and publishers are fond of saying that the growth of one-newspaper cities has been accompanied by an increased sense of duty to their communities among the dailies which have survived. Spokesmen for the Cowles newspapers in Des Moines and Minneapolis have said that the one daily in a city has a greater responsibility than ever to "help society inform itself and act intelligently" and that the editorial page is an important medium for supplementing and complementing the reporting of news. In both editorial content and advertising, the monopolistic trend in the newspaper field has put new responsibilities on publishers, according to Edward Lindsay of the Lindsay-Schaub Newspapers. "They have a responsibility to minorities in the publication of complete and objective news accounts," he wrote in one of his papers. "They have a responsibility at the business level. Newspaper publishers are denied the luxury of refusing to deal with those whom they dislike or of using their control of a medium of communication to punish those who patronize a competitor. . . ." In their code, broadcasters speak of exerting every effort to insure equality of opportunity in the discussion of public issues; and the television code advises stations to "give fair representation to opposing sides of issues which materially affect the life or welfare of a substantial segment of the public."

A third requirement of the press, the Commission states, is that it "provide a representative picture of the constituent groups in society." Closely related to the preceding two, this requirement would have the press accurately portray the social groups, the Chinese and the Negroes, for example, since persons tend to make decisions in terms of favorable or unfavorable images and a false picture can subvert accurate judgment. In principle if not in practice, most media operators would perhaps concur with the Commission. The movie, radio, and television codes all contain statements urging the media to respect national feelings and the sensitivity of racial and religious groups. Newspaper and magazine workers probably would say that this requirement is implicit in their conscientious effort to report the day's intelligence truthfully and impartially.

A fourth requirement mentioned by the Commission is that the press be responsible for "the presentation and clarification of the goals and values of the society." Again, practitioners would probably accept this requirement with little hesitation. Newsmen would perhaps respond, for instance, that one function of a good editorial page is just such presentation and clarification. Movie producers and broadcasters could point to their codes of performance, which urge the media to respect accepted values and to portray the traditional virtues.

The final requirement mentioned by the Commission is that the press provide "full access to the day's intelligence." Since the citizen today requires more current information than in any earlier day, the Commission notes, there must be a wide distribution of news and opinion. The press would certainly agree. Apart from the attempts of the press to reach as wide an audience as possible, there is evidence of the agreement, for example, in the evolution of the concept of "freedom of information." As newsmen became imbued with a sense of responsibility, they contended that the public had a right of access to information, had a basic right to be informed, and that the press was the agent of the public in breaking down barriers to the free flow of news. . . .

The social responsibility theory of the press rests on a foundation of thought which has amended certain fundamental assumptions of libertarian theory and which has largely rejected others. The concept of liberty which it represents is fundamentally different from that which traditional theory represented. Libertarian theory was born of a concept of negative liberty, which we can define loosely as "freedom from" and more precisely as "freedom from external restraint." The social responsibility theory, on the contrary, rests on a concept of positive liberty, "freedom for," which calls for the presence of the necessary implements for the attainment of a desired goal. Let us explore this point more fully.

In sum, negative liberty consisted of leaving the individual free to work out his own destiny. If he were free from outside forces, he could do so by using his reason to discover the unchanging laws of nature which governed the universe and by bringing his institutions into harmony with them. It was enough, then, to remove the restrictions on man. And it was enough to remove all but a minimum of restrictions on the press; for if the press were unhampered, it would feed information and ideas into the market place, and from their interchange truth would emerge triumphant.

The social responsibility theory is grounded in a school of thought which sees a purely negative liberty as insufficient and ineffective. Negative liberty, according to this view, is an empty liberty; it is like telling a man that he is free to walk without first making sure that he is not crippled. To be real, freedom must be effective. It is not enough to tell a man that he is free to achieve his goals; one must provide him with the appropriate means of attaining those goals. . . .

Pause, Now, and Consider Some Tentative Conclusions About the Meaning of This Mass Perversion Called Porno-violence: What It Is and Where It Comes From and Who Put the Hair on the Walls

Tom Wolfe

Keeps His Mom-in-law in Chains, meet *Kills Son and Feeds Corpse to Pigs.* Pleased to meet you. *Teenager Twists Off Corpse's Head . . . To Get Gold Teeth,* meet *Strangles Girl Friend, then Chops Her to Pieces.* Likewise, I'm sure. *Nurse's Aide Sees Fingers Chopped Off in Meat Grinder,* meet. . . .

In ten years of journalism I have covered more conventions than I care to remember. Podiatrists, theosophists, Professional Budget Finance dentists, oyster farmers, mathematicians, truckers, dry cleaners, stamp collectors, Esperantists, nudists and newspaper editors—I have seen them all, together, in vast assemblies, sloughing through the wall-to-wall of a thousand hotel lobbies (the nudists excepted) in their shimmering grey-

From *Esquire Magazine,* July 1967. Reprinted by permission of Tom Wolfe, c/o Marvin Josephson Associates, Inc. Copyright © 1967 by Esquire, Inc.

metal suits and Nicey Short Collar white shirts with white Plasti-Coat name cards on their chests, and I have sat through their speeches and seminars (the nudists included) and attentively endured ear baths such as you wouldn't believe. And yet some of the truly instructive conventions of our times I seem to have missed altogether. One, for example, I only heard about from one of the many anonymous men who have labored in . . . a curious field. This was a convention of the stringers for *The National Enquirer.*

The Enquirer is a weekly newspaper that is probably known by sight to millions more than know it by name. In fact, no one who ever came face-to-face with *The Enquirer* on a newsstand in its wildest days is likely to have forgotten the sight: a tabloid with great inky shocks of type all over the front page saying something on the order of *Gouges Out Wife's Eyes to Make Her Ugly, Dad Hurls Hot Grease in Daughter's Face, Wife Commits Suicide After 2 Years of Poisoning Fails to Kill Husband. . . .*

The stories themselves were supplied largely by stringers, i.e., correspondents, from all over the country, the world, for that matter, mostly copy editors and reporters on local newspapers. Every so often they would come upon a story, usually via the police beat, that was so grotesque the local sheet would discard it or run it in a highly glossed form rather than offend or perplex its readers. The stringers would preserve them for *The Enquirer,* which always rewarded them well and respectfully.

In fact, one year *The Enquirer* convened and feted them at a hotel in Manhattan. It was a success in every way. The only awkward moment was at the outset when the stringers all pulled in. None of them knew each other. Their hosts got around the problem by introducing them by the stories they had supplied. The introductions, I am told, went like this:

"Harry, I want you to meet Frank here. Frank did that story, you remember that story, *Midget Murderer Throws Girl Off Cliff After She Refuses To Dance With Him.*"

"Pleased to meet you. That was some story."

"And Harry did the one about *I Spent Three Days Trapped at Bottom of Forty-foot-deep Mine Shaft and Was Saved by a Swarm of Flies.*"

"Likewise, I'm sure."

And *Midget Murderer Throws Girl Off Cliff* shakes hands with *I Spent Three Days Trapped at Bottom of Forty-foot-deep Mine Shaft,* and *Buries Her Baby Alive* shakes hands with *Boy, Twelve, Strangles Two-year-old Girl,* and *Kills Son and Feeds Corpse to Pigs* shakes hands with *He Strangles Old Woman and Smears Corpse with Syrup, Ketchup and Oatmeal* . . . and. . . .

. . . There was a great deal of esprit about the whole thing. These men were, in fact, the avant-garde of a new genre that since then has become institutionalized throughout the nation without anyone knowing its proper name. I speak of the new pornography, the pornography of violence.

Pornography comes from the Greek word *porne,* meaning harlot, and pornography is literally the depiction of the acts of harlots. In the new pornography, the theme is not sex. The new pornography depicts practitioners acting out another, murkier drive: people staving teeth in, ripping guts open, blowing brains out and getting even with all those bastards. . . .

The success of *The Enquirer* prompted many imitators to enter the field, *Midnight, The Star Chronicle, The National Insider, Inside News, The National Close-up, The National Tattler, The National Examiner.* A truly competitive free press evolved, and soon a reader could go to the newspaper of his choice for *Kill the Retarded! (Won't You Join My Movement?)* and *Unfaithful Wife? Burn Her Bed!, Harem Master's Mistress Chops Him with Machete, Babe Bites Off Boy's Tongue,* and *Cuts Buddy's Face to Pieces for Stealing His Business and Fiancée.*

And yet the last time I surveyed the Violence press, I noticed a curious thing. These pioneering journals seem to have pulled back. They seem to be regressing to what is by now the Redi-Mix staple of literate Americans, plain old lust-o-lech sex. *Ecstasy and Me (By Hedy Lamarr),* says *The National Enquirer. I Run A Sex Art Gallery,* says *The National Insider.* What has happened, I think, is something that has happened to avant-gardes in many fields, from William Morris and the Craftsmen to the Bauhaus group. Namely, their discoveries have been preempted by the Establishment and so thoroughly dissolved into the mainstream they no longer look original.

Robert Harrison, the former publisher of *Confidential,* and later publisher of the aforementioned *Inside News,* was perhaps the first person to see it coming. I was interviewing Harrison early in January of 1964 for a story in *Esquire* about six weeks after the assassination of President Kennedy, and we were in a cab in the West Fifties in Manhattan, at a stoplight, by a newsstand, and Harrison suddenly pointed at the newsstand and said, "Look at that. They're doing the same thing *The Enquirer* does."

There on the stand was a row of slick-paper, magazine-size publications, known in the trade as one-shots, with titles like *Four Days That Shook the World, Death of a President, An American Tragedy* or just *John Fitzgerald Kennedy (1921–1963).* "You want to know why people buy those things?" said Harrison. "People buy those things to see a man get his head blown off."

And, of course, he was right. Only now the publishers were in many cases the pillars of the American press. Invariably, these "special coverages" of the assassination bore introductions piously commemorating the fallen President, exhorting the American people to strength and unity in a time of crisis, urging greater vigilance and safeguards for the new President, and even raising the nice metaphysical question of collective guilt in "an age of violence."

In the three and a half years since then, of course, there has been an incessant replay, with every recoverable clinical detail, of those less than five seconds in which a man got his head blown off. And throughout this deluge of words, pictures and film frames, I have been intrigued with one thing. The point of view, the vantage point, is almost never that of the victim, riding in the Presidential Lincoln Continental. What you get is . . . the view from Oswald's rifle. You can step right up here and look point-blank right through the very hairline cross in Lee Harvey Oswald's Optics Ordinance four-power Japanese telescopic sight and watch, frame by frame by frame by frame by frame, as that man there's head comes apart. Just a little History there before your very eyes.

The television networks have schooled us in the view from Oswald's rifle and made it seem a normal pastime. The TV viewpoint is nearly always that of the man who is going to strike. The last time I watched *Gunsmoke*, which was not known as a very violent Western in TV terms, the action went like this: The Wellington agents and the stagecoach driver pull guns on the badlands gang leader's daughter and Kitty, the heart-of-gold saloonkeeper, and kidnap them. Then the badlands gang shoots two Wellington agents. Then they tie up five more and talk about shooting them. Then they desist because they might not be able to get a hotel room in the next town if the word got around. Then one badlands gang gunslinger attempts to rape Kitty while the gang leader's younger daughter looks on. Then Kitty resists, so he slugs her one in the jaw. Then the gang leader slugs him. Then the gang leader slugs Kitty. Then Kitty throws hot stew in a gang member's face and hits him over the back of the head with a revolver. Then he knocks her down with a rock. Then the gang sticks up a bank. Here comes the sheriff, Matt Dillon. He shoots a gang member and breaks it up. Then the gang leader shoots the guy who was guarding his daughter and the woman. Then the sheriff shoots the gang leader. The final exploding bullets signals The End.

It is not the accumulated slayings and bone-crushings that make this porno-violence, however. What makes it porno-violence is that in almost every case the camera angle, therefore the viewer, is with the gun, the fist, the rock. The pornography of violence has no point of view in the old sense that novels do. You do not live the action through the hero's eyes. You live with the aggressor, whoever he may be. One moment you are the hero. The next, you are the villain. No matter whose side you may be on consciously, you are in fact with the muscle, and it is you who disintegrate all comers, villains, lawmen, women, anybody. On the rare occasions in which the gun is emptied into the camera—i.e., into your face—the effect is so startling that the pornography of violence all but loses its fantasy charm. There are not nearly so many masochists as sadists among those little devils whispering into your ears.

In fact, sex—"sadomasochism"—is only a part of the pornography of violence. Violence is much more wrapped up, simply, with status. Violence is the simple, ultimate solution for problems of status competition, just as gambling is the simple, ultimate solution for economic competition. The old pornography was the fantasy of easy sexual delights in a world where sex was kept unavailable. The new pornography is the fantasy of easy triumph in a world where status competition has become so complicated and frustrating.

Already the old pornography is losing its kick because of overexposure. In the late Thirties, Nathanael West published his last and best-regarded novel, *The Day of the Locust,* and it was a terrible flop commercially, and his publisher said if he ever published another book about Hollywood it would "have to be *My Thirty-nine Ways of Making Love by Hedy Lamarr.*" *Ecstasy and Me* is not quite that . . . but maybe it is. I stopped counting. I know her account begins: "The men in my life have ranged from a classic case history of impotence, to a whip-brandishing sadist who enjoyed sex only after he tied my arms behind me with the sash of his robe. There was another man who took his pleasure with a girl in my own bed, while he thought I was asleep in it."

Yawns all around. The sin itself is wearing out. Pornography cannot exist without certified taboo to violate. And today Lust, like the rest of the Seven Deadly Sins—Pride, Sloth, Envy, Greed, Anger and Gluttony—is becoming a rather minor vice. The Seven Deadly Sins, after all, are only sins against the self. Theologically, the idea of Lust-—well, the idea is that if you seduce some poor girl from Akron, it is not a sin because you are ruining her, but because you are wasting your time and your energies and damaging your own spirit. This goes back to the old work ethic, when the idea was to keep every able-bodied man's shoulder to the wheel. In an age of riches for all, the ethic becomes more nearly: Let him do anything he pleases, as long as he doesn't get in my way. And if he does get in my way, or even if he doesn't . . . well . . . we have *new* fantasies for that. *Put hair on the walls.*

Hair on the walls is the invisible subtitle of Truman Capote's book, *In Cold Blood.* The book is neither a who-done-it nor a will-they-be-caught, since the answers to both questions are known from the outset. It does ask why-did-they-do-it, but the answer is soon as clear as it is going to be. Instead, the book's suspense is based largely on a totally new idea in detective stories: the promise of gory details, and the withholding of them until the end. Early in the game one of the two murderers, Dick, starts promising to put "plenty of hair on them-those walls" with a shotgun. So read on, gentle readers, and on and on; you are led up to the moment before the crime on page 60—yet the specifics, what happened, the gory details, are kept out of sight, in grisly dangle, until page 244.

But Dick and Perry, Capote's killers, are only a couple of lower-class bums. With James Bond the new pornography has already reached dead center, the bureaucratic middle class. The appeal of Bond has been explained as the appeal of the lone man who can solve enormously complicated, even world problems through his own bravery and initiative. But Bond is not a lone man at all, of course. He is not the Lone Ranger. He is much easier to identify than that. He is a salaried functionary in a bureaucracy. He is a sport, but a believable one; not a millionaire, but a bureaucrat on expense account. He is not even a high-level bureaucrat. He is an operative. This point is carefully and repeatedly made by having his superiors dress him down for violations of standard operating procedure. Bond, like the Lone Ranger, solves problems with guns and fists. When it is over, however, the Lone Ranger leaves a silver bullet. Bond, like the rest of us, fills out a report in triplicate.

Marshall McLuhan says we are in a period in which it will become harder and harder to stimulate lust through words and pictures—i.e., the old pornography. In an age of electronic circuitry, he says, people crave tactile, all-involving experiences. The same thing may very well happen to the new pornography of violence. Even such able craftsmen as Truman Capote, Ian Fleming, NBC and CBS may not suffice. Fortunately, there are historical models to rescue us from this frustration. In the latter days of the Roman Empire, the Emperor Commodus became jealous of the celebrity of the great gladiators. He took to the arena himself, with his sword, and began dispatching suitably screened cripples and hobbled fighters. Audience participation became so popular that soon various *illuminati* of the Commodus set, various boys and girls of the year, were out there, suited up, gaily cutting a sequence of dwarves and feebles down to short ribs. Ah, swinging generations, what new delights await?

II · Individual Media

How extensive is the power of the press? In the first selection of this section, a veteran journalist and editor, T. S. Matthews, takes a good look at this cliché and defines the limits of its meaning and the limits of the power of the press.

Another cliché of the newspaper profession is re-examined by the late Elmer Davis, one of the most intelligent and courageous reporters in the business. In Davis' view, the long-held belief in the value of completely objective reporting is not only mistaken, but also dangerous; he poses against this belief an interpretive form of journalism that he thinks can better fulfill the functions of the newspaper.

Emmet John Hughes, another professional journalist, uses the famous Kennedy-Nixon debates as a touchstone for a broader study of the specific ways in which television reporting has already begun to affect the world of politics.

Similarly, John Gregory Dunne deduces implications from a particular form of television reporting—coverage of a riot—about the way television actually interacts not only with its audience, but also with the very events it is reporting.

Looking at radio from a broader point of view, Paul Lazarsfeld derives several basic effects that regular radio listening has upon the audience and its conception of the world.

The Power of the Press?

T. S. Matthews

The biggest piece of clap-trap about the press is that it deals almost exclusively, or even mainly, with news.

And the next-biggest piece of clap-trap is that the press has enormous power. This delusion is persistent and widespread. It is taken for granted by the public-at-large, who are apt to be impressed by anything that is said three times; it is continually advertised by the press itself, and it is cherished by press lords, some of whom, at least, should know better. The Hutchins Commission of the Freedom of the Press, which represented a more-than-usually-intelligent public-at-large in the United States, not only took the power of the press at the press's own valuation, but thought it very alarming:

> We have the impression that the American people do not realize what has happened to them. They are not aware that the communications revolution has occurred. They do not appreciate the tremendous power which the new instruments and the new organization of the press place in the hands of a few men.

In what way is the press supposed to be so powerful? The general notion is that the press can form, control or at least strongly influence public opinion. Can it really do any of these things? Hugh Cudlipp, editorial director of *The London Daily Mirror,* and a man who should know something about the effect of newspapers on public opinion, doesn't share this general notion about their power. He thinks newspapers can echo and stimulate a wave of popular feeling, but that's all. "A newspaper may successfully accelerate but never reverse the popular attitude that common sense has commended to the public." In short, it can jump aboard the bandwagon, once the bandwagon's under way, and exhort others to jump aboard too; but it can't start the bandwagon rolling, or change its direction after it's started.

Like other habit-forming pills, the press can stimulate or depress, but it cannot cure. It can fan fear and hatred of another nation (when the fear and hatred are there, waiting to be fanned) but it cannot make peace. As more and more people have painful reason to know, the press has a nasty kind of power—the same kind of power a bully has, of hurting somebody smaller and weaker than himself. An individual's only defense against the press is the law of libel, but considerable harm and much pain can be caused without going as far as to commit an actionable libel. Journalists themselves generally have a horror of being interviewed, "written up" or even noticed by the press—they know too well from their own experience how inept and cruel a distortion the result is likely to be. Nine times out of ten, as they know, ineptness is to blame rather than conscious cruelty; but there is always that tenth case. And a blundering friendly hand can be as heavy as an unfriendly fist. The press is often like a clumsy giant who gives you a pat on the back and knocks the wind out of you, if he doesn't cause internal injuries. I remember once coming upon an elderly professor of my university who had just been "written up" by the paper I worked on. When he saw me, tears came into his eyes, and he said, "What have I done to them? What have I done to deserve this?" He was deeply wounded by the article, and regarded it as an extremely unkind caricature. Knowing that it had been written by one of his former students who liked and admired the professor, I tried to reassure him that it was at least kindly meant; I don't think I succeeded.

The press has a negative power—to titillate, alarm, enrage, amuse, humiliate, annoy, even to drive a person out of his community or his job. But of the positive power to which is pretends, and of which the press lords dream—to make and break governments, to swing an election, to stop a war or start a revolution—there is no tangible evidence. Its vaunted might is a gigantic spoof. Professor David Mitrany, speaking in 1932 on "The Press and International Relations," put the case with delicate irony:

> There is no need to spend time in an attempt to show how great is the influence of the press. It is greater in certain fields than in others. It is greater, one could say, in any field in which the knowledge and interest of the man in the street is lesser. For in that case the reading public is apt to think that the press speaks with the voice of authority; while the authorities are apt to assume that the press is speaking with the voice of the people. . . .

Everyone has heard of the "power of the press"; no one has seen it. The greatest believers in this exaggerated "power" and the loudest promoters of it are, naturally, the press lords themselves. One of the most deluded of these, not even excepting Northcliffe or Beaverbrook, was Robert McCormick, publisher of The Chicago Tribune (still emblazoned with his modest motto: "The world's greatest newspaper"). McCormick, and of course his paper, were always in bitter opposition to the Roosevelt Democrats, as well as to the liberal element in his own Republican Party.

A story used to be told about the *Tribune*—no doubt apocryphal but in essence true—that one of the janitors in the *Tribune* building always bet against any political candidate the paper supported, and gave odds to boot; and that he found this sideline so profitable that he was able to buy two sizable blocks of flats.

The people in Chicago who bought the *Tribune* didn't buy it to find out how to cast their votes: they bought it in spite of its advice and its bias, because on the whole they liked its personality and found it entertaining. Does this seem to argue a too shrewd, calm and sensible attitude on the part of the ordinary newspaper reader? The press is generally appreciated by the public for what it is rather than for what it pretends to be. They don't feel it as a power in their lives, but as a working-day prerequisite.

The Need for Interpretive Reporting

Elmer Davis

This striving for objectivity was in its beginnings a good thing, but it went a little too far. From holding that newspapers ought to present both sides, it went on to the position that it was right to present only one side, if nobody happened to be talking on the other; and it was not the business of the newspaper to tell the reader if that one argument happened to be a phony.

This is not quite so bad now as it used to be; it reached its peak, I think, some twenty-five years ago—in the administration of Calvin Coolidge, when it was the opinion of the great majority of American citizens that things are what they seem. In those days, if the Hon. John P. Hoozis was important enough to be interviewed, you might see half or two-thirds of a column embodying the views of the Hon. John P. Hoozis on some topic or other, with no indication that what he said was a lie from beginning to end—even if the editor who printed the story happened to know it—and no indication that the Hon. John P. Hoozis might have a

Excerpts from "Must We Mislead the Public?" by Elmer Davis, in *The Press in Perspective,* edited by Ralph B. Casey. Copyright 1963. Reprinted by the permission of Louisiana State University Press.

powerful personal interest, financial or otherwise, in getting that view over to the public. He had said it, and if he was important enough to be news, it would not have been objective not to print it. . . .

Consider Senator McCarthy; not a single one of his charges has ever been proved, most of them have been pretty conclusively disproved in public hearings—yet he can repeat those same charges and still get space in the papers, sometimes on the front page. And not always merely in papers which find him a useful stick with which to beat the political opposition; very often in papers whose editors may know that this is old stuff, may know that none of it has been proved and much of it has been refuted, yet who feel that if a United States Senator keeps on saying it, it would not be objective to refuse to print it. . . .

This kind of dead-pan reporting—So-and-so said it, and if he is lying in his teeth it is not my business to say so—may salve the conscience of the reporter (or of the editor, who has the ultimate responsibility) as to his loyalty to some obscure ideal of objectivity. But what about his loyalty to the reader? The reader lays down his nickel, or whatever, for the paper, in the belief that he is going to find out what is going on in the world; and it does not seem to me that the newspaper is giving him his nickel's worth if it only gives him what somebody says is going on in the world, with no hint as to whether what that somebody says is right or wrong.

Well, what is the answer? One answer of course has been the rise of the syndicated columns. Who started them I do not know—whether Paul Mallon, or Ray Tucker (for both of whom the honor has been claimed —not by themselves), or, as I am inclined to suspect, a man now almost forgotten, Clinton Gilbert.

At any rate they first came into prominence back in the Coolidge days, when there began to be newspaper readers who were not sure that things are what they seem and who wanted somebody to try to figure things out for them; and they proliferated in the early New Deal, when government had all at once become infinitely more complex, and its problems needed more explanation than ever before. Certainly, over all, the columns have been a good thing for public enlightenment—especially in newspapers which are willing to print columns representing different opinions, instead of sticking to those that back up the editorial page.

Along with the columns, of course, came the radio news commentary, which, like the column, is a mixture of news and interpretation—opinion, if you like—but which differs from the column in that it usually covers at least the high spots of a day's news, while the syndicated column, written as a rule a day or so in advance, is likely to deal only with a single topic. It would ill beseem me to try to estimate the influence or importance, actual or relative, of the trade in which I myself am engaged; all I can say—and this might be said of columns too—is that some radio commentaries admirably illuminate and explain the news for the customer, some seem likely to leave him in a state of total confusion.

But whatever the impact of the news broadcaster or the syndicated columnist, I doubt that either of them has materially supplanted what remains the principal source of news to the general public, the front page of the paper. And it makes a difference, a vast difference, to the health of the republic whether what is on that front page is what is so, to the best of the editor's and the reporter's capacity to ascertain it, or only what somebody falsely alleges to be so. Objectivity, a necessary and useful ideal in its day, has been carried so far that it leans over backward and often obscures the truth instead of revealing it. How can we cure that? . . .

I believe the present tendency is toward more interpretation. But just how it can effectively be done—not in the columns or the radio commentary or on the editorial page, but on the front page—that is something that must still be worked out, and present American newspaper techniques offer little help. . . .

The good newspaper must walk a tight rope between two abysses—on the one side the false objectivity which takes everything at face value and lets the public be imposed upon by the charlatan with the most brazen front; on the other, the interpretive reporting which fails to draw the line between objective and subjective, between a reasonably well-established fact and what the reporter or the editor wishes were the fact. This is primary-school stuff, of course; everybody knows it, and if few people practice it, that is because practicing it is very hard. It is easier to pick out the nearest exit—to fall back on the incontrovertible fact that the Hon. John P. Hoozis said, colon quote, without going into the question whether he was lying or not.

What makes it hard to do anything else is partly the increasing complexity of the news, and partly the traditions of the trade. There is the headline; it must simplify, and simplification is often distortion; but its general pattern is fixed and it seems hopeless to try to change it now. It is permissible for the syndicated column to interpret; but if a man of enough importance to be quoted on the front pages says something this is known to be false—if Pat Hurley, for instance, blames the Atomic Energy Commission for something that happened before the Commission was created or even thought of—it would be an outrageous innovation to interrupt his reported discourse with a bracketed paragraph pointing out that this is not true. I believe I have seen that done, during the war, with some

speeches of Hitler; it may have been done since the war with some statements by Stalin; but I cannot recall that I have ever seen it done with one
of our own people. If it was ever done, any time, anywhere, it has certainly been done very seldom indeed.

Interpretive and corrective journalism not only entails the risk of
confusing opinion with fact—a statement which could easily be documented out of certain newspaper columns, and certain radio commentaries. It is also extremely hard work—increasingly hard these days in
Washington, when we get the same old subjects gone over, again and
again, with the same old witnesses coming up and telling stories something like, but not exactly like, what they told before.

The Impact of TV on American Politics

Emmet John Hughes

Has the power of television—now dramatized by the device of debate
—really revolutionized the democratic process? Is the change more apparent than real? For better or for worse?

So stunning are the factors of size of audience and speed of communication on the grand scale that the very rhythm of political life does seem
revolutionized. And a case can be at least plausibly argued that American
political history has been decisively affected, these last eight years, by this
revolution in technique.

Three witnesses—three of America's political giants—can be summoned
to lend evidence to that case.

Richard M. Nixon in 1952 dramatically appeared on national television
to explain to all the homes of America how he had financed his home, his
career, his whole life—in a performance that made Checkers the nation's
most famous dog since F. D. R.'s Fala. Hours, even minutes before that
telecast, Mr. Nixon stood an excellent chance of making history as the first
candidate on a national ticket ever to be stricken from the lists in mid-
campaign as an insufferable embarrassment to his own party.

So nearly definite was this stern verdict of the party leaders that it is not enough to note that television remarkably served the man: it saved him. No other kind of apologia—nothing but television, with impact both massive and instantaneous could have spared Mr. Nixon swift retirement to the little town of Whittier, California, whose residents thronged the streets, just a few weeks ago, to hail the 1960 Presidential nominee.

Dwight D. Eisenhower in 1956 spent an agonizing late spring in slow recovery from major surgery, following his earlier heart attack. His decision to run for re-election trembled in doubt for weeks; even the thought of it would have made a weaker man tremble. But it is hardly conceivable that even he would have elected to wage a national campaign were it not for the fabulous facilities of television to ease and simplify the ordeal.

John F. Kennedy in 1960 found his spring offensive for the Democratic nomination fatefully committed to the primary battle for West Virginia. His most ominous problem was the state's massive and pervasive hostility to a Catholic candidate. Only the most full and personal kind of campaign —directly reaching and affecting tens of thousands—could counter popular passions so diffuse, so widespread. And only television made such an effort conceivable.

Three different men, in three different years: for all of them, the road to this political moment took its crucial turning around the same extraordinary fact.

Towering personalities and dramatic incidents aside, the impact of television on American political life can be reckoned in a number of other ways. These are ways less crisply clear, yet perhaps more seriously historic and lasting.

First, TV makes political life itself more fluid and more volatile. Men can surge or stumble with astonishing speed—either triumphing over obscurity or tripping over a hasty or graceless public word or gesture. And issues can become as mercurial as individuals: A single performance before a sufficiently massive audience can virtually end an issue or precipitate one.

In the golden days of radio, the nightmare of performers in the studio was the mumbling of some indiscretion or vulgarity a moment before the microphone was dead. Now the politician almost lives before a live "mike" and camera. His world is tapped.

Second, TV forces much of the backstage machinery of political life to endure the same exposure. Conventions tend to become not national caucuses of politicians, but public spectacles, designed less for deliberation (or dealing) among the participants than the delight (or entertainment) of an audience. It is at least debatable whether this makes the event itself more sober or merely more contrived.

It is equally debatable whether the effect upon the audience is one of visual education, in a serious sense, or one of visual enjoyment just a notch or two above the level of the peepshow. What is not in doubt is the fact that the people *see* more.

Third, TV dramatically tends to nationalize political life. The citizen who can watch and hear Presidential candidates from his easy chair feels understandably less excitement than his father at the prospect of a "live" appearance in the local auditorium of a Congressman or even a Senator. Local political clubs—as centers of political life—tend to suffer and sag in appeal.

The firing of local partisan zeal, then, requires ever more prestigious names—as close to the top of the ticket as one dare demand. Ultimately, this could dictate, of course, greater dependence of all local tickets upon the national ticket.

Fourth, TV can strikingly shift political advantage toward those office-holders with easiest access to a national medium; these are national office-holders. It seems hardly an accident that 1960 has been notable for the fact that three of the four candidates on the national tickets come from the U.S. Senate—traditionally inferior to state governorships as sources of national candidates—while the fourth candidate, Henry Cabot Lodge, has enjoyed unique exposure on national television.

In the future of television, it would seem doubtful if the most distinguished governor, whatever his record or his personality, could come close to national candidacy without finding a way, first, to establish his identity as nationally as Washington leaders.

Fifth, accenting the person and the personal, TV both imposes new demands and offers new opportunity to the individual politician. This transcends the level of a Kennedy's concern with his hair or a Nixon's anxiety about his eyebrows (both appropriately adjusted for the current campaign). In the meeting—or the muffing—of issues, it puts new and heavy stress on the man himself.

Thus, for example, one astute political commentator, watching last spring's West Virginia primary, anticipated Senator Kennedy's massive victory on the basis of one response, discovered universally among all citizens queried a fortnight before election. This was the simple fact that all who had seen the Senator on television had reacted favorably, even if grudgingly. Enough television, then, logically would prevail. It did. But it underscored the fact that there could have been no effective substitute for this entirely personal attack on the political problem.

Sixth, TV obviously quickens the tendency of big politics to resemble big business. The cost of campaigning, of course, soars: the relatively easy political struggle of 1956 cost the G. O. P. some $2 million for television and radio. The eager novice, in this televised political life, can afford to start unknown—but not unfinanced.

A Riot on TV

John Gregory Dunne

No one wants to impugn the courage, ingenuity, and virtuosity of the broadcast journalists in Watts. But the very nature of television, with its pressing need to fill the gaping maw of dead air, mitigates against reasoned analysis of a running civil disturbance. Consciously or not, electronic journalism is essentially show business, and show business demands a gimmick. With its insatiable appetite for live drama, television turned the riots into some kind of Roman spectacle, with the police playing the lions, the Negroes the Christians. The angle, in this case, was that the Christians were winning.

Not only did television exacerbate an already inflammatory situation, but also, by turning the riots into a Happening, may even have helped prolong them. One channel went so far as to score its riot footage with movie "chase" music. The situation was made to order for the late-night call-in shows, which cater to what one critic calls "a twilight world of the lonely, the subliterate, the culturally deprived." The riots gave these disembodied voices in the night a chance to vent their private furies against "these people," a euphemism for "Negroes" on station after station. "What do these people want. . . . Why don't they get jobs like decent people. . . . These people remind me of animals." . . .

No rumor, however unsubstantiated, went unreported. Hovering over the riot scene in a helicopter, a reporter for KTLA suddenly announced, "There's a report that one or two policemen are surrounded, so we're going up that way for a look." The report was unfounded, but by the time that was established, there were other unconfirmed stories on the air. The Shrine Auditorium was on fire, the Minute Men were invading

Watts, a contingent of Hell's Angels was even now careening down the Harbor Freeway toward the riot area; all were false alarms. Even when there was nothing new to report, the pitch was maintained—looting at Vermont and 83rd, a shooting at Central and 39th, a car gunned down running a roadblock at Broadway and 47th—until quite isolated events blurred into holocaust and a riot became a massacre.

In fact broadcast coverage of the riots only deepened my own conviction that a thousand words are worth one picture. The most disturbing effect of televised news coverage is that, like LSD, it tends to create a heightened and often spurious reality of its own. No newspaper, no magazine has television's awesome ability to maintain the momentum of an event. Watts is a vast sprawling ghetto, fifty miles square. Normally the dweller in such a peculiarly horizontal slum, in such an immense area, would hear of an incident with the police only the next day, if at all, when he read it in the newspaper. With 24-hour on-the-spot news coverage, however, reality for the viewer in the eye of the storm became not the quiet outside his own bungalow, but the place, often miles away, where the action was.

And the screen affected as well the viewer who was not in the storm at all, the man who could sit in his family room 30 miles away and watch a continuous and indiscriminate feast of violence, death, and destruction. Since only high points are reported, an incident soon becomes a skirmish, a skirmish a full-scale war. Moreover, a microphone tends to create news, often where there is none. . . .

By virtue of the microphone in his hand, an electronic journalist is automatically a participant in any story he covers, particularly in one as volatile and fluctuating as a riot. There is no rewrite man to temper his immediate emotions, no time to reflect before a typewriter upon what he has seen. He is forced to shoot from the lip, as are those he interviews. When a microphone is thrust before an official's face, there is nothing off the record, no chance for a later strategic retreat. He is frozen in the position of defending himself at all costs, giving blanket absolution to his adherents, accepting no blame at all.

Because it is so dependent upon action, television runs the risk of being manipulated far more than the other news media. Who can blame a picket for alerting the networks before going out on the line? . . .

The Effects of Radio

Paul Lazarsfeld

One of the effects of radio is to carry on the trend from detailed information—suited to the interests of a small, well-educated minority—to the barest essentials of current news—designed for the larger masses of people, who are not interested in the details. There are many other fields in which the effect of radio is to increase prevailing trends toward standardization and simplification of communications.

In the political field this effect of radio probably makes people more class conscious. If people for the most part listen to what fits their own frames of reference, and if radio brings more material to their attention, then the effect should be to make their own political decisions more consistent with their class situation and less dependent upon incidental local issues. In an elaborate study of the last presidential campaign, conducted by the Office of Radio Research, it was surprising to see how, as the campaign progressed, the political decisions of most of the people were determined more and more by a few of their social characteristics—religious affiliation, amount of schooling, and economic level. . . .

A corollary of this trend effect of radio is a new "radio type" of consumer in many cultural areas. Radio has helped to bring to the attention of the American people the important events in Europe and thus has contributed to the generally increased interest in news. However, it has been shown in special studies that this new type of news-consumer created by radio has a more hazy knowledge and a less acute interest in those events than the traditional and smaller groups of people with long-established news interests. A similar audience has been developed in the field of serious music. There is no doubt that the broadcasting of good music over hundreds of stations in this country has enlarged the number of those who like it. Still, a more detailed study of their tastes and attitudes has shown that the musical world of these new music lovers is different, if not inferior, to that of the musical élite of past decades and as judged by classical standards.

The second group of situations in which an effect of radio can be traced are those in which radio is used to supplement other forms of influence, especially face-to-face contact. Experiences in the field of educational broadcasting, for instance, have definitely shown that programs are most effective when they promote the activities of organizations like farm bureaus or adult education groups, which have an independent status of their own and use radio to supplement other means of promoting their aims. The technical term applied to this cooperation between social institutions and radio for cultural purposes is "audience-building." For one intending to use radio for promotional purposes of any kind, nothing is more important than to know that it is most effective when used in conjunction with other stimuli for which radio provides, so to say, the background. . . .

The mediated effect of radio deserves much further study. In the presidential-campaign investigation it was found that in the county studied about 15 per cent of the citizens acted as so-called opinion leaders. It was they who listened to the radio and read the newspapers and then through various forms of personal contact conveyed what they learned to the large masses of the population. The opinion leaders need not necessarily have social prominence in the community; a temperamental aptitude for the role of go-between is sufficient.

The last group of effects may be called the monopolistic effects of radio. Such have attracted most public attention because of their importance in the totalitarian countries. If a government monopolizes the radio, then by mere repetition and by exclusion of conflicting points of view it can determine the opinions of the population. We do not know much about how this monopolistic effect really works, but it is important to note its singularity. No inference should be drawn regarding the effects of radio as such. It is often forgotten that Hitler did not achieve control through radio but almost despite it, because at the time of his rise to power radio was controlled by his enemies. The monopolistic effects have probably less social importance than is generally assumed. . . .

III · Critiques and Cases

IN RECENT YEARS, the newspapers, radio, and television have been subject to constant and close analysis, not only of their treatment of the news of the world generally, but also of their treatment of specific events and different kinds of events. Martin Kreisberg's investigation of the effectiveness of the media in bringing the news of foreign affairs to the audience illustrates the common approach of using audience analysis to trace the results of the reporting.

Two examples of foreign news coverage are provided for further analysis in the next pair of selections. Here, the same general subject—the threat posed by Communist China in the Far East—is treated in two magazine articles (the second of these is part of a longer article). The differences between the two pieces can help to illustrate the distinctions between publications in terms of such basic questions as the method and intellectual level of discussions, the audience addressed, the results sought and achieved, the breadth of fact employed, and the basic purposes of magazines.

The selection by Theodore Draper focuses on the treatment by the press of one phase of the Dominican Republic crisis of 1965 and questions the reliability and motives of the coverage of significant news events. Draper's piece is followed by two sets of cases: first, two immediate newspaper accounts of the revolt and, second, two magazine accounts of the events which, most importantly, consider the causes of the events. Again, the differences in the accounts in each case can illustrate some of the basic questions involved in newspaper and magazine reporting.

Martin Grodzins' study about how the coverage of Japanese-American news in the California press changed during the early periods of World War II provides another example of these problems and another indication of the importance of an alert, critical public.

In his analysis of the Army-Senator McCarthy hearings, Gerhart D. Wiebe, like Kreisberg, focuses on the effects on the audience. He is concerned with the lasting effects achieved by these hearings, which at the time seemed to have had the strongest impact to date of any television coverage.

The excerpt from an article on radio news by Leila Sussmann provides a sample of the quantitative analysis that is regularly made, not only of the radio, but of all the mass media. Although the media's attitude toward labor may have since changed—and whether it has and/or how it has would be a worthwhile subject for further study—the basic problem involved in this kind of structuring of news content is still present and deserves constant attention.

Dark Areas of Ignorance

Martin Kreisberg

What do the polls disclose about popular knowledge of foreign policy? Those who analyze and interpret polls classify people in three categories: (1) the *unaware*, the people who freely confess that they have neither heard nor read of important issues in American foreign policy; (2) the *aware*, the people who have heard or read the issues but who have only rudimentary knowledge about them; (3) the *informed*, the people who are not only *aware* of the issues but who also know their meaning and their implications. Usually both the *unaware* and the *aware* are regarded as *uninformed*. Using these definitions public opinion analysts over a period of years have established the following:

About 30 percent of the electorate, on the average, is *unaware* of almost any given event in American foreign affairs.

About 45 percent of the electorate is *aware* of important events in the field but cannot be considered *informed*. These people retain little information. Although they may follow discussions of the issues of foreign policy, they cannot frame intelligent arguments about them.

Only 25 percent of the electorate consistently shows knowledge of foreign problems.

These averages do not hold for all issues. When an aspect of foreign policy is the big news of the moment, the number of the *unaware* is likely to drop somewhat, and the number of the *aware* but *uninformed*, as well as the number of the *informed*, will increase. But even when an issue has received widespread publicity, a large proportion of the electorate remains unaware of it, and substantially less than half is found to be *informed*. . . .

Being aware of an event seems to require only exposure (e.g., through newspapers or the radio), whereas being informed requires an active interest. People are more interested in domestic affairs because they directly affect their lives; foreign affairs seem remote. When asked what specific issues interested them, 67 percent of the electorate mentioned

Excerpts from "Dark Areas of Ignorance" by Martin Kreisberg, in *Public Opinion and Foreign Policy* by Lester Markel, published by Harper & Row for the Council on Foreign Relations. Copyright 1949. Reprinted by permission of the Council on Foreign Relations, Inc.

such things as inflation control and food shortages, while only 60 percent mentioned issues of foreign policy, such as atomic control and relations with Russia. Similarly, people talk more about domestic than foreign matters. Approximately 45 percent of the voters reported that they discussed domestic issues, while only 36 percent said they discussed foreign policy issues. . . .

When information is related to personal or group interest, it is more readily understood and retained. For example, 80 percent of the people were able to give reasonable arguments for continuing the OPA; only 44 percent could give reasonable arguments for making the British loan. In the same way, while 66 percent could give cogent reasons against continuing OPA, only 49 percent supplied reasons for opposing the British loan.

There are definite areas of ignorance in the popular mind which are traceable to social, economic, educational and geographical conditions. . . .

Sex. Of 45 million women eligible to vote, some 38 million are uninformed about the most important issues and events in American foreign policy; almost 10 million never even heard or read about them. For example, 19 percent of the women polled, compared with 13 percent of the men, had never heard of the Marshall Plan. Only 12 percent of the women polled could state its purpose.

Income. The lower a person's income the less is his information. Eighty-eight percent of voters with less-than-average incomes, compared to 82 percent with above-average incomes, could not cite the purpose of the Marshall Plan. Why are the poor more uninformed? Primarily because they lack the interest, the time and the background to become informed. Few of them consider knowledge of foreign affairs either necessary or helpful. One unskilled worker replied to an interviewer, "Foreign affairs! That's for people who don't have to work for a living."

Education. About 29 percent of Americans with grammar schooling or less are unaware of the Marshall Plan, compared with 3 percent of the college graduates. The uneducated are, by and large, the same persons who fall into the low-income group. Their ignorance can be explained partly by their occupations and partly by their lack of facility in reading and in piecing together the information they obtain either from newspapers or the radio. Hence, they accept without question the simpler, and often the more superficial, reporting on foreign matters.

Rural-urban. Urban residents are generally better informed than people in the country for a variety of reasons. Educational facilities are frequently better in the cities. Cities prosper on commerce, which is itself a branch of foreign affairs. Often, as we shall see later, the channels of information, newspapers, radio, television, are more accessible and do a better job of information in the cities.

Region. The regional data confirm generally accepted notions. Persons living on the West and East Coasts seem to be better informed than those in the Midwest and in Southern hinterlands. On the coasts, where the ties to foreign lands are more keenly felt, people take a greater interest in international affairs than in the hinterland. You may argue that agricultural prosperity depends on foreign trade, but it is still hard to persuade the Middle West farmer that he is concerned with what goes on in Trieste. Three thousand miles of water plus 1,500 miles of American soil give him, in spite of the atom bomb, a sense of security. In the South, information is less than in the coastal regions, owing to poorer educational facilities and a lower standard of living. . . .

How well then has the press discharged its responsibility? The answer is "not too well." The desire to sell their wares has a powerful influence on the selection of what newspapers print and on the programs of radio and TV stations. Although there are publishers and stations that try to fulfill their responsibilities faithfully, the tendency in too much of the press is to try to please as many people as possible. . . .

For example, . . . few listeners hear the serious programs provided by radio round-tables and forums; less than two-thirds of them regularly listen to news reports. Radio news reports are brief, and besides only a fraction of each report is devoted to foreign affairs.

Although more than 80 percent of the American people regularly read newspapers, only 50 percent spend a half hour or more in perusing them. In this brief space the reading is likely to be superficial; foreign news may be passed over entirely or given merely a cursory glance. Also, many people have time to read only one newspaper, and thus have no basis for judging either the adequacy or the objectivity of its foreign coverage.

Moreover, the press generally gives its readers too little information about what is going on abroad, or about the problems with which the State Department has to deal. Also, too many newspapers and radio programs, when they do treat foreign affairs, emphasize feeling and emotion rather than thought and reason. . . .

Thus we seem to be caught in a vicious circle. Newspapers do not emphasize foreign affairs because the people are not interested, and the people are not interested because they do not find much foreign news in their papers.

In this connection, the political apathy of the uninformed is an important factor. The uninformed usually believe that no political event can greatly affect their personal fortunes. While foreign policy issues agitate the informed, the world of the uninformed is circumscribed by the daily cares of a child's cough, a boss's gripe, an unexpected frost. They are too immersed in the details of daily living to make the effort to inform themselves on what is happening in Yugoslavia or Germany. . . .

COMMUNIST CHINA: A CASE FOR ANALYSIS

China's Strategy: A Critique

Donald S. Zagoria

The revolutionary recipe offered up by Marshall Lin is not new in the sense of reflecting any major departures in Chinese thinking. The idea of "surrounding" North America and Western Europe—the "cities" of the world—by fomenting Communist and nationalist revolution in the former colonial areas—the "countryside"—has been implicit in Chinese strategic writing since 1958 and was explicitly stated on behalf of Peking by the Indonesian Communists more than a year ago. Nor, as we have already seen, is there anything very new in the revolutionary strategy itself. The only significant difference between past Chinese statements and Lin's is the unusual stress Lin places on armed conflict. In the past it was usually made clear that while armed struggle is the main and highest form of revolution, peaceful political struggle could become the main form in a certain period and under certain circumstances. The

Excerpt from *Commentary*, November 1965. Reprinted by permission of the author.

absence of any such qualification in Lin's article, and his heavy emphasis on the virtues of armed conflicts—no matter how successful or who leads them—seem to reflect Peking's growing interest not merely in promoting revolution but in tying the United States down in a series of debilitating protracted wars against local guerrillas throughout Asia, Africa, and Latin America.

This is not to suggest that Peking has in the past or will in the future indiscriminately foster armed revolution and civil war. Their main objective is to weaken their principal national enemy, the United States, and they will foment armed struggles wherever by so doing they can achieve that objective as a contribution to the ultimate aim of forcing a total withdrawal of the Americans from Asia and the rest of the underdeveloped world. Thus they will continue to concentrate, as they have in the past, on fostering armed struggles primarily in countries tied to the American alliance system—that is, on getting several "South Vietnams" going at once. In addition, they will try to fan the flames of any local war that might prove embarrassing to the Americans or implicate them (this was clearly their intention during the abortive Indo-Pakistani war). There is a double advantage here. First, if successful armed struggles can be launched in these countries, there is a good chance that the Americans will come in and get bogged down in an unpopular war against a colored people. Second, an incentive is provided for pro-American governments to accommodate themselves to Peking. For Peking is in effect blackmailing these governments by telling them to get rid of the Americans or else prepare for a protracted war led by local Communists.

This strategy, Peking believes, is already bearing fruit. The Americans are deeply bogged down in South Vietnam and therefore cannot afford to become involved so deeply elsewhere. To keep the Americans in this dilemma, the Chinese are, with some success, using all their influence in North Vietnam to prevent a negotiated settlement, while selectively fanning the flames of war elsewhere, most recently in the Indo-Pakistani conflict. Moreover, a strategy of overextending and exhausting a great power is ideally suited to the limited material resources of an inferior one like China: it requires no large investment either of Chinese manpower or material. And indeed, Lin Piao pointedly asserts that local revolutionaries cannot and should not expect much outside help, that they must win largely on their own resources.

Why was Lin's article released at this particular time? It is now clear that a decision was taken about a year ago by Hanoi and the Liberation Front to step up the battle in the South from a guerrilla to a conventional war. This effort has failed, and the question for Hanoi now is whether to go back to guerrilla tactics and fight a protracted struggle or to negotiate and try to take over South Vietnam by political means. Lin's argument is designed to support the former alternative. He is in effect telling Hanoi and the Front that, no matter how great the difficulties may seem now that massive American air and fire power have been introduced, they will triumph in the end. "Difficulties are not invincible monsters," says Lin: our liberated areas faced great difficulties from "savage attacks" by the Japanese and Kuomintang; we survived encirclement and the economic blockade; and we did this all by relying on our own resources.

The extraordinary importance Lin attaches to the virtues of self-reliance suggests an effort both to rationalize the lack of any substantial Chinese support to the Vietnamese Communists and to bolster those in Hanoi who argue that the Americans can be defeated even without much outside aid. In a particularly pointed passage, Lin says that reliance even on Socialist countries still committed to revolution—that is, China as opposed to Russia—is no substitute for self-reliance.

More generally, the Chinese are also seeking to reassure Communist revolutionaries not only in Vietnam but throughout the emerging areas that they can defeat the United States and its allies by protracted violence even though the price will be high and the path tortuous. Peking has persistently claimed, and Lin reiterates, that Vietnam is a crucial testing ground for the strategy of people's war.

Lastly, the fact that China's top military leader rather than a political figure was chosen to deliver a statement of such importance indicates that the statement has implications for the dialogue which has been going on for some time within the Chinese military between the "modernizers" and the "guerrillas." There have been a number of recent attacks on "modernizers" who want more professional, up-to-date armed forces equipped with the latest weapons as a deterrent against American attack. Lin's article could in part be the party's response to these critics, for it in effect says that China itself must in any case be prepared to fight a protracted guerrilla war in the event of an American attack on the mainland.

But if the Chinese strategy seems to be bearing fruit at the moment, in tying the United States down in Vietnam, is it in the long run realistic? My own belief is that it is not. Without denying the considerable Chinese capacity for mischief-making in the underdeveloped countries, I would say that their global strategic thinking is crude and growing more and more dogmatic.

The truth is that Mao's strategy has serious weaknesses on both of the two levels at which it operates. On the first level—where it is designed to turn Afro-Asian nationalism against the United States and optimally to foment war between the new nations and the U.S.—the strategy assumes that the American role in the underdeveloped areas can plausibly be equated with Japanese expansionism in Asia before and during World War II. Now it is obvious that both the interests and policies of the developing countries are sometimes in conflict with those of the United States. Moreover, in a world where tensions between rich and poor nations are likely to grow, nationalist leaders will always be tempted to use the richest country on earth as a scapegoat. But American policy in the emerging areas is not static and is not dictated by the rapacious needs of an "imperialist" system, as the Chinese believe. Nor, by and large, do the nationalists in the Third World view the United States as their main enemy, and neither are they anxious to see a complete American military, economic, and political withdrawal. The best recent indication of this is that the Chinese have not been successful in getting the majority of the Afro-Asian powers to condemn American "imperialism"—as distinguished from ritualistic condemnations of "imperialism" and colonialism in general—as the main enemy. In an implicit confession of failure, Peking's Foreign Minister asserted not long ago that if the second Afro-Asian conference, due to be held in Algiers early this month, does not condemn American imperialism by name, it will not succeed; if the conference cannot succeed, he went on to say, it should be postponed "until conditions are ripe"—that is, until the anti-American tide grows. The Chinese, embittered by their own grievances against the Americans, and seeing the United States as the major obstacle to the achievement of their ambition to dominate the Third World, mistakenly think that they can easily transfer their anti-American animus to others. But although it is certain that tensions between the United States and various emerging countries will persist and perhaps increase, it is unrealistic to assume, as the Chinese do, that these tensions must eventually lead to an anti-American alliance of the colored nations.

On its second level—where it is a design for local Communists to capture the nationalist movement during an armed struggle against the Americans or an American-supported government—the Maoist strategy has up to now worked only in China itself and in Vietnam. Two crucial factors were common to both these cases. First, there was an armed struggle with an outside enemy—the Japanese in China and the Japanese and then the French in Vietnam—which gave the Communists an opportunity to make a nationalist appeal against an imperialist or colonial power. Second, the nationalist opposition to the Communists both in China and Vietnam was divided, unimaginative, and without effective organization at the rice-roots level. Current Vietcong successes in South Vietnam are inextricably related to the fact that Ho Chi-minh, like Mao, was able to capture a weak nationalist movement during World War II.

Communist successes in China and Vietnam should not, however, obscure the more fundamental point that the Communists have been unable to seize control of a nationalist movement anywhere else in Africa or Latin America since the start of World War II. (Castro was not a Communist when he took power; he converted to Communism afterward in order to obtain Soviet protection against American attack.) This is not a mere historical accident. It suggests that the Chinese and Vietnamese successes are not easy to duplicate even in the favorable circumstances of an anti-colonial armed struggle. Witness the fact that in none of the recent or current instances of such a struggle—Algeria and Angola, for example— have local Communists played an important role. All this means that Communist prospects of creating another "South Vietnam" are not as good as either Mao or the American adherents of the "domino theory" believe them to be.

In those Afro-Asian countries which have already achieved independence—and these, of course, constitute the vast majority—Maoist strategy runs into a number of even greater difficulties. First, the Chinese cannot woo nationalist leaders in order to turn them against the United States while simultaneously trying to subvert them: Chou En-lai cannot wear a diplomatic topper and a guerrilla beret at the same time. (Peking has already alienated a number of African leaders by supporting efforts to topple them.) Second, many of the Afro-Asian states have established one-party regimes which make it all but impossible for the local Communists to build up independent power bases. Third, even the local Communists in these areas are becoming increasingly aware that the Maoist revolutionary model cannot be mechanically adapted to their own situations.

In India, for example, the Communists are irrevocably split into pro-Soviet and pro-Chinese parties and the latter has been critically, if not mortally, wounded by the Chinese-Indian border conflict—which has robbed it of the chance to pick up the banner of Indian nationalism. In Indonesia, the local Communists have as of this writing been dealt a severe blow after participating in a premature coup directed against the army. In Thailand and Cambodia, the local Communists are extremely weak. In Burma, although the local Communists have been waging an armed struggle against the government for more than a decade, they are not now a serious threat to Ne Win's military government, and without substantial help from China (which they have not been getting), they are unlikely to become such a threat. In what remains of Malaysia, Communist influence is confined largely to the overseas Chinese, who are very unpopular with the Malays. A Communist-led insurrection there would thus most likely lead to a communal war between the Malays and that portion of the Chinese under Communist influence. This strategy failed in 1948 and there is no reason why it should meet with success now. What is more, in none of these Asian countries, with the exception of Indonesia, do the local Communists have a strong base among the peasantry, an indispensable prerequisite for launching a Maoist-style guerrilla war.

As for Africa and Latin America, one decisive fact stands out—great physical limitations on the Chinese ability to intervene directly or by proxy on behalf of local guerrillas. For all the Chinese talk about self-reliance, the truth is that their own aid to the North Vietnamese was decisive in Ho Chi-minh's victory over the French in 1954 and that external Communist aid is a necessity for any guerrilla force which wants to move from guerrilla to conventional war.

But not only do most of the Communist parties in the former colonial areas lack the capability to launch protracted wars against the Americans or American allies; many of them may not have the will. Indeed, they must now be wondering about the desirability of a Chinese strategy for fighting the United States with Vietnamese and other Asian and African lives.

In addition to all this, Peking's attempts to export protracted war are inhibited by the fact that Moscow is putting its still considerable influence in the world Communist movement largely on the side of evolutionary rather than violent change. The vehemence with which Lin denounces Soviet "arguments against people's war" and efforts to "undermine it," suggests that the Soviet influence is having a considerable impact on local Communist parties. It is noteworthy in this connection that in the past year, the North Koreans, North Vietnamese, and Cubans have all veered away from Peking toward a neutral position in the Sino-Soviet conflict.

All of which points up a general weakness in the Chinese approach—its almost obsessive preoccupation with violence and war as the key to social change. This may reflect the mood of desperation of an aging leadership in Peking, but it is doubtful that it accurately reflects the mood in most African and Asian countries, even among the radicals. There are large sections of the Asian Communist movement, for example, that are simply not psychologically prepared to fight in the swamps for twenty or thirty years. Moreover, some of these parties, notably the PKI in Indonesia, have made impressive gains by following a peaceful path. The results from South Vietnam are not yet in, but whatever the outcome, Peking will never be able to argue that Communist successes were purchased cheaply.

So far as the Soviet Union is concerned, its recent efforts to bring a quick halt to the Indo-Pakistani war were in sharp contrast to Chinese attempts to throw gasoline on the fire. Clearly, Moscow is increasingly committing itself to stability in the underdeveloped areas. Not that it has given up hope of tilting the unaligned countries toward the East or eventually even of installing pro-Soviet Communists in power. But the Russians are more and more counseling non-violent revolutionary paths to Afro-Asian nationalists and Communists alike. In Vietnam, the Russians, unlike the Chinese, have been eager for a negotiated settlement from the beginning. They have given enough aid to Hanoi to maintain their credentials as Communists but have done little more. Indeed, Soviet restraint in Vietnam has been remarkable and has not been exercised without considerable cost to Moscow's worldwide prestige. Even its moderate Communist allies in Eastern Europe, who are not at all in sympathy with Chinese tactics, have been shocked by Soviet impotence in the face of an American attack against a "socialist" country. This Soviet humiliation in Vietnam could eventually produce strong pressures in Moscow, particularly among the military, to "stand up" to the Americans.

On the other side, the Soviets have their hands full at home in modernizing the economy and increasing what for the past few years has been an extremely slow rate of growth. To do this, and to raise their standard of living, is not compatible with an arms race or support of Communist-led protracted wars against the Americans. Nor is there any reason for Moscow to mortgage its foreign policy to Communist guerrillas in Africa and Asia.

What then are the implications of Mao's theory of people's war for American foreign policy? The Chinese are undoubtedly right in believing that armed violence in the form of civil, revolutionary, or local wars will occur in the future as it has in the past twenty years. But the experience of the past twenty years also suggests that such conflicts are not necessarily incompatible with American interests even when the Chinese themselves label them "people's wars." The Algerian war is a case in point. More important, recent experience also indicates that it will be very difficult for local Communists to take over the leadership of such armed struggles, which means that there is no reason for Washington to rush in with American military power out of fear of a possible Communist takeover whenever violence erupts in the underdeveloped countries (the Dominican Republic is a good example).

On the other hand, in countering the Chinese strategy, the United States would do well to help educate nationalist leaders and nationalist armies in the underdeveloped countries to subvert people's-war tactics by taking the appropriate military and socio-political preemptive measures early enough. To accomplish this, and in the long run to promote the stability and independence of these newly emergent countries, the United States cannot withdraw from these areas. Its continued presence is vital. At the same time, however, while reiterating its intention to remain in Asia, to protect allies and friends from attack, and to take serious steps to bridge the widening gap between rich and poor nations, the United States ought to begin laying the basis for a realistic relationship with Communist China (recognition, a seat in the UN, limitation of the trade embargo to strategic materials only) once the present leaders pass from the scene. Such a policy would in all likelihood be denounced by Mao and his comrades as an imperialist trick. But it would at least have the virtue of putting the onus for the impasse in American-Chinese relations on Peking's present leadership. More important, it would make available an alternative to Mao's anti-American policy for those who will come to power in China after his death.

Why We Are Fighting in Asia

Francis Vivian Drake

The Chinese communists are embarking on a plan of unparalleled audacity. Their scheme: to turn the Pacific into a communist lake fronting the shores of North and South America.

Korea was the site of the first surge. It failed. South Vietnam is the latest. The enemy—North Vietnam, led by Ho Chi Minh, the communist-supported dictator—is driving south. The war is being fought in a place

so unfamiliar that thousands of Americans are asking: Why are we fighting in this remote land? Why can't we leave and let the Asians fight it
out among themselves?

High Stakes. It would make millions extremely happy if it were in the
interests of our country to order our boys home. The war, however, does
not concern merely South Vietnam or even Southeast Asia. It concerns
the future of the whole Pacific and the security of the Western hemi-
sphere, especially the United States. At stake are worldwide issues still
not fully understood by the public.

South Vietnam is the key to the safety and independence of nations
made up of 325 million free people, possessed of some of the greatest
riches in the world. Burma, Laos, Cambodia, Thailand, the Philippines
could all be forced into serfdom with the collapse of South Vietnam and
the expulsion of the United States.

Even more critical, however, is the fact that Southeast Asia leads to
the ultimate, little understood objective of the present conflict—control
of the Strait of Malacca. This strategic waterway, dominated by the great
port of Singapore, is one of the prime shipping bottlenecks of the world.
Six hundred miles long, 60 miles wide at its narrowest point, studded with
islands, it is a thoroughfare even more important to the United States
than the Strait of Gibraltar, the Suez Canal or the English Channel, for
it is the shortest and safest route from the Pacific to the Indian Ocean.
About 98 percent of the trade of the Orient flows through the Strait in a
procession of ships carrying billions of dollars' worth of merchandise to
and from world markets. In one year more than 12,000 ships drop anchor
in Singapore and more than 10,000 at ports in Indonesia. Thousands
more go on through the Strait for Japan, Taiwan, the Philippines,
Australia. On any given day, as many as 200 ships pass through the Strait
in a line so continuous that a vessel steams under the smoke of the one
ahead.

Next Targets. Communist conquest of South Vietnam would almost
certainly trigger the downfall of neighboring Thailand and Malaysia and
yield control of the Strait of Malacca to the Reds, permitting them to seal
off trade routes, east, west and south. It would also put the communists
within easy reach of their next targets of expansion: Indonesia, Australia
and Japan.

Indonesia, with a population of 100 million, is an archipelago of more
than 3000 islands which stretch like pieces of a jigsaw puzzle from the
Asian mainland to New Guinea on the threshold of Australia. Already

it leans heavily to the left. Its president, Sukarno, who makes no secret of his dislike of the United States, has accepted 650 million dollars proffered in aid from Russia, plus two heavy cruisers, four destroyers, six submarines and 175 MIG planes. While Indonesia is still fence-straddling, awaiting the outcome of the Vietnam conflict, the country has been strategically infiltrated by three million members of the People's Communist Institute, waiting the word to seize power.

If they do so, this would leave Australia facing a solid Red rampart to the north—a perilous predicament for a country the size of continental United States, with only 11 million inhabitants, slight defenses and some of the greatest mineral resources in the world.

Japan, too, will be vulnerable and a rare prize, for her productive genius has developed the world's fifth-largest industrial complex. China reached for Japan via Korea and was defeated. But if China should gain control of both sides of the Strait of Malacca it would be another story. Without striking a blow she could constrict the great artery of Pacific trade. Ships attempting to use other Indonesian straits would not only have a far longer way to travel but could just as easily be stopped by hostile planes, torpedo boats and minefields.

Such a blockade would be catastrophic for Japan, which must import all her raw materials and export much of her manufactured goods. The Red Chinese, themselves without food to export or money to pay for imports, have long hoped to force Japan into their sphere in order to use Japan's productive genius to build up a communist economy. Perhaps the most effective way to do this would be to shut off the supply of oil on which Japanese industry is almost wholly dependent. Ninety-two percent of this passes through the Strait of Malacca. Were the Strait shut off, Japanese industry would grind to a halt. The price of survival would be union with Red China.

In fact, everywhere China peers in the Pacific she sees items she needs desperately—lead, zinc, nickel, manganese, rice from the Philippines; rubber, oil, tin from Indonesia and Malaysia; ships, iron, steel, machinery, tools from Japan; sugar, wood, chemicals from Taiwan; gold, silver, copper, teak from Burma. Everywhere she sees rice, wheat, barley in profusion to feed perpetually undernourished Chinese stomachs.

The Reason Why. Virtually all of these countries are party to defense treaties with the United States and with each other. The United States is honor-bound to come to their aid in case of aggression. Furthermore, without them we would be at a great disadvantage. Our planes would be deprived of forward bases, our ships would have to fight their way

through treacherous narrows under a hail of communist bombs. At the
least we would suffer heavy losses; at the most we would be drawn into
a third world war.

This is why we are trying to stop at its source the projected conquest
of the Pacific. This is why we have great naval forces, planes and men
resisting the Vietcong puppets in Vietnam. This is why the British Commonwealth has nearly half its navy and 75,000 men at Singapore athwart
the route to Australia. It is also why the communists have refused to
"negotiate," for they feel themselves close to realizing their dream of
world domination.

Balance Sheet. Are we militarily strong enough to block the conquest
of Southeast Asia and the Pacific? Are we strong enough to withstand the
"escalation" constantly threatened by the communists? The answer is:
Yes.

From Pearl Harbor we can move great forces to any point in the circle
of the Pacific quicker than the communists can move along the rim. In
the Pacific our Navy comprises 400 warships, spearheaded by nine carrier
task forces. Our Army numbers over 200,000 men, and we can increase
it at will. Our Air Force has 50,000 men and, with the Navy and Marines,
nearly 2000 combat jets in the Pacific, with thousands more on call. These
jets are likely to be of decisive use, for they can fly at 1500 miles per hour,
carry cannon and missiles, and some have a bombload three times that carried in our World War II Flying Fortresses. But they have one great need:
a place to sit down, refuel, take on weapons. This is why our aircraft
carriers and stepping-stone bases—Midway, Wake, Guam, Kwajalein,
Taiwan, the Philippines—have become vital as never before. A fortress
today is not a Rock of Gibraltar but a runway with supplies.

In addition to our own forces we have allies and potential allies whose
lands, populations and planes add up to a formidable total: some 325
million people in Japan, Australia, the Philippines, Malaysia, Thailand,
South Vietnam, Taiwan, Okinawa, South Korea and free Indonesia.
Their combined armies total 2,175,000 men, supported by a total of 1800
jet aircraft.

Arrayed against this force is the population of China, some 750 million
strong. The numbers are daunting, but masses of men need ships, trains
and trucks to transport them and their supplies. China does not have
these. Most Chinese battalions still move on their feet. The army is composed of 2,500,000 men and millions of militia, but has scant transport,
artillery and tanks. The Chinese navy has 28 old submarines and a lot
of small craft. The air force has 2400 planes but nearly all are partially

obsolescent. Maintenance is poor, fuel is short. The whole force lacks quality. In a brush a few years ago with the Chinese Nationalists from Taiwan, the Nationalists inflicted a kill rate of 20 to one.

Thus the Chinese threat to "escalate" the war in Vietnam by sending in its own troops does not stand up to realistic military examination. For one thing, North Vietnam possesses a natural dam against a flood of men from China, a rampart of mountains. The only rail ingress is through two long and deep ravines, with bridges that could be destroyed from the air. Roads are few and poor. Moreover, escalation can run two ways, and China dreads retaliation into her own territory. Lop Nor, the atomic center where she proposes to build nuclear weapons with which to blackmail the Pacific, would be the first target in an expanded war, and its destruction would throw China into a Great Leap Backward in nuclear plans. When she calls the United States a "paper tiger," she is gazing in a mirror.

The final comparison of the forces in the Pacific is therefore as follows, including United States and British Commonwealth units in the area, plus some 1500 U.S. Navy, Air Force and Marine planes on land or the carriers:

	Free Countries	China
Populations	325,000,000	750,000,000
Armies	2,700,000	2,500,000
Ships	500	50
Jets	4000	2000

Such is the balance sheet on which victory or defeat in the Pacific now depends. It shows that we have supreme power on the sea and in the air. We can transport ample troops to meet the enemy if we do not invade China itself. It does seem, therefore, that we are equipped to make a stand now in Southeast Asia, to come to grips with the enemy before he grows stronger, to try and limit the conflict to an area where he cannot bring all his forces to bear, and we can. Time is on our side. If we can stop the communist invasion before it reaches the Pacific islands, they will have time to build up their own defenses and decrease their dependence on the United States. The facts cry for *combination*, for some kind of Pacific Union not subject to communist veto.

The Challenge. To beat the communist drive in the Pacific we have much to learn. We have been ignorant and naïve. We backed into South Vietnam with a handful of "advisers" and a few obsolete planes. We

did not recognize it as the start of a very big thing. We suffered humiliat-
ing defeats. Now we are putting in desperately needed military power;
but the ultimate solution will demand more than arms.

It will demand that millions of our people be able to feel a measure
of *self-identification* with millions in the Pacific who are eager to be
our friends, if we will but trouble to understand them.

They know that the Chinese want to take them over. They have yet to
learn that we don't, that our people rightly consider foreign possessions
as so many liabilities, and that we want the Pacific nations to be free,
independent and self-protecting. The challenge in the Pacific has already
begun. It is as great as any we ever faced.

Contaminated News of the Dominican Republic

Theodore Draper

The classic case of contaminated news is undoubtedly Ambassador
Bennett's briefing on April 29. It was Bennett's first meeting with the
newly arrived correspondents, none of whom could yet circulate freely
in the city. The ambassador devoted most of the meeting to the "Communist takeover" and rebel atrocities. The first list of 53 Dominican
Communists was passed out. The ambassador horrified the assembled
correspondents with some of the reports that he had received: the rebels
were shooting people against walls to the accompaniment of the Castroite cry, *"Paredón!"* (To the wall!); they had severed heads and paraded
them on spikes; Colonel Caamaño had machine-gunned Colonel Calderón,
the aide-de-camp of Reid Cabral. Tad Szulc tells us that a telegram from
Bennett to the State Department that same day reported that Caamaño
had "personally killed" Colonel Juan Calderón. The message said that
"Caamaño had gone berserk" and had committed numerous atrocities.

This is how Ambassador Bennett's briefing was worked into the story
in *Time* magazine of May 7:

> No one had an accurate count of the casualties as frenzied knots of soldiers
> and civilians roamed the streets, shooting, looting and herding people to their

Excerpt from "The Dominican Crisis" by Theodore Draper, in *Commentary*,
December 1965. Reprinted with permission of the author.

execution with cries of "Paredón! Paredón!" (To the wall! To the Wall!) . . .
The rebels executed at least 110 opponents, hacked the head off a police officer
and carried it about as a trophy.

Here is the version in the *U.S. News & World Report* of May 10:

Victims were dragged from their homes and shot down while angry mobs
shouted, "To the wall!"—the same cry that marked the mass executions in
Cuba in the early days of Fidel Castro. The assassinated Dominicans were
dumped into crude graves right at the execution spots.

Other reports from the embassy found their way into President Johnson's speeches: there were "1,000 to 1,500 bodies that are dead in the
street" and "six or eight of the embassies have been torn up" (May 4);
"some 1,500 innocent people were murdered and shot, and their heads
cut off," and "six Latin American embassies were violated" (June 17).
Ambassador Ellsworth Bunker went the President one better and told
the O.A.S. he understood that the El Salvador embassy had been sacked
and burned.

None of these atrocity stories turned out to be true. When the correspondents were able to see for themselves and talk to Dominicans in
the street, they quickly learned that the mass executions and cries of
"Paredón!" had never taken place. No one had ever seen heads on spikes.
Colonel Calderón was found in a hospital suffering from a slight neck
injury and was soon released. Since President Johnson told of 1,000–1,500
dead bodies in the street on May 4, the correspondents could go right
out to look for them; they found, as Barnard L. Collier later put it, "no
more than 6 to 10 bodies in the streets at one time." There had been no
looting in the rebel zone. No embassy was torn up, and the El Salvador
embassy had not been sacked or burned.

Ambassador Bennett never expressed regret for his horror stories of
April 29. Instead, embassy officers have blamed the press for having reported these admittedly unverified "rumors" or "reports received" as if
they were "known facts." Whatever sins the press may have committed,
this is surely the grossest injustice to a group of hard-pressed correspondents who had just arrived on the scene, were getting their first briefing
from the ambassador, and were still totally dependent on him for their
information. They were certainly entitled to assume that no responsible
and experienced diplomat in these circumstances would stand before
them and feed them not one but a succession of atrocity reports implicat-
ing by name the main military leaders of the revolt. It is also hard to
believe that Mr. Bennett was not aware of the dubious journalistic prac-

tice of leaving out the source and passing off information as if the correspondent had first-hand knowledge of it himself. As the versions in *Time* and *U.S. News & World Report* show, the worst offenders were precisely the "news" organs that most crudely took their lead from the ambassador: not only did they themselves assume responsibility for some of his stories but they never did inform their readers that the stories had started out as unverified rumors and had ended up as verified myths. There must be thousands of readers who depend on *Time* or *U.S. News & World Report* for their news, and still think that *"Paredón! Paredón!"* was the theme song of the Dominican revolution. After all, President Johnson still brought up the 1,500 people who had been "murdered and shot, and their heads cut off" at a news conference on June 17, over six weeks after he should have known better.

I do not mean to suggest that the correspondents did not find enough death, destruction, and suffering to be appalled. What they found, however, was the result of the civil war, not of a lust for blood peculiar to Colonel Caamaño and his supporters. If there were any true atrocities in the entire struggle, they were committed by the Dominican air force and navy which repeatedly bombed, shelled, and strafed the city. The most reprehensible air attacks came on June 15 and 16 in flagrant violation of the cease-fire. If shooting "innocent people" was so disturbing to President Johnson, it is hard to understand how he was able to resist speaking out against this crime, especially since he chose to recall the 1,500 "innocent people" who had allegedly been murdered and shot and had their heads cut off between April 24 and April 28, on June 17, the day after the utterly indefensible Dominican air force attacks on "its own" defenseless city.

It is difficult, if not impossible, in a country like the United States to separate what anyone, even the President, says U.S. policy is and how that policy is transmitted to and through the press. The way our Dominican policy was transmitted to and through the press in the last week of April 1965 indicates that what this country needs at least as much as anything else is a pure news law. . . .

THE DOMINICAN AFFAIR: TWO CASES FOR ANALYSIS

U.S. TRIES TO BAR PRO-REDS FROM DOMINICAN CONTROL; MARINES KILL TWO SNIPERS

ATTACK REPULSED

70 Defend Embassy—Insurgents Enlarge Grip on Capital

BY TAD SZULC

Special to The New York Times

SANTO DOMINGO, Dominican Republic, April 29. United States Marines guarding the American Embassy here repulsed an attack by snipers today.

Two snipers were killed by marine bullets, United Press International reported. An embassy official said a third sniper was "probably" killed and a fourth "possibly" killed.

The sniping was by members of the Communist-infiltrated rebel forces favoring the return to power of Juan D. Bosch, who was ousted as President of the Dominican Republic in 1963.

A high-ranking United States Navy officer said earlier today that the function of the marines who had been landed here was not only to protect the evacuation of Americans and other nationals but also "to see that no Communist government is established in the Dominican Republic."

Heavy Firing at Embassy

The snipers fired profusely at the embassy from nearby houses. The 70 marines at the embassy responded with machine-gun and rifle fire.

The incident came as the rebel forces appeared to be strengthening their position in the continuing fighting in downtown Santo Domingo. It occurred less than 24 hours after 520 United States Marines had been landed here.

The marines were restricted up to now to a small perimeter around the Embajador Hotel, from where evacuees were being flown by helicopter to the carrier Boxer standing about 10 miles offshore.

There were indications, however, that more marines would be landed, and it could not be excluded that in the end United States forces would become more directly engaged in fighting the rebels.

Planes Strafe Downtown

The rebels, who included army units as well as armed civilians and militiamen, were in control of most of the central part of the city this afternoon.

Aircraft belonging to the counterrevolutionary forces commanded by Brig. Gen. Elias Wessin y Wessin, strafed the downtown headquarters of the riot police this morning. Firing continued through the day in what had become a virtual no man's land.

Food and medicine were running short, and United States Marine helicopters delivered shipments of both to the Red Cross and the Wessin y Wessin headquarters at the San Isidro Airforce Base.

While the marines occupied the Embajador Hotel earlier, the United States activity here was being directed by Ambassador W. Tapley Bennett Jr. He was in continuing radio communications with the marines at the hotel, with the Boxer and with the San Isidro Base.

There was no question that the United States was fully supporting the three-man military junta even though it could not control the city.

This afternoon, a marine helicopter flew Antonio Imbert, an influent Dominican politician, to the Boxer in an apparent attempt to use him as a potential mediation figure in the civil war.

Marines dug in around the Embajador Hotel perimeter, and others patroled the sun-drenched garden and swimming-pool area. Marines stood guard inside the hotel lobby.

Marine helicopters kept up a busy shuttle between the hotel and the Boxer. Navy jets flew along the shore.

Fighting has been under way here since last weekend, when supporters of Mr. Bosch overthrew the civilian junta that had succeeded him in 1963. That junta was headed by Donald Reid Cabral.

The current Dominican junta is composed of representatives of the army, navy and air force.

Two Snipers Dead Confirmed

SANTO DOMINGO, April 29 (UPI)—United States Marines guarding 1,000 Americans here today shòt and killed two Dominican snipers firing on the American Embassy.

Two of the snipers were confirmed killed by marine bullets. An embassy official said another sniper was "probably" killed and a fourth "possibly" killed.

Besides the thousand Americans living in the capital, another thousand were elsewhere in the country.

Embassy officials said 1,400 more marines were available for duty here if and when needed. They included 1,000 men from the battalion landing team here and 200 more in the helicopter squadron used to fly out refugees.

The civil war has taken 400 Dominican lives so far.

Twelve hundred Dominicans have been wounded, and there were reports that the toll was rising. Hospitals were reported jammed with wounded and dead.

ANARCHY IN DOMINGO:
CITY WITHOUT FOOD,
WATER, MEDICINE
IN CIVIL WAR

BY PAUL BETHEL

Special to the Herald-Examiner

SANTO DOMINGO, April 30—Anarchy—bloody anarchy—was on the loose in Santo Domingo today, littering the streets with dead and dying as Communist-led rebels plunged the Dominican Republic into civil war.

At least 50 top Communists are in this island republic, 27 of whom were trained in Fidel Castro's Red Cuba. And eight of the top Communists are known to be directly involved in the attempted rebel takeover.

One Western diplomat declared:

"Peking Communists, Moscow Communists and Castro Communists are in league in subverting this country."

While battles rage across the island, a Russian trawler is riding offshore from Santo Domingo, bristling with electronic gear, watching and monitoring everything.

Reds Behind Revolt

It is no secret here that Castro guerrillas have been infiltrating the island over the past year. The Communists and their followers are considered the principal movers behind the insurrection.

From *The Los Angeles Herald-Examiner,* April 30, 1965. Reprinted by permission of Hearst Headline Service and *The Los Angeles Herald-Examiner.*

Santo Domingo is a scene of terror, violence and death.

American Ambassador W. Tapley Bennett Jr. and his staff described conditions as being in "a state of anarchy."

For observers here, it is like Madrid during the Spanish civil war all over again. There is no food, no water, no medicine, no sanitation, no lights or power, no transportation, and precious few telephones to the outside world.

There are about 2000 casualties, and about half of them are dead.

In one street alone, there were at least 90 people dead or dying.

There are children dying on the streets with their stomachs ripped open, and nobody to bury their bodies.

It is carnage. It is real civil war. The streets are almost literally running with blood.

Among the dead are about 600 policemen who were loyal to the government. They were dragged to walls by rebels and shot down.

At 2 A.M. today, planes of the counter revolutionary forces of Brig. Gen. Elias Wessin y Wessin dropped lighted flares over the city and strafed pockets of Communist resistance.

Paratroops Land

The Communist led rebels retaliated by rounding up the wives, mothers and children of the Wessin y Wessin forces and dragged them into the target zones.

Even as Gen. Wessin y Wessin's planes roared over the heart of the capital, U.S. paratroopers were arriving at the San Isidro Air Force base, which is headquarters for the counter revolutionary forces.

The paratroopers are expected to carry out the mandate of the Organization of American States, which is to restore peace and order in this strife-torn country with the help of U.S. Marines.

First Encounter

If they move to put down the revolt, it would be the first solid encounter between American military forces and the Communist rebels.

The issue is still in doubt, but it was hoped that the American show of military force in Santo Domingo would have the effect of restoring the balance of power in the Caribbean.

As the paratroopers arrived, 70 U.S. Marines were already dug in around the American embassy in the heart of the city, and another 536 Marines ringed the Embajador Hotel on the eastern edge of the capital.

American civilians in Santo Domingo were evacuated yesterday from the Embajador by helicopter to the aircraft carrier USS Boxer, which is standing about 10 miles off-shore as part of a four-vessel American flotilla.

Yesterday afternoon, snipers opened up on the American embassy from nearby rooftops, pouring bullets into the building.

The Marine guard responded with machinegun and rifle fire, raking the rooftops with withering volleys and killing at least two of the rebel snipers.

By early today, almost all American civilians had been evacuated, leaving only about 100 Americans in the huge Embajador Hotel—many of them correspondents here by choice—and only American officials in the embassy.

Among the most tragic situations here has been the lack of medicine and surgical instruments to treat the wounded. Doctors have been able to do little for the victims of violence.

Ambassador Bennett managed to get 14,000 pounds of food and medicine into the city yesterday, and has promised to bring in another 15,000 pounds later today if he can get the supplies through rebel lines.

Power—and the Ticking of the Clock: How Did It Happen?

There is no foreseeable end to the chronic turmoil that besets much of the Caribbean. Economics, history, and human pride and passion will see to that. There is also no foreseeable end to the responsibility the U.S. must bear there. Cuba saw to that.

It was these political realities that prompted the U.S. to move swiftly and powerfully last week to put down the bloody revolt in the Dominican Republic, the proud but chaotic little nation (population 4 million) that occupies the eastern half of the island of Hispaniola. In the four years since assassins freed the Dominican Republic of the tyranny of dictator Rafael Leonidas Trujillo, the government in Santo Domingo has known one free election, eight different governments, and at least half a dozen assorted coups and countercoups.

Last week's revolt got off to a faltering start, but before it was over more than 2,000 Dominicans had been killed or wounded, and U.S. Marines and Army troops had been landed in a Latin American nation for the first time in three decades.

The Rebels Act. The revolt began shortly before 3 P.M. on a quiet Saturday, when eighteen soldiers and civilians, led by nominal supporters of exiled President Juan Bosch, stormed Radio Santo Domingo in the heart of the capital. They promised the overthrow of the military-backed triumvirate headed by Donald Reid Cabral, the return from Puerto Rico of Bosch, and urged Dominicans to turn out in the streets and demonstrate. Simultaneously, the rebels seized two government arms depots outside Santo Domingo and began distributing arms and ammunition to their immediate supporters.

The first call to revolt brought little response. Dominicans had been through it all before, or so they thought at the time. A few hours later they hear Radio Santo Domingo announce that the station had been retaken, and the rebels were issued an ultimatum to "surrender or die." And that seemed to be that.

But it wasn't. At dawn the next day, a detachment of rebels stormed the National Palace, overpowered the guards, and ousted Reid. The rebels retook the radio station and announced that the ex-President of the Congress would be Chief of State pending Bosch's return from Puerto Rico. "We want," said Col. Francisco Caamaño Deno, a rebel leader and a confidant of many Dominican and Cuban Communists, "to return to the people what was taken from the people." In Puerto Rico, white-haired ex-President Bosch did his best to rise to the occasion. He would return, he said, "within the hour."

By now, the rebels totaled about 1,000 men, mostly soldiers like Caamaño. Not all the Dominican military units were willing to join in. But scores of pro-Bosch partisans, finally convinced that the revolt was in earnest, and hundreds of youthful hooligans, known locally as "tigers," joined the rebel forces. Arms were passed freely to all comers. They poured out into the streets of the capital, shooting at random, looting, and occasionally pausing to link arms with bands of citizens and shout, "Viva Bosch!"

Counterattack. Almost from the outset, the rebels were opposed by the navy and air force and, more important, by Gen. Elias Wessin y Wessin. The burly, black-browed son of a Lebanese immigrant, Wessin y Wessin had helped overthrow Bosch in the first place (in 1963) because he was convinced that Bosch's well-meaning but lackluster liberalism was setting the country up for a Communist take-over.

The air force began strafing rebel positions intermittently Sunday afternoon. One prime target: the two-lane Duarte Bridge over the Ozama River. Rebel soldiers at the bridge fired back at the planes; some used mirrors to try to blind the attacking pilots by reflecting the bright tropical sun into their eyes. Now, at his military center at the sprawling San Isidro army base 20 miles east of Santo Domingo, General Wessin y Wessin prepared his infantry and armor for the attack on the rebels' ground positions within the city. There, anarchy was in full cry, and slowly the dead began to pile up at the city's morgues and hospitals.

In Washington, the progress of the coup was watched closely from the first day. The State Department's Dominican desk telephoned U.S. Ambassador W. Tapley Bennett, who had arrived in the capital for consultations only two days before. Tap Bennett, an incisive, quietly brilliant Georgian, had been recalled to discuss the Dominican Republic's worsening economic and political situation. Bennett returned to Santo Domingo, arriving scant hours before the U.S. Embassy there came under fire for the first time. At first, in Washington as in Santo Domingo, the reading was that the revolt would be short-lived, and that General Wessin y Wessin's forces would carry the field in a matter of hours.

Enter the Navy. He didn't. On Monday, Wessin y Wessin tried to send his tanks across the Duarte Bridge, and was repulsed twice. From offshore, the tiny Dominican Navy supported the general's attacks with shells and flares. At the U.S. Embassy, Bennett and his staff prepared for the evacuation of as many of the 2,000 U.S. citizens in Santo Domingo as wished to leave.

By now Washington's crisis machinery was in full gear. President Johnson had been notified of the revolt almost as soon as it began. In the U.S. Navy's Pentagon war room, the maps and charts on Vietnam were moved to one side, and the maps on the Caribbean and the Dominican Republic rolled to the center of the stage. Throughout the day, the President met with State, CIA, and Pentagon officials. By Monday nightfall, Ambassador Bennett had advised the President he wanted to evacuate Americans, and the aircraft carrier USS Boxer hove to off the Dominican port of Haina, 8 miles from Santo Domingo.

On Tuesday morning, Tap Bennett issued the evacuation order in Santo Domingo. "We were given twenty minutes' notice," said New York Attorney Charles Carroll. "We could take one suitcase. Everything else had to be left behind. At 5:30 A.M., there were 1,000 Americans in the lobby of the Embajador Hotel. Then a group of Dominican civilians drove up. They shouted, 'Everyone line up against the wall.' Then they began firing machine guns. I hit the dirt along with everyone else." But no one was hurt. The Dominicans were firing at their opponents on the hotel's roof. Ambassador Bennett, meanwhile, had managed to arrange a temporary cease-fire, and by that afternoon some 1,100 Americans had been evacuated by launch and helicopter to the Boxer.

Across the Bridge. The fighting raged unabated. Wessin y Wessin's troops finally forced the Duarte Bridge, and fought into the center of the capital. Bosch's deputy fled the National Palace for the Colombian Embassy, but rebel forces fought on, entrenching themselves in Ciudad Nueva, a low-cost public housing project downtown. By nightfall, unofficial reports placed the Dominican dead at more than 400.

Wednesday was the day of decision—in Santo Domingo and in Washington. While the fighting continued, Wessin y Wessin swore in a new military junta headed by Air Force Col. Pedro Bartolomé Benoit. The U.S. Embassy evacuated 200 more Americans, and Ambassador Bennett asked for an assurance that U.S. lives and property (total investments of $110 million, chiefly by Alcoa, the Southern Puerto Rico Sugar Corp., and United Fruit) would be protected. But the new junta could promise nothing. That afternoon, Tap Bennett got on the telephone to Washington to recommend that the Marines be sent in. "Even while the Ambassador was talking," an Embassy aide recalled later, "small-arms fire came in, shattering the windows, and the Ambassador was yelling, 'Duck, or you'll get your heads cut off by the glass!'"

President Johnson had already decided to follow his ambassador's recommendation. Though the fog of war prevented any definitive attempts at classifying all the rebels who fought on—the pro-Bosch officers by now had sought asylum—both Defense Secretary McNamara and the CIA's new boss, Adm. William F. Raborn Jr., believed there was clear danger that the Communists were ascendant. Some OAS ambassadors heard reports from their embassies in Santo Domingo that Castro-style uniforms were being worn by rebel leaders. At 8:45 P.M. Wednesday, President Johnson went on national television to announce his decision to send the Boxer's contingent of 556 Marines in to protect the lives of U.S. and other foreign nationals.

Rape and Pillage. Throughout the next day LBJ conferred constantly. An emergency session of the Organization of American States met at the Pan American Union and ultimately sent in a five-nation peace mission.

From Santo Domingo, snippets of intelligence trickled to Washington; leaders of three Communist factions were identified among the leaders of the rebel street fighters. The beleaguered city was now without water or electricity. There were reports of rape, pillage, and mass executions. The dead lay in the streets.

That afternoon, a State Department briefing for reporters was postponed, put off repeatedly into the night, then canceled at 3:15 A.M. Soon after 2 A.M. Friday, the White House announced that 2,500 combat troops of the U.S. 82nd Airborne division had been landed in the Dominican Republic. Friday night, Mr. Johnson went on television again. "There are signs," the President said, "that people trained outside the Dominican Republic are seeking to gain control. Thus the legitimate aspirations of the Dominican people . . . are threatened . . . Loss of time may mean that it is too late . . ."

But in Santo Domingo, the rebels fought on. At a conference held between Wessin y Wessin's troops and the rebels, Papal Nuncio Msgr. Emanuele Clarizio and Ambassador Bennett finally obtained agreement on a cease-fire. But the agreement was hardly reached before it was broken, apparently by both sides. U.S. casualties stood at four or five killed and nearly two score wounded as the week ended. . . .

The reason the troops landed on April 28 was that President Johnson ordered them to, and Mr. Johnson had to act almost entirely on the advice of a soft-spoken professional diplomat from Georgia, W. Tapley Bennett Jr. The lanky, 48-year-old Bennett started his diplomatic career in Santo Domingo as a political and economic analyst from 1941 to 1943. "After I was appointed Ambassador to the Dominican Republic last year," Bennett recalled last week, "I warned President Johnson that the Dominicans had fortunately not had a blood bath after dictator Rafael Trujillo was assassinated in 1961, but that they might still have it."

Warnings. Bennett insists that although his embassy did not specifically predict the rebels' recent coup, it had reported that the military-backed junta led by Donald Reid Cabral was in serious political and economic trouble. Reid's opponents staged several abortive coups, and the embassy noted stepped-up Communist activities early this year. Bennett passed on to Washington the reports from Peace Corps volunteers that drought was causing bitterness among the working classes, incited by agitators' tales that the wealthy people had all the water they wanted. The ambassador personally wrote Under Secretary of State Thomas Mann: "We are almost on the ropes in the Dominican Republic."

And early in April, in a curiously Aesopian message for an official with access to ciphering devices, Bennett telegraphed Washington: "Little foxes, some of them red are chewing at the grapes. It is impossible to guarantee a good harvest in view of many unfavorable aspects of local scene. It is, however, fair to say that a diminution of our effort or failure to act will result in a bitter wine."

But despite the warnings, the fact remains that on April 24, the day the rebels seized Radio Santo Domingo and called for the return of exiled President Juan Bosch, Tap Bennett was in Georgia visiting his mother, and eleven key members of his military staff were at a conference in Panama.

Bennett immediately flew to Washington for consultations, but his absence from Santo Domingo contributed to the initial policy confusion. He flew back to the Embassy on Tuesday morning, on a Navy helicopter that had already been evacuating American refugees. That afternoon, some fifteen pro-Bosch leaders trooped into his office to try to persuade him to join the Papal Nuncio in helping them negotiate a cease-fire with the junta backed by General Wessin y Wessin. Bennett's military aides had already informed him the rebels had lost, and as he remembers the group they struck him as "an utterly dejected crew, defeated and down." He told them he had no authority for such intervention in Dominican affairs.

Countercharges. The exiled, irascible Juan Bosch, who has been fighting the rebel cause with bitter words from San Juan, disputes Bennett's version. He says Bennett told the rebels that although they had won up to that point, he was bringing in U.S. troops to crush them. Bosch's wife Carmen carried her husband's battle to Washington last week. "Mr. Bennett was so committed to the aristocracy and Wessin y Wessin that he threw his career on the side of these people," she told a press conference.

At any rate, the Ambassador's refusal on that Tuesday to participate in negotiations changed the entire complexion of the rebel organization. Four rebel military commanders defected immediately and most of the key civilian politicians took asylum in embassies. But Colonel Caamaño refused to give up. By default, the rebellion slipped into the hands of the radicals and suspected Communists. And within a few hours, the rebel military, which the Ambassador thought to be defeated, was firing on the embassy.

Bennett's initial decision not to participate in a settlement led irrevocably to his second principal move. Wednesday afternoon, with the embassy under attack, Bennett called for U.S. troops to protect Americans, although 1,100 refugees had already been evacuated. Under Secretary of State Mann, Mr. Johnson's onetime "Mr. Latin America," didn't like the idea, but with Bennett on the spot, nobody in Washington could afford to say no.

Threat. Last week members of the OAS committee generally accepted Bennett's argument that the call for troops "was absolutely essential to avoid a massacre." The British Ambassador himself had coolly sent a final message to London saying "All is well, have food and Scotch, please send bagpipes," but he and other diplomats also supported Bennett's decision. The danger, they agreed, was not only from the organized rebel forces but from civilian mobs, who had been given 10,000 small arms from a captured munitions dump.

On CBS's "Face the Nation" program, ex-President Bosch charged that the arrival of the Marines Wednesday evening changed the course of the revolt. "When they landed," he declared, "Wessin y Wessin's forces were defeated. Twenty-four hours more and the Dominicans would have solved their own problems."

At what point the U.S. military intervention shifted its chief objective from protecting civilians to preventing a Communist take-over cannot yet be documented. But under the stress of rebel firing, with water and electricity cut off, and with the rebel-controlled radio spouting propaganda so reminiscent of Castro's early days, it was easy to believe that a Fidelista revolution was just around the corner. One Latin American diplomat said bluntly: "We were within 48 hours of a Communist take-over." Honest and good men still insist passionately this was the belief.

And yet, two weeks later, the United States has not made its case. After the paratroopers arrived, the U.S. Embassy distributed a poorly documented list of 58 names of "identified and prominent Communist and Castroite leaders" among the rebel forces, and described "three Communist political organizations involved." But the analysis suffered from a lack of hard information. The three parties listed were unquestionably leftist, nationalist, and anti-U.S.—and one printed pamphlets containing Communist slogans. But to what degree that made them Communist or Castro-dominated could not be proved. Several of the 58 people were also observed to be armed with guns—but so were thousands of Dominican patriots. One suspected Communist not on the list is Rafael Tavares, former propaganda chief of a leftist party, who is working on propaganda for Caamaño. Last week, the embassy released the names of thirteen Communists who met with Colonel Caamaño the day he was sworn in as Provisional President and supposedly received his assurances of a role in his government.

OAS Study. Both Bosch and Caamaño admit there are a few Communists in the rebel movement but deny they have any influence. (Bosch says the Americans have an "obsession with anti-Communism.") Certainly none of the five top people around Caamaño is even alleged to be a Communist. And an OAS on-the-spot study of the rebel movement lent some support to their contention by reporting that although Communists had infiltrated the rebel ranks, it was difficult to measure just how strong they were.

The military leaders are genuinely pro-Bosch, and were convinced that Reid Cabral, the man who was deposed by the coup, would never permit a free election. These officers have turned out to be excellent negotiators and first-rate military planners—so good, in fact, that U.S. Gen. Bruce Palmer suspects they could only have learned at Castro's knee. But many of them, like Caamaño, are U.S.-trained. The embassy failed generally to convince the 156 foreign correspondents in Santo Domingo that "the 58" were a menace. . . .

Full Story of Caribbean War:
How Reds Plotted a Take-over

SANTO DOMINGO. This is the story of a Communist plot that turned into America's war in the Caribbean.

It started six months ago when mimeographed handbills began to appear, telling people how to make Molotov cocktails, how to build street barricades, plant bombs, how to seize arms.

It advanced carefully, step by step.

And by April 28 the Dominican Republic was in chaos, Communist plotters were on the verge of seizing power. The first of thousands of American marines and paratroopers arrived to protect Americans and prevent this country from becoming a "second Cuba."

Reprinted from *U.S. News & World Report,* May 10, 1965, published at Washington. Copyright 1965 U.S. News & World Report, Inc.

Two days later—on April 30—marines found themselves in a fire fight with rebels in Santo Domingo. One marine was killed, at least six others wounded.

Sugar prices a big factor. The plotting began against a background of discontent on the part of the workers. Sugar prices have been low, and sugar is the base of the island economy.

This forced upon the President, Donald Reid Cabral, the need to impose a program of austerity. He acted to break a strike of sugar workers. Businessmen were forced to deposit with the Government 40 per cent of the cost of goods they imported.

At the same time, some high-ranking officers were fired from the Army out of fear that there might be plotting against the regime.

The result is that businessmen, workers and key elements of the military all had become disgruntled.

Complicating the situation was the fact that the President was not a good speaker—he did not have the ability to go on television and radio and make a convincing argument in favor of the austerity he was trying to impose.

Communist leaders, aware of the discontent, speeded their plans.

Two weeks ago 52 trained Communist agents slipped into the country —32 of them from Castro's Cuba where they had been trained in guerrilla-warfare schools. The rest were from similar training schools in Russia, China and other Communist countries.

Some came on forged passports. Others slipped in by boat at night.

In touch with Bosch. Months before, the leaders of the plot had been working with Juan Bosch, former President who had been overthrown in September, 1963, and had taken refuge in San Juan, Puerto Rico.

Bosch was not known as a Communist, but he knew that Communists were in on the plot to restore him to power, and he worked with them. All details for the revolt were being worked out in secrecy. Timing became the key element. Everything was in readiness.

On Saturday morning, April 24, action was taken to crack down on three colonels in the Army whom the Government suspected of disloyalty.

The colonels were ordered fired. Instead of accepting the order, the three officers seized and disarmed the Army Chief of Staff.

Communists found out about this half an hour after it happened. They managed to broadcast a report that the military was in revolt.

By some means, the plotters then got hold of the Government radio

and television for 35 minutes and broadcast a false report that the regime
of President Reid Cabral had fallen.

The broadcasters who appeared on the TV screen wore the beards and
berets that are standard equipment of Castro Communists. They ex-
horted their listeners to take to the streets.

Every possible device was used to capitalize on the growing unpop-
ularity of the Government. People started dancing in the streets. They
were inspired, and led, by known Communists.

The President went on the air Saturday night to show that he still
was in power. He told the people that loyal troops were surrounding the
two camps in which there were disloyal colonels.

He announced that unless the disloyal elements surrendered by 5
o'clock Sunday morning, April 25, they would be attacked by Government forces.

It seems, however, that Brig. Gen. Elias Wessin y Wessin, a friend of
the President's, had been convinced by the Communist-led mobs in the
streets that this was a true uprising of the people. He failed to carry out
the attack the President had ordered.

When the attack did not come, the Reds moved out in the open. Their
months of careful plotting was triggered into action with split-second
timing.

Arms began to be passed out to civilian toughs on Sunday. The three
colonels, working with the Reds, had access to military equipment.

What soldiers did. Lower echelons in the Army had been thoroughly
infiltrated by the plotters, and they went over with the colonels to the
Communist side.

Juan Bosch, in Puerto Rico, packed his bags on that Sunday and prepared to move back to Santo Domingo. Rebel forces, by then, had chased
President Reid into the Israeli Embassy and were in control of parts of
the city.

Before Mr. Bosch could make his move, dissension developed in the
ranks of his supporters.

Mr. Bosch claimed the right to move back and serve out the unfilled
portion of the term from which he had been ejected. Others in the group
insisted that new elections be held.

When Reds moved in. While the squabbling went on, the Communists
took over the uprising. Something close to panic spread through the ranks
of the non-Communists among the plotters.

The Air Force, most of the Navy and some elements of the Army—as well as Santo Domingo's 10,000 armed police—remained loyal to the Government.

General Wessin y Wessin had led the move that overthrew Bosch in 1963 and was not ready to accept his return.

Fighting between the loyal troops and the rebels became intense. Casualties were high on both sides.

By Monday, some followers of Juan Bosch were seeking asylum in foreign embassies. The open take-over of the rebel movement by Castro-type Communists proved more than they were willing to accept.

There were defections from the Communist cause, too, by some of the Army officers when they discovered that what they had thought to be a true uprising against an unpopular Government was, in fact, a Red move to take power.

By this time rebel leaders and Communists had fanned out through the city, distributing rifles, Molotov cocktails, other weapons to aroused civilians.

Many thus armed were known Communists.

As for the others, the armed, trigger-happy populace offered the sort of civilian unrest that Communists always hope to capitalize on.

Those in the rebellion ranged all the way from known Communist agents—carbon copies of Castro's revolutionaries—to bands of criminals intent on looting. Many wore the green fatigue uniforms popular with Castro Communists.

The violence that spread through Santo Domingo gave the appearance of utter chaos. Actually, it was cut to a standard Communist pattern.

Bands of young toughs—called "tigers"—roamed the streets, carrying burp guns and other weapons. Others sat on rooftops, sniping.

"To the wall." Victims were dragged from their homes and shot down while angry mobs shouted, "To the wall!"—the same cry that marked the mass executions in Cuba in the early days of Fidel Castro. The assassinated Dominicans were dumped into crude graves right at the execution spots.

Anti-Communist pilots of the Dominican Air Force added to the toll with their strafing and bombing attacks on rebel strongholds in the capital. The rebels tried to stop the air attacks by putting the families of the pilots out in the streets where they became targets.

Much of the gunfire appeared to be for no other purpose than to terrorize the city. There were reports of bands of young rebels dashing through the streets spraying shots wildly from their machine guns and rifles.

The result was chaos.

On Tuesday, April 27, there seemed to be a turn against the rebels and a lull in the fighting. But it was misleading.

That day, the U.S. Ambassador, W. Tapley Bennett, visited the Presidential Palace. He found it largely deserted. The rooms were strewn with wreckage.

The island now was without any effective Government. Anarchy prevailed in Santo Domingo.

American citizens, in this period, began to be in real danger.

On Wednesday, April 28, civil order broke down completely.

Two to three hundred armed rebels stormed into the Ambassador Hotel, where 1,100 Americans and some other foreigners were awaiting evacuation.

The rebels seized many of the Americans, separated the men from the women and children, marched them off out of sight of their families, fired shots over their heads. The purpose was terror. Ambassador Bennett asked for marines to protect the lives of U.S. citizens, after Dominican military leaders had told him they could no longer guarantee the safety of Americans.

Among the Americans on the island at the time were many tourists, a University of Michigan jazz band, and delegates to a brewers' convention.

Advance warning. Two weeks before the Ambassador called for protective troops, the U.S. had learned through intelligence sources that trouble was impending in the Dominican Republic. The U.S. had moved the aircraft carrier Boxer, with a contingent of 1,100 Marines, to a point within easy reach of the island.

On Thursday, April 29, the Marines—first of thousands of U.S. troops —came in by helicopter.

The announced purpose of the landing was to protect American lives and to help with the evacuation of the foreigners.

Actually, the U.S. seemed to have made up its mind that it would not permit another Cuba on its doorstep.

On Thursday, the fighting had become heavy. The U.S. Embassy was fired upon. Marine guards returned the fire. Several rebel snipers were killed.

The war, itself, became more intense in the city, but the countryside outside Santo Domingo seemed quiet.

In the capital, the well-armed rebels had concentrated their attack on the 10,000-man police force. One estimate was that hundreds of police were killed in the first three days of fighting.

The Communists captured Radio Patrola, the police network station. That made it almost impossible for officers to direct police reinforcements to areas where they were needed most.

There was no mistaking the Communist pattern of the revolution. One worried diplomat told me: "All types of Communists are in this thing—Peiping Communists, Moscow Communists, Castro Communists."

By Thursday night most of downtown Santo Domingo was in the hands of the rebel forces. By then, they had seized the international telephone exchange. Estimates of the dead and wounded passed the 2,000 mark. U.S. flew in 15,000 pounds of medical supplies.

By Friday, April 30, the U.S. had built up a total of 4,200 American fighting men—1,700 Marines and 2,500 paratroopers of the Army's 82nd Airborne Division.

There was no slowing in the fighting. At noon on Friday a Marine armored column drove into the heart of the city to seal off a zone around the American Embassy, and drew rebel fire. The Marines had their first casualties.

The State Department announced that "law and order had ceased to exist" and it was clear now that the U.S. was prepared to take any action necessary.

Said a high-ranking U.S. naval officer: "It is our intention to prevent a Communist take-over."

Slanted Coverage of Japanese-American News

Martin Grodzins

Measurements and tabulations of news stories with respect to the Japanese problem were made for five large daily newspapers: the *Chronicle* and *Examiner* of San Francisco, the *Times* and *Examiner* of Los Angeles, and the *Bee* of Sacramento. The period covered was from December 8, 1941, through March 8, 1942. . . .

News stories about resident Japanese were divided according to a simple four-fold classification:

1. Stories "favorable" to resident Japanese, e.g., publicizing their pledges of loyalty to America and their enlistment in the armed forces.

2. Stories "unfavorable" to resident Japanese, e.g., describing FBI arrests, accusing Japanese of incipient fifth-column activities, urging mass evacuation.

3. Stories of government regulations and compliance with those regulations, e.g., describing contraband regulations.

4. Stories of a miscellaneous character not falling in any of the previous categories, e.g., giving statistics on Japanese population and the effect of evacuation on school enrollment; describing Japanese suicides.

In the first days of the war, newspapers were liberal in devoting space to stories that painted resident Japanese in a favorable light. The *Los Angeles Times,* for example, publicized pledges of loyalty and condemnations of the Pearl Harbor attack made by citizens of Japanese ancestry on the five consecutive days after war began (December 8–12) and again on December 14. Stories in the same paper emphasized the Americanism of residents of that city's Little Tokyo (December 8); commented in a picture underline on the loyalty of a group of resident Japanese reading war bulletins (December 8) gave large amounts of space to pleas of local officials and church spokesmen that Japanese-American students be treated fairly (December 9, 10); noted Japanese contributions to the Red Cross (December 14); and publicized the efforts of several Japanese-Americans to enlist in the armed forces (December 14, 15). Other papers followed a similar news line. The *Los Angeles Examiner* printed six declarations of loyalty by Japanese-American groups and individuals within an eight-day period (December 8–15).

The decrease in both the number of favorable news stories and the space devoted to them was rapid after the first days of the war. The *Los Angeles Times* carried thirteen "favorable" stories from December 8 to 12; five from December 13 to 17; one from December 8 to 22; none from December 23 to 27; and none from December 28 to January 1.

In more revealing terms, the five metropolitan dailies devoted approximately 17 columns of news space to favorable Japanese news in the first week of the war; 3.6 columns in the next week; and 1.3 columns from December 22 through 28.

Even during the brief era of good feeling, favorable news constituted only a little more than 21 per cent of all news. Total news devoted to resident Japanese decreased after the excitement of the first days of war, and the percentage of favorable to total news remained at almost 20 per cent from January 5 to 25. At that time there was no concomitant rise of favorable news to match the fifth-column accusations or to oppose the evacuation demands. As a consequence, the ratio of favorable to total news changed radically, the percentage of favorable news being squeezed to 4 per cent of total news (January 26–February 8). It subsequently remained below this point. . . .

The tense war situation and the sensational character of "unfavorable" news made it naturally more newsworthy than the milder type of reported events that were classified as "favorable." Despite the underweighting of unfavorable news in the tabulations, its preponderance was apparent at all times. Even in the first days after the war, when favorable news reached its absolute peak, the ratio of unfavorable to favorable was more than two to one. During only one week (January 5–11) did favorable exceed unfavorable news, the excess being trivial. The early unfavorable peak during the first week of the war, resulting almost entirely from the large number of alien arrests, was not exceeded until February 2–8. The interim period, from the middle of December past the middle of January, was one of general lack of interest, punctuated from time to time with official and unofficial reports on Pearl Harbor sabotage and sundry features reflecting suspicion of resident Japanese. During this period of little interest, even the small amount of unfavorable news occupied more than twice the space given to favorable news.

The violent upswing of unfavorable news that started on January 26 followed publication of the Roberts report, coincided with the first organized attempts to bring about mass evacuation, and was accompanied by new waves of arrests and new control measures of the Justice Department. For the period between January 26 and March 8, unfavorable news occupied an average of more than 48 columns weekly for the five newspapers compared with 2.7 columns devoted to favorable news. In other terms, for every 9.5 column *inches* of favorable news during this period there was printed more than a full *page* of unfavorable news.

Whereas news favorable to resident Japanese-Americans varied between 2 and 21.6 per cent of the total, the range of unfavorable news was from 44.7 to 69.1 per cent, the highest percentages being achieved in February. Of the total news, 56.7 per cent was unfavorable; 6.9 per cent favorable. The disparity of front-page space was even greater: of all news about resident Japanese on the first page, 57.9 per cent was unfavorable; four-fifths of 1 per cent favorable. Between January 10 and February 23 there was not a single favorable item of front-page news printed in any of the five newspapers.

For more than a month after Pearl Harbor, no word of mass evacuation appeared in the news columns. On January 10 a former president of the Los Angeles Realty Board was reported to have suggested that Japanese could raise food at inland points for the armed services, and a similar idea was expressed by a California state senator nine days later. Congressman Leland Ford was the first person to make the news with an outright program of "concentration camps" for Japanese. This was followed by a barrage of similar demands by individuals and groups. Very wide publicity was given the activities of the western bloc of congressmen who had organized themselves for the purpose of fostering evacuation.

Compared to the fact that there were no demands for evacuation in the news columns during the first thirty days of the war and only three during the next fifteen-day period, there were fifty-one between January 22 and February 5 and fifty-six between February 6 and 20. Even after evacuation was clearly portended in Executive Order 9066 (which was announced on February 20), forty demand stories appeared in the next fifteen days. The high point, however, was reached before the executive order and prior to General DeWitt's recommendation for evacuation: twenty-three demand stories appeared in the five papers in the five-day period, February 6–10.

. . . For the peak period, February 9–15, evacuation demands constituted 53 per cent of all unfavorable news. From the week of January 5–11 (when the first demand appeared) to March 8, there were almost five inches of space devoted to evacuation demands to every single inch devoted to favorable news. All told, there were 138 demand stories in the five newspapers, with the two Los Angeles papers accounting for more than two-thirds of the total. . . .

Nevertheless, even the pre-evacuation period was characterized by a type of reporting that frequently subordinated facts to fancy. The direction in which the stories turned was invariably unfavorable. The *Los Angeles Examiner,* for example, capitalized on some of the early sentiment in favor of evacuation: "Los Angeles officials and citizens, confronted with the footloose presence here of 33,000 Japanese, moved yesterday to establish a control program to satisfy swelling public demand." The companion Hearst paper of San Francisco (December 24) turned a set of census tabulations on Japanese population on the point that it illustrated "fifth column possibilities." Later (February 21), a reporter of this paper wrote about an FBI raid in the Fresno area: "What local authorities regard as indisputable evidence of organized fifth column activity was uncovered in three San Joaquin Valley counties today, as public feeling against the Japanese continued to rise." And again (March 13), a feature story on funds sent to Japan by resident Japanese read: "The Japanese war machine . . . might with a fair degree of accuracy bear the label 'Made in California.' " The editorially liberal *San Francisco Chronicle* noted on February 26 that the governor's office had been "flooded" with telegrams from people "screaming" for the evacuation of all Japanese and on March 6 embellished a story about the acquisition of Manzanar as a reception center with the comment that "several citizens claimed the Japanese couldn't leave fast enough to satisfy them."

The *Los Angeles Times* was the most consistent news column editorialist. Its Washington correspondent, Kyle Palmer, identified himself with the western congressional bloc, and his frequent dispatches were colored with their point of view. On January 29, for example, he wrote:

> Reassurance that Army and Navy authorities have been actively moving toward a solution of the Japanese problem . . . has now been given only because of clamor for action emanating from Los Angeles and other coastal cities.
>
> Military heads continued to cloak their proposals and plans in secrecy, but were quite willing to have it known that they have profited by the lessons of Pearl Harbor and do not propose hereafter to be too trustful or to be caught napping.

In later articles the correspondent of the *Times* characterized the Attorney-General's policy as "leisurely" and described Congress as believing that the Department of Justice "failed to take a realistic view of the Japanese problem." The real reason for the government's failure to act was "official Washington's state of mind. Or, at least, that part of it represented by Mr. Biddle." Mr. Palmer wrote: "Perhaps it is unkind to conjecture as to whether it is the kind of state of mind that preceded events at Pearl Harbor on December 7."

News served an editorial function in at least one other aspect, i.e., the prominence given fifth-column rumors and fears. The Pearl Harbor charges appeared as early as December 10; though later proved false, they were printed in detail and with an assurance of authenticity. Descriptions were given of false air-raid alarms and flashing lights to guide bombing planes and of an actual exchange of gunfire between Japanese fifth-columnists and American soldiers. The official Knox report on the Pearl Harbor disaster, made public on December 16, was variously headlined "Fifth Column Treachery Told," "Fifth Column Prepared Attack," and "Secretary of Navy Blames 5th Column for the Raid." Subsequent stories were even more specific: a Manila shopkeeper had donned his Japanese major's uniform and had been made a provincial military governor by the invading forces; Japanese fliers shot down over Pearl Harbor were wearing class rings of the University of Hawaii and Honolulu High School; a Japanese resident taken to a hospital after the December 7 attack had been painted green, and "hospital attendants guessed he had camouflaged himself so he could hide in the foliage and aid attacking Japs"; Hawaiian Japanese had aided attacking planes by cutting arrows in sugar-cane fields that pointed to strategic installations.

Pearl Harbor stories were matched by the space given to alleged evidences of sabotage intent on the mainland. These stories were given official credence by the large quantity of contraband material gathered in police raids and by the statements of political and civic leaders that sabotage was planned. Congressman Martin Dies, for example, made large headlines on five occasions in three months, each time stressing the potential fifth-column danger and the need for summary action. The publication of *The Yellow Book* of the Committee on Un-American Activities was displayed with great prominence. More than six full columns were devoted to it by the *Los Angeles Times,* a page-one banner reading: "Children Born to Nippon Soil," a page-six headline reading: "Pacific Coast Jap Spying Exposed; Dire Peril Told in Dies Report." Other papers gave the story almost equal prominence and similar headlines. Less spectacular announcements of oil industry leaders, California congressmen, local officials, and "unnamed authorities" appeared with regularity. The total effect was an assumption of sabotage guilt in every paper and in almost every edition.

The Effects of the Televised
Army-McCarthy Hearings

Gerhart D. Wiebe

The more interesting findings relate to the frame of reference in which the hearings were perceived. Our interviews took place some 60 days after

Excerpts on pp. 236–239 from "The Effects of the Televised Army-McCarthy Hearings" by Gerhart D. Wiebe, in *Journalism Quarterly,* Fall 1959. Reprinted with permission of the publisher.

Excerpts on pp. 239–240 from "The Army-McCarthy Hearings and the Public Conscience" by Gerhart D. Wiebe, in *Public Opinion Quarterly,* Winter 1958–1959. Reprinted with permission of the publisher.

the end of the hearings. You know how fresh two-month-old news is under ordinary circumstances. Yet people responded as if the hearings were last week's fight in the local PTA. . . .

We mentioned three characteristics of the intimate frame of reference. The first was the sense of an informal, face-to-face relationship. Listen to what the owner of a shoe-repair shop said:

> There was nothing that I can remember that had all the people talking and taking sides over so long a time as this. When they came into the shop they didn't discuss the weather like they do now till I wish they wouldn't mention it again but they always had some angle to tell about and ask how you felt about it, you just had to take a stand and there was no way to say you didn't care. That isn't so good for business but it wasn't like local politics where they wouldn't come in and trade anymore, this seemed far away enough to make it exciting and very emotional for men and women and we surely listened and talked it and only way we got away from it was to get to bed.

The close approach to the intimate frame of reference is clear. The personal involvement even pushed aside the weather.

The proprietor of a paint store spoke of the fellows on our side versus the guys on their side when he said:

> It seemed on TV that you could see McCarthy was surrounded by young men whispering and talking all the time while on the other side they were much older.

A more general index to the illusion of face-to-face acquaintance that people experienced is the memory for names. Some 60 days after the hearings, here are the names that were spontaneously mentioned among our 30 interviews: McCarthy, Schine, Stevens, Adams, Cohn, Mundt, Jenkins, Symington, Eisenhower, J. Edgar Hoover, Nixon, Flanders, Fisher, Welsh, Brownell, Carr and General Laughton.

Seventeen of them.

The second characteristic of the intimate frame of reference is the sense of a "responsive other."

A female office manager said:

> The arguments between McCarthy and Symington were exciting. Symington brought up all the old charges that McCarthy had never answered, but McCarthy parried them all.

A filling station owner laughed as he said:

> The thing that impressed me was the time John Edgar Hoover told McCarthy that no one was going to tell him how to run his job, that he worked directly

under the judicial body and was only responsible to them and to the President, no one else. I got quite a kick out of that retort.

Such references to the techniques of argument, skill in repartee, the personal talents of the antagonists repeatedly point up consciousness of, and interest in the "responsive other."

It is interesting to observe that when respondents were asked to think back to *before* the hearings and tell how they felt *then* about Senator McCarthy and his work, they spoke briefly, and often in terms of general concepts. "Somebody has got to clean up Washington," "He was doing a good job of ferreting out Communists," "They seem to be against him," etc. "Washington," "Communists," "they," general concepts—not flesh and blood human beings, not "responsive others."

General Zwicker, who was certainly a key figure in the events that led up to the hearings, and whose name and situation certainly were publicized, was mentioned only once in the 30 interviews. Annie Lee Moss was not mentioned. J. B. Matthews was not mentioned. The responses about *before* the hearings featured collective nouns. But responses shifted from these basket terms, characteristic of a distant frame of reference, to specific names when people were asked to talk about the hearings.

Finally there is the matter of a sensitive, intuitive system of ethics that characterizes the intimate frame of reference.

An upper-middle-class housewife said:

McCarthy didn't care who he stepped on to get to the top. He may have known Fisher was OK now, but he tried to hurt him to save himself.

A lower-middle-class sales clerk said:

I felt that they both had something to hide for they worked at it so seriously. It wasn't like people who were proud of their accomplishments. . . .

A lower-class housewife who turned against Senator McCarthy during the hearings said:

I don't know just what it could be that changed my feelings about him, I just started to know more about him really and saw him in action as a lawyer and I became afraid of such a man, that the power he had was terrible to make other men feel uncomfortable.

There was no talk here of communists, who might well be made to feel uncomfortable. Although this woman indicated her anti-communism earlier in the interview, what she finally reacted to was an intuitive feeling *in herself* that this man is to be feared. The same woman showed her personal intuitive involvement at another point when she said:

I think he is a son of a gun, not the other word for I wouldn't say that about anyone's mother, and I just bet that his mother and his poor wife are embarrassed to be related to him.

The responses add up to a dramatic illustration of mass communication on a national issue being perceived in an intimate frame of reference.

Perhaps you have noticed that among these comments, none mentioned what are assumed to be the basic issues in the hearings. Although the hearings were less than orderly, a number of issues were repeatedly stated in the hearings themselves, and in the reporting of the hearings.

1. Did Stevens and Adams use improper means in trying to stop McCarthy from investigating the Army?

2. Did McCarthy and Cohn use improper means in trying to get preferred treatment of Private Schine?

3. Was the President justified in refusing to divulge certain confidential executive information to a legislative group?

4. Should a Senator encourage government employees to divulge classified information to persons unauthorized to receive it?

There was very little mention of these issues. These are official types of issues, and people didn't react in terms of a controversy taking place at a high official level. They reacted as if it took place at the neighborhood level. Their responses showed little concern with questions of policy. They were concerned about whether Senator McCarthy won or lost. Incidentally, only one of our 30 respondents mentioned the fact that the report on the hearings had not yet been submitted at the time of the interviews. . . .

. . . Following the hearings, our 46 respondents divided as follows: 25 were pro-McCarthy, 20 were anti-McCarthy, and 1 seemed to be genuinely neutral. According to their own reports of previous sentiment, only 2 had definitely changed their minds. Both had become anti-McCarthy as a result of the hearings, one because "Senators . . . shouldn't set themselves up as bigger than the government. . . ." and the other because Senator McCarthy wanted ". . . to have things in his own way like a spoiled child." There is a possibility that some respondents withheld their former feelings if the hearings changed their minds, but the social milieu would appear to have minimized this pattern. It had only gradually become apparent to the public that President Eisenhower, who enjoyed very high status as a national hero, was against the Senator. Numerous conservative Senators had turned against Senator McCarthy. So there was ego support in moving to an anti-McCarthy position. Furthermore, it is not easy to deceive an experienced interviewer during the whole of a discursive interview lasting thirty to forty-five minutes.

Although editorial opinion in the mass media had much to say about public opinion having been aroused and about a ground swell of protest, our small sample showed no such shift of position. Nor was this sample atypical in this regard. A nationwide poll by George Gallup in April 1954, before the hearings, showed 38 per cent Favorable to Senator McCarthy, 46 per cent Unfavorable, and 16 per cent No Opinion. In August, some two months after the hearings and at about the time our 46 interviewers were conducted, Gallup reported 36 per cent Favorable, 51 per cent Unfavorable, and 13 per cent No Opinion. The hearings did not cause a definitive turnabout among the public. The Senator's supporters did not collectively turn their backs on him.

Some three years later, several months before Senator McCarthy's brief illness and death, Elmo Roper and Associates asked a nationwide sample this question: "Several years ago we heard a lot about Senator Joseph McCarthy of Wisconsin and his activities. But recently he has been much less prominent in the news. How do you feel now about Senator McCarthy and what he stands for? Do you approve, disapprove, or are you neutral about him?" The results were: Approve 16 per cent, Disapprove 20 per cent, Neutral 40 per cent, Don't know 24 per cent. So even at this late date, when Senator McCarthy's prestige, prominence, and power had long since disappeared, the relative proportions of pro and con opinion among the rank and file had changed little. The big shift was that more than half the pros and the cons had moved to the Neutral or No Opinion categories. What public spokesmen and the nation's leaders called a general repudiation of Senator McCarthy by the public was for the most part a repudiation among themselves. The dominant shift among the rank and file was that they turned their attention elsewhere. Although the hearings were fascinating to millions, they appear to have caused little change in position. . . .

Labor in the Radio News

Leila A. Sussmann

The thirty-three programs which were monitored made 665 broadcasts between September 17 and November 5, 1944. They carried in all 212 items of news and comment on labor during these seven weeks. Nearly all (three-fourths) of the programs had at least one labor item; one in every five broadcasts had such an item. However, the items were not evenly distributed among the programs; five programs accounted for more than half. In other words, an important item of labor news was likely to hit most of the programs, but there were a few broadcasts which hammered away at labor questions constantly.

Twenty-one per cent of the 212 items on labor were straight factual reports. The remaining 79 per cent were evenly divided between *Opinion* (commentators' own views), 40 per cent, and *Quoted Opinion,* 39 per cent. *Opinion* was the heaviest category during three of the seven weeks and *Quoted Opinion* during four. *Fact* was the smallest category during every week but one.

How much of the attention to labor is concerned with the strength and weakness of labor forces and how much with the right and wrong, in the moral sense, of labor policies?

Morality items (bearing on the right and wrong of labor policies) were three times as frequent as *Strength* items. That is to say, in conflict situations involving labor, news commentators devoted much more attention to the question of who was right and who wrong than to the question of who was most likely to win out. This typical concern of American political discourse with moral rather than power issues has often been remarked by social scientists. . . .

Taking *Morality* items alone, *there were five items unfavorable to labor for every one which was favorable.*

Strength items were distributed quite differently. *There were as many favorable Strength items as unfavorable ones.*

Translated, this means that labor was presented as being morally wrong five times as often as it was morally right; on the other hand, it was presented as being strong just as often as it was presented as being weak.

Excerpts from "Labor in the Radio News: An Analysis of Content" by Leila A. Sussmann, in *Journalism Quarterly,* September 1945. Reprinted with permission of the publisher.

Furthermore, the predominance of unfavorable *Morality* items held for all three categories of *Fact, Opinion* and *Quoted Opinion*. That is, factual reports (usually of strikes in war plants) were nearly all about something morally wrong which some labor group or leader had done; opinion quoted was nearly always unfavorable-to-labor opinion; and the commentators themselves nearly always expressed unfavorable-to-labor views.

Very interesting also are the findings on *who* was quoted for and against labor. Against labor, there were quotations from government officials, prominent Republicans, business men, and anonymous rank-and-file union members. Pro-labor quotations came almost exclusively from labor leaders themselves.

The image of labor which must emerge from content structured in this way is plain. Labor is sometimes strong, sometimes weak, but what it does is nearly always morally wrong; no one approves of labor except the labor leaders themselves. . . .

PART THREE

FOR FURTHER
STUDY, ANALYSIS,
AND RESEARCH

I · Topics and Questions

1. The mass media provide a wide variety of comedy and comedians, each with different bases and approaches to humor, and different social significance. Define and analyze either one type of comedy or one particular comedian. Discuss the basis of the humor and the reasons for popularity, and show its relationship to society and the times. Compare two different types of comedians in these same terms.
2. Many critics have worried about the relative lack of serious drama on television. What accounts for the absence of serious drama and, conversely, why are the types of dramatic programs that are regularly produced as popular as they are?
3. What image of the American family is projected by the many domestic comedies and dramas on television? Does this image accurately reflect the contemporary relationships between husbands and wives, and parents and children? Is the image projected on television similar to that conveyed by current family-situation movies? Why or why not?
4. What is the basis for the popularity of certain basic genres or types of movies and television programs—such as the Western, the family comedy, the secret agent or science fiction thriller? What (possibly in an indirect manner) do the elements of these popular genres reveal about the audience?
5. What changes are taking place in the form, techniques, and contents of movies? What is the relationship between these changes and the changes in society, personal relationships, morals, the world of ideas?
6. Define and analyze the current approaches to television commercials. On what do they base their appeals? What techniques, both psychological and artistic, do they employ?
7. What do the contents, styles, and techniques of today's popular music (as illustrated by a general type of music, or a specific performer or group) represent? Do they reflect any deep changes in society? How do they compare to the elements of popular music of an earlier period?
8. Protest songs are one flourishing form of popular music. What types of protests are embodied in these songs? What contemporary problems

do they reflect? Do they reflect these problems honestly and meaning-
fully?

9. Much has been written about current forms of dancing. What attitudes and feelings are expressed in these dancing styles? How do they
differ from earlier styles? Why?

10. What is the reason for the wide appeal of Charles Schulz' comic
strip, "Peanuts" (or any other popular comic strip)?

11. One of the most popular and pervasive forms of radio programs is the
"telephone call-in" program. What is the appeal of this type of
program? What is its value?

12. Do you agree with the critics who contend that there is excessive
violence on television? What effects can this violence, excessive or
otherwise, have?

13. What is the basis for the appeal of certain major television, movie,
or recording stars (or groups)? What do they represent to the public,
or that segment of the public to whom they appeal?

14. Analyze the degree of realism in the treatment of "love" in various
kinds of films and television programs. Can these films and programs
have any effect on the emotional lives of audiences?

15. Write a review of a film or television program. Be sure to go beyond
a mere citation of plot and characters. Analyze and evaluate the
themes and discuss their implications. Describe the techniques used to
achieve these elements.

16. Analyze two or more works by a single movie director by tracing the
unifying threads of situation, theme, character analysis, social comment, and technique.

17. Do you agree that the mass media tend to alienate people from personal experience and impoverish responsiveness, or do you believe
they tend to enrich consciousness? Approach this subject in terms of
either a personal response to specific media materials or an investigation of the writings of authorities in the field.

18. What are the advantages of the current forms of mass media? What
are their disadvantages? Which are dominant?

19. Is there a conflict between entertainment and art in the media today?
What is the effect of the size of the audience involved?

20. Which medium do you think is best fulfilling its potentials? Why?
Which one is lagging in this regard?

21. Has the stereotyping produced by the mass media affected your life
personally? Which of your values, concepts, and attitudes have been
influenced by the media and in what ways have they been affected?

22. Apply Marshall McLuhan's concept of hot and cold media to your

own experience of a particular form of media presentation or one specific film, program, or performance. Do you agree with McLuhan's definition of the psychological attributes of specific media?

23. What are the results of the media's need to appeal to large audiences? What effects, for example, do television ratings have? What are the alternatives to this approach?

24. Analyze the newspaper and/or magazine critics' reviews of a particular movie or television program. Note the agreements and disagreements of the critics and also interpret the assumptions and approaches that underlie these similarities and differences.

25. What has been the single most significant experience you have had as a member of the audience of a mass media presentation? What effect and/or influence did it have on you and what were the reasons for this?

26. In his famous defense of the freedom of speech entitled *The Areopagitica,* the British poet, John Milton, asked, "What wisdom can there be to choose, what continence to forebear without the knowledge of evil?" Apply his statement in an analysis of the problem of censorship of the mass media. For a research project, find sources that support and explain your position as well as the opposing positions.

27. Which of the media is the most influential in shaping the opinions, attitudes, values, and beliefs of its audience? What functions, characteristics, and situations produce this strength of influence?

28. Which functions and roles of the media—or any one medium—are the most valuable for the public?

29. What problems are created by the fact that media are both private business enterprises and public services? What is the best solution of these problems or how can these problems be ameliorated?

30. Analyze and evaluate the purposes, format, functions, coverage, and techniques of a particular local newspaper (or newspapers).

31. Compare and contrast the treatment of a specific news event or situation in two magazines or newspapers. Show the relation of that treatment to the general purposes, positions, and roles of the publication. Determine the extent of the bias or slanting involved.

32. Analyze and evaluate the problem of government secrecy and publicity (or one or the other) in the field of information and opinion.

33. Can media objectivity become a problem? Is more interpretive journalism needed to balance completely objective reporting?

34. Do advertising and the pressures of advertisers affect the content of the media? Are the possible effects the same in all media? Why?

35. Compare and contrast the level, methods, and purposes of movie

or book reviews in newspapers and magazines. Relate these to the general purposes of the publications.

36. Define the extent, the value and, if necessary, the remedies of the influence and effects of television on children.

37. Analyze the similarities and differences among the variety of magazines published in a single field—such as news and opinion magazines, sports magazines, and men's or women's magazines.

38. Analyze the differences in the handling of news as typically practiced in two of the media—such as television and newspapers.

39. Is sensationalism a problem in the media?

40. Analyze the stereotypes projected by a single publication in one or several of its issues.

41. What are the current problems of the laws and regulations governing radio and television? How do these compare with those governing newspapers and magazines? With those governing movies?

42. By analyzing a specific movie or group of movies, or by finding secondary sources that have done this analysis, discuss the possible influences of movies on ideas, attitudes, and beliefs.

43. What are the conditions, the values, and the problems of the rating systems in the television industry?

44. Does the television audience get what it wants to see? Does it get what it should see? *Should* it get what it should see?

45. Do the media tend to strengthen conformity in a society? If so, in what ways?

46. Analyze the advertisements of one issue of a publication in terms of the following: implied or stated values, kinds of appeals, methods, use of connotation, audience, style and level of language, relation to contents of the publication.

47. In the press, what are some of the problems of the relationship between freedom and responsibility?

48. Compare the treatment of a significant news story in magazines during and immediately after the event with its later treatment in books or magazines.

49. How has television affected the conduct of political affairs and campaigns? And with what result?

50. Compare the tables of contents of three different magazines for the significance of what is revealed about their different functions, purposes, audiences, and so forth.

II · Bibliography

Books

Agee, James. *Agee on Film*. New York: Ivan Obolensky, Inc., 1958.

Alsop, Joseph, and Stewart Alsop. *The Reporter's Trade*. New York: Reynal & Company, Inc., 1958.

Arnheim, Rudolf. *Film as Art*. Berkeley, Calif.: University of California Press, 1957.

Bainbridge, John. *Little Wonder and How It Grew*. New York: Reynal & Company, Inc., 1946.

Barnouw, Erik. *Mass Communications*. New York: Holt, Rinehart and Winston, Inc., 1956.

Berelson, Bernard, and Morris Janowitz. *Reader in Public Opinion and Communication*. New York: The Free Press, 1953.

Bird, George, and Fred Merwin. *The Press and Society*. Englewood Cliffs, N.J.: Prentice-Hall, Inc., 1951.

Blum, Eleanor. *Reference Books in the Mass Media*. Urbana, Ill.: University of Illinois Press, 1962.

Blumberg, Nathaniel B. *One-Party Press*. Lincoln, Neb.: University of Nebraska Press, 1954.

Bogart, Leo. *Age of Television*, 2d ed. New York: Frederick Ungar Publishing Co., 1958.

Cantril, Hadley, and Gordon W. Allport. *The Psychology of Radio*. New York: Harper & Row, Publishers, 1935.

Carpenter, Edmund, and Marshall McLuhan. *Explorations in Communication*. Boston: The Beacon Press, 1960.

Casey, Ralph D. (Ed.) *The Press in Perspective*. Baton Rouge, La.: Louisiana State University Press, 1965.

CBS. *The Eighth Art*. New York: Holt, Rinehart and Winston, Inc., 1962.

Chaffee, Zechariah. *Government and Mass Communication*, 2 vols. Hamden, Conn.: The Shoe String Press, 1947.

Cohen, Bernard. *The Press and Foreign Policy*. Princeton, N.J.: Princeton University Press, 1963.

Cross, Harold L. *The People's Right To Know*. New York: Columbia University Press, 1953.

Dale, Edgar. *How To Read a Newspaper*. Glenview, Ill.: Scott, Foresman and Company, 1941.

Davis, Elmer. *But We Were Born Free.* Indianapolis: The Bobbs-Merrill Company, Inc., 1954.

DeMott, Benjamin. *Hells and Benefits.* New York: Basic Books, 1962.

Denny, Reuel. *The Astonished Muse.* Chicago: University of Chicago Press, 1957.

Dexter, James Anthony, and David Manning White. *People, Society, and Mass Communication.* New York: The Free Press, 1964.

Elliott, William Y. *Television's Impact on American Culture.* East Lansing, Mich.: Michigan State University Press, 1956.

Emery, Edwin, Philip Ault, and Warren Agee. *Introduction to Mass Communication.* New York: Dodd, Mead & Company, Inc., 1960.

Fenin, George N., and William K. Everson. *The Western: From Silents to Cinerama.* New York: Grossman Publishers, Inc., 1962.

Gerald, J. Edward. *The Social Responsibility of the Press.* Minneapolis: University of Minnesota Press, 1963.

Greenberg, Bradley, and Edwin Parker. *The Kennedy Administration and the American Public.* Stanford, Calif.: Stanford University Press, 1965.

Hall, Stuart, and Paddy Whannel. *The Popular Arts.* New York: Random House, Inc., 1964.

Head, Sidney. *Broadcasting in America.* Boston: Houghton Mifflin Company, 1956.

Hocking, William. *Freedom of the Press.* Chicago: University of Chicago Press, 1947.

Houston, Penelope. *The Contemporary Cinema.* Baltimore: Penguin Books, Inc., 1963.

Howe, Quincy. *The News and How To Understand It.* New York: Simon and Schuster, Inc., 1940.

Innis, Harold. *The Bias of Communication.* Toronto: University of Toronto Press, 1951.

Jacobs, Lewis. *The Rise of the American Film.* New York: Harcourt, Brace & World, Inc., 1939.

———. *Introduction to the Art of the Movies.* New York: The Noonday Press, 1960.

Jacobs, Norman. *Culture for the Millions.* Boston: The Beacon Press, 1962.

Johnson, Gerald W. *Peril and Promise: An Inquiry into Freedom of the Press.* New York: Harper & Row, Publishers, 1958.

Kael, Pauline. *I Lost It at the Movies.* Boston: Little, Brown & Company, 1965.

Kauffmann, Stanley. *A World on Film.* New York: Harper & Row, Publishers, 1966.

Kelley Jr., Stanley. *Public Relations and Political Power.* Baltimore: The Johns Hopkins Press, 1956.

Key, Vladimir O. *Public Opinion and American Democracy.* New York: Alfred A. Knopf, 1961.

Klapper, Joseph T. *The Effects of Mass Communications.* New York: The Free Press, 1960.

Knight, Arthur. *The Liveliest Art*. New York: Crowell-Collier and Macmillan, Inc., 1957.

Kostelanetz, Richard. *The New American Arts*. New York: Horizon Press, Inc., 1965.

Lasswell, Harold, and Ralph D. Casey. *Propaganda, Communication, and Public Opinion*. Princeton, N.J.: Princeton University Press, 1946.

Laws, Frederick. *Made for Millions*. London: Contact Publications, 1947.

Lazarsfeld, Paul F., and Harry Feld. *Radio and the Printed Page*. New York: Duell, Sloan & Pearce-Meredith Press, 1940.

Lazarsfeld, Paul F., and Patricia Kendall. *Radio Listening in America*. Englewood Cliffs, N.J.: Prentice-Hall, Inc., 1948.

Liebling, A. J. *The Wayward Pressman*. New York: Doubleday & Company, Inc., 1948.

———. *The Wayward Pressman's Casebook*. New York: Doubleday & Company, Inc., 1949.

Lindstrom, Carl E. *The Fading American Newspaper*. New York: Doubleday & Company, Inc., 1960.

Lippmann, Walter. *Public Opinion*. New York: Crowell-Collier and Macmillan, Inc., 1922.

———. *The Phantom Public*. New York: Harcourt, Brace & World, Inc., 1925.

Lowenthal, Leo. *Literature, Popular Culture, and Society*. Englewood Cliffs, N.J.: Prentice-Hall, Inc., 1961.

MacCann, Richard Dyer. *Film: A Montage of Theories*. New York: E. P. Dutton & Co., Inc., 1966.

MacDonald, Dwight. *Against the American Grain*. New York: Random House, Inc., 1962.

Marx, H. L. *Television and Radio in American Life*. New York: The H. W. Wilson Company, 1953.

McLuhan, Marshall. *The Gutenberg Galaxy*. Toronto: University of Toronto Press, 1962.

———. *Understanding Media*. New York: McGraw-Hill, Inc., 1964.

Mehling, Harold. *The Great Time Killer*. Cleveland: The World Publishing Company, 1962.

Merton, Robert. *Mass Persuasion*. New York: Harper & Row, Publishers, 1946.

Mott, Frank L. *The News in America*. Cambridge, Mass.: Harvard University Press, 1952.

Nossiter, Bernard. *The Mythmakers*. Boston: Houghton Mifflin Company, 1964.

Pollard, James. *The Presidents and the Press*. New York: Crowell-Collier and Macmillan, Inc., 1947.

Pool, Ithiel de Sola. *The Prestige Papers: A Survey of Their Editorials*. Palo Alto, Calif.: Hoover Institute Studies, 1952.

Reston, James. *The Artillery of the Press*. New York: Harper & Row, Publishers, 1967.

Rivers, William. *The Opinion Makers*. Boston: The Beacon Press, 1965.

Rosenberg, Bernard, and David Manning White. *Mass Culture*. New York: The Free Press, 1957.

Rotha, Paul, and Richard Griffith. *The Film Till Now*. New York: Funk & Wagnalls, 1949.

Rowse, Arthur. *Slanted News*. Boston: The Beacon Press, 1957.

Schramm, Wilbur. *Communications in Modern Society*. Urbana, Ill.: University of Illinois Press, 1948.

———. *Responsibility in Mass Communications*. New York: Harper & Row, Publishers, 1957.

Seldes, Gilbert. *The Great Audience*. New York: The Viking Press, Inc., 1951.

———. *The Public Arts*. New York: Simon and Schuster, Inc., 1956.

Siebert, Frederick, Theodore Peterson, and Wilbur Schramm. *Four Theories of the Press*. Urbana, Ill.: University of Illinois Press, 1956.

Siepmann, Charles. *Radio, Television, and Society*. New York: Oxford University Press, 1950.

Skornia, Harry J. *Television and Society*. New York: McGraw-Hill, Inc., 1965.

Steinberg, Charles S. *Mass Media and Communication*. New York: Hastings House, Publishers, Inc., 1966.

Talbot, Daniel. *Film*. New York: Simon and Schuster, Inc., 1960.

Thompson, Denys. (Ed.) *Discrimination and Popular Culture*. Harmondsworth, England: Penguin Books, Inc., 1965.

Tyler, Parker. *Magic and Myth of the Movies*. New York: Holt, Rinehart and Winston, Inc., 1947.

———. *Three Faces of the Film*. New York: A. S. Barnes & Company, Inc., 1960.

van den Haag, Ernest, and Ralph Ross. *The Fabric of Society*. New York: Harcourt, Brace & World, Inc., 1957.

Warshow, Robert. *The Immediate Experience*. New York: Doubleday & Company, Inc., 1962.

Waugh, Coulton. *The Comics*. New York: Crowell-Collier and Macmillan, Inc., 1947.

Wertham, Frederick. *Seduction of the Innocent*. New York: Holt, Rinehart and Winston, Inc., 1954.

White, David Manning, and Robert Abel. (Eds.) *The Funnies: An American Idiom*. New York: The Free Press, 1963.

Wilkinson, Morris. *Public Opinion and the Spanish-American War*. Baton Rouge, La.: Louisiana State University Press, 1932.

Wolfe, Tom. *The Kandy-Kolored-Tangerine-Flaked Streamline Baby*. New York: Farrar, Straus & Giroux, Inc., 1965.

Wolfenstein, Martha, and Nathan Leites. *Movies: A Psychological Study*. New York: The Free Press, 1950.

Wolseley, Roland E. *The Magazine World*. Englewood Cliffs, N.J.: Prentice-Hall, Inc., 1951.

Wood, James P. *Newspapers in the United States*. New York: The Ronald Press Company, 1949.

————. *Magazines in the United States*. New York: The Ronald Press Company, 1956.

Wylie, Max. *Clear Channels: TV and the American People*. New York: Funk & Wagnalls, 1954.

Periodicals

Alpert, Hollis. "Sexual Behavior in the American Movies," *Saturday Review*, 39 (June 23, 1956), 9–10.

Anders, Gunther. "The Phantom World of TV," *Dissent*, 3 (Spring 1956), 14–24.

Bagdikian, Ben. "The Newsmagazines," *New Republic*, 40 (February 2, 16, and 23, 1959), 11–16.

Bartlett, Kenneth G. "Social Importance of the Radio," *Annals of the American Academy of Political and Social Science*, 250 (March 1947), 89–97.

Barzun, Jacques. "Kind Words for Pop, Bop, and Folk," *The Reporter*, 14 (May 17, 1956), 36.

Bauer, R. A., and H. A. Bauer. "America, Mass Society, and Mass Media," *Journal of Social Issues*, 16, No. 3 (1960), 3–66.

Bestor, Alfred. "The New Age of Radio," *Holiday*, 33 (June 1963), 56–65.

Block, Mervin. "The Night Castro 'Unmasked'," *Columbia Journalism Review*, 1 (Summer 1962), 5.

Bogart, Leo. "American Television," *Journal of Social Issues*, 18 (July 1962), 36–42.

Bradshaw, Michael. "Slanting the News," *Atlantic Monthly*, 174 (August 1944), 79–82.

Brucker, Herbert. "Mass Man and Mass Media," *Saturday Review*, 48 (May 29, 1965), 14–16.

Brustein, Robert. "The New Faith of the *Saturday Evening Post*," *Commentary*, 16 (October 1953), 367–369.

————. "Reflections on Horror Movies," *Partisan Review*, 25 (Spring 1958), 288–296.

Bush, Chilton R. "The Press, Reader Habits, and Reader Interest," *Annals of the American Academy of Political and Social Science*, 219 (January 1942), 7–10.

Carey, James W. "Harold Adams Innis and Marshall McLuhan," *Antioch Review*, 27 (Spring 1967), 5–39.

Chaffee, Zechariah. "An Outsider Looks at the Press," *Neiman Reports*, 7 (January 1955), 5.

Childs, Marquis. "The Interpretive Reporter's Rule in a Troubled World," *Journalism Quarterly*, 27 (Spring 1950), 134.

Coffin, Thomas E. "Television's Impact on Society," *American Psychologist*, 2 (October 1955), 630.

Cohen, Eliot. "The Film Drama as a Social Force," *Commentary*, 4 (March 1947), 110–118.

Draper, Theodore. "A Case of Defamation: U.S. Intelligence versus Juan Bosch," *New Republic*, 154 (February 19 and 26, 1966), 13–19; 15–18.

Dudley, Drew. "Moulding Public Opinion through Advertising," *Annals of the American Academy of Political and Social Science*, 250 (March 1947), 105–112.

Elkin, Frederick. "The Value Implications of Popular Films," *Sociology and Social Research*, 38 (May 1954), 320–322.

Friedrick, Otto. "There are 00 Trees in Russia: The Function of Facts in News Magazines," *Harper's Magazine*, 229 (October 1964), 59–65.

Galbraith, John Kenneth. "The Age of the Wordfact," *Atlantic Monthly*, 206 (Summer 1960), 287.

Gieber, Walter. "Do Newspapers Overplay Negative News?," *Journalism Quarterly*, 32 (Summer 1955), 311.

Goldman, Ralph. "How Republican Is the Press?," *New Republic*, 127 (September 15, 1952), 10–12.

Gruenberg, Sidonie M. "The Comics as a Social Force," *Journal of Educational Sociology*, 18 (Spring 1944), 204–213.

Gundlach, Ralph. "The Movies: Stereotypes or Realities?," *Journal of Social Issues*, 3 (Summer 1947), 26–32.

Guthrie, Tyrone. "Can TV Be Saved?," *Esquire*, 60 (December 1963), 211.

Hauser, Arnold. "Can Movies Be Profound?," *Partisan Review*, 15 (April 1948), 69–73.

Hayakawa, S. I. "Popular Songs versus the Facts of Life," *Etc.*, 12 (Spring 1955), 83–95.

Holland, Norman. "Puzzling Movies: Three Analyses and a Guess at Their Appeal," *Journal of Social Issues*, 20 (January 1964), 71–96.

Houseman, John. "Today's Hero," *Hollywood Quarterly*, 2 (Summer 1947), 161.

Howe, Irving. "Notes on Mass Culture," *Politics*, 5 (Spring 1948), 120–123.

Jensen, Jay. "A Method and a Perspective for Criticism of the Mass Media," *Journalism Quarterly*, 37 (Spring 1960), 261.

Kelley Jr., Stanley. "Elections and Mass Media," *Law and Contemporary Problems*, 27 (Spring 1962), 307–326.

Klapper, Joseph. "Mass Media and the Engineering of Consent," *American Scholar*, 17 (Spring 1948), 419.

Klonsky, Milton. "Along the Midway of Mass Culture," *Partisan Review*, 16 (Summer 1949), 348–365.

Koch, Christopher. "The Cool Totalitarian, or 'The McLuhan Megillah'," *Ramparts*, 4 (October 1966), 55–58.

Lyress, Paul. "The Place of Mass Media in the Homes of Boys and Girls," *Journalism Quarterly*, 29 (Fall 1952), 3.

MacDougall, Curtis D. "The American Press: Influence on Public Opinion," *International Journal of Opinion and Attitude Research*, 3 (Summer 1949), 251.

Markel, Lester. "The Real Sins of the Press," *Harper's Magazine,* 225 (December 1962), 85–87.

Markham, James W. "Foreign News in the United States and South American Press," *Public Opinion Quarterly,* 25 (Summer 1961), 249.

Mayer, Martin. "How Good Is TV at Its Best?," *Harper's Magazine,* 221 (August–September 1960), 82–86.

Miller, William Lee. "Can Government Be Merchandized?," *The Reporter,* 9 (October 27, 1953), 11–16.

Mizener, Arthur. "The Elizabethan Art of Our Movies," *Kenyon Review,* 4 (Spring 1942), 108.

Otto, Herbert. "Sex and Violence on U.S. Newsstands," *Journalism Quarterly,* 40 (Winter 1963), 16.

Peterson, Theodore. "Why the Mass Media Are That Way," *Antioch Review,* 23 (Winter 1963–1964), 405.

Podhoretz, Norman. "Our Changing Ideals as Seen on TV," *Commentary,* 16 (June 1953), 534–540.

Read, Herbert. "Toward a Film Aesthetics," *Cinema Quarterly,* 1 (Autumn 1932), 7–10, 11.

Riesman, David. "Listening to Popular Music," *American Quarterly,* 2 (Fall 1950), 365–371.

Saerchinger, Cesar, "Radio as a Political Instrument," *Foreign Affairs,* 16 (January 1938), 244–259.

Schein, Harry. "The Olympian Cowboy," *The American Scholar,* 24 (Summer 1955), 309–320.

Schwartz, Delmore. "Masterpieces as Cartoons," *Partisan Review,* 19 (July–August 1952), 461–471.

Seldes, Gilbert. "The News on TV," *New Republic,* 130 (January 18, 1954), 7–10.

Shannon, Lyle. "The Opinions of Little Orphan Annie and Her Friends," *Public Opinion Quarterly,* 18 (Spring 1954), 169.

Shils, Edward. "Daydreams and Nightmares: Reflections on the Criticism of Mass Culture," *Sewanee Review,* 65 (Autumn 1957), 597–608.

Sisk, J. P. "Exposé Magazines," *Commonweal,* 64 (June 1, 1956), 223.

Smith, Desmond. "American Radio Today," *Harper's Magazine,* 229 (September 1964), 58–63.

Smith, Henry Ladd. "The Rise and Fall of the Political Cartoon," *Saturday Review,* 37 (May 29, 1954), 7.

Stern, Philip. "The TV Debates in Retrospect," *New Republic,* 143 (November 26, 1960), 18.

Talley, William. "Newspapers Reveal but Part of the Facts," *Syracuse University School of Journalism Publications,* Series 2, No. 7 (September 1948), 17–21.

Tannebaum, Percy H. "The Effect of Headlines on the Interpretation of News Stories," *Journalism Quarterly,* 30 (Spring 1953), 189–197.

Tebbel, John. "Rating American Newspapers," *Saturday Review,* 44 (May 13, 1961), 60–62.

Thrasher, Frederick M. "The Comics and Delinquency: Cause or Scapegoat?," *Journal of Educational Sociology,* 23 (Spring 1949), 195–205.

Wagner, Philip. "What Makes a Really Good Newspaper?," *Harper's Magazine,* 224 (June 1962), 12.

White, William S. "Trying To Find the Shape—If Any—of the News in Washington," *Harper's Magazine,* 217 (August 1958), 76–80.

Wiebe, G. D. "Merchandising Commodities and Citizenship in Television," *Public Opinion Quarterly,* 15, No. 4 (1951), 679.

Wilensky, H. L. "Mass Society and Mass Culture: Interdependence or Independence?" *American Sociological Review,* 29 (April 1964), 173–197.

Wilson, Elmo. "Effectiveness of Documentary Broadcasting," *Public Opinion Quarterly,* 12 (Spring 1948), 19–29.

Wolfenstein, Martha, and Nathan Leites. "The Unconscious versus the 'Message' in an Anti-Bias Film," *Commentary,* 10 (March 1950), 380.

Wylie, Evan M. "Violence on TV—Entertainment or Menace?," *Cosmopolitan,* 134 (February 1953), 34–39.

Index of Authors and Titles

Index of Authors and Titles*

*Titles are italicized.

259